IMAGES
of America

HUDSON RIVER LIGHTHOUSES

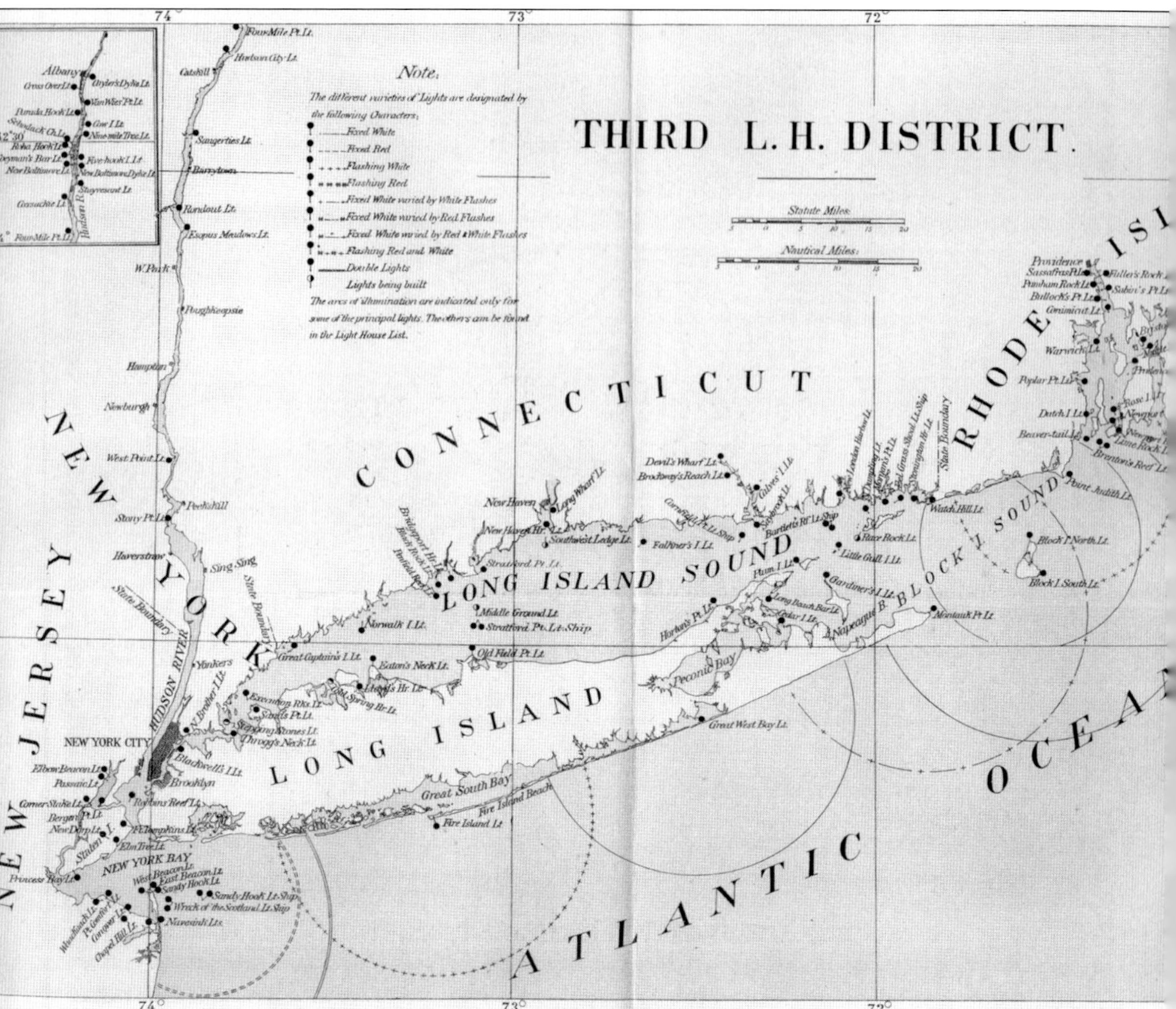

This map, from the 1876 *Annual Report of the US Lighthouse Service*, shows the Third Lighthouse District, which includes the Hudson River (at left). The Third District stretched from the shores of Rhode Island along the coasts of Connecticut, Long Island, and northern New Jersey before traveling up the Hudson River to Albany. This book will focus on the Hudson River, from the Verrazzano-Narrows Bridge to just north of Albany, New York.

On the Cover: Saugerties Lighthouse, located at the mouth of Esopus Creek in Saugerties, New York, was completed in 1869. This lighthouse is the second structure at that location and was part of an effort in the 1860s to replace older, 1830s lighthouses. Four such replacement lighthouses were constructed at Rondout, Saugerties, Stuyvesant, and Coxsackie between 1867 and 1869, all built from identical architectural plans. The Saugerties Lighthouse remains today and is operated by the nonprofit Saugerties Lighthouse Conservancy as a bed-and-breakfast.

IMAGES
of America

HUDSON RIVER LIGHTHOUSES

Hudson River Maritime Museum

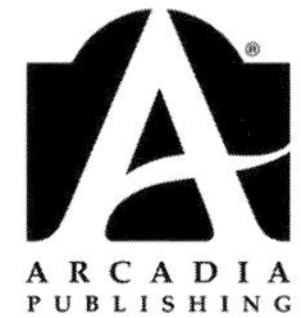

ARCADIA
PUBLISHING

ISBN 978-1-4671-0330-5

Published by Arcadia Publishing
Charleston, South Carolina

Printed in the United States of America

Library of Congress Control Number: 2018961456

For all general information, please contact Arcadia Publishing:
Telephone 843-853-2070
Fax 843-853-0044
E-mail sales@arcadiapublishing.com
For customer service and orders:
Toll-Free 1-888-313-2665

Visit us on the Internet at www.arcadiapublishing.com

To the lighthouse keepers and their families who lost their lives in service of safe navigation.

Contents

Acknowledgments

Books never come together on their own, and rarely are they the work of a single person. This particular book was the result of a great deal of cooperation, and the staff and board of the Hudson River Maritime Museum would like to thank the following people for providing access to their images, writing captions, and assisting with research: members of the Hudson River Lighthouse Coalition, including the Hudson-Athens Lighthouse Preservation Society, particularly Athens town historian Lynn Brunner and Greene County historian David Dorpfeld; the Saugerties Lighthouse Conservancy, especially lighthouse keepers Patrick and Anna Landewe; the Save the Esopus Lighthouse Commission, especially director Barbara Ralston; the Stony Point Battlefield State Historic Site, including site manager Julia Warger, historian Michael Sheehan, and special projects coordinator Jennifer Plick; and Village of Sleepy Hollow Recreation and Parks Department supervisor Matthew Arone. Additional thanks to Carol Weiss and Myra Starr of the Nyack Library for assistance in research, and Dr. Sara Mascia, executive director of the Historical Society Inc. Serving Sleepy Hollow and Tarrytown, for assistance in locating photographs. Special thanks to Billy Wade, supervisory archivist of the Still Picture Branch, Special Media Records Division, National Archives and Records Administration, for his cheerful and prompt delivery of many very high-resolution images for use in this book. Thanks also to Patrick Kaufmann, Richard Sharp, and Warren Mumford for contributing images from their private collections.

Special thanks also go to Hudson River Maritime Museum volunteer researchers George Thompson for his incredible newspaper research; Joan and Carl Mayer for their willingness to travel, dogged quest for rare images, research, extensive written contributions, and modern photographs; and intern Jade Mitchell, who found the hand-annotated historic map and newspaper articles that revealed so many "lost" lights and lighthouses.

This book was compiled, written, organized, and edited by Hudson River Maritime Museum director of education Sarah Wassberg Johnson, with assistance from board member Mark Peckham (who also contributed modern photographs of "lost" lighthouses), collections manager and digital archivist Dr. Carla R. Lesh, and curator emerita Allynne Lange.

Finally, we wish to thank you, the reader, for purchasing and enjoying this book. All royalties from the sale of this book will benefit the education and preservation mission of the Hudson River Maritime Museum.

The images in this volume appear courtesy of the Hudson River Maritime Museum (HRMM), National Archives and Records Administration (NARA), Library of Congress (LOC), www.archive.org (ARC), Save the Esopus Meadows Lighthouse Commission (EML), Saugerties Lighthouse Conservancy (SLC), Stony Point Battlefield State Historic Site (SPB), Nyack Public Library (NPL), and the Historical Society Inc. Serving Sleepy Hollow and Tarrytown (HSISHT). Images from private collections are credited individually.

Introduction

The image of towering coastal lighthouses standing like sentinels on rocky islands surrounded by heaving seas is familiar to many people, but hundreds of lighthouses mark the inland waterways of the United States as well. In the Hudson River Valley of New York, dozens of lighthouses and light beacons, of all different architectural styles, were built between 1826 and 1921.

The purpose of any lighthouse is to offer mariners a visual aid in identifying shorelines and warning of dangerous obstructions in the navigation channel or the approaches to ports. Submerged sandbars (often called shoals), small islands, submerged rocks, shallow areas including marshes, mudflats, rock shelves, and other obstructions were common reasons to install a lighthouse.

Lighthouses can be traced back to the Tower of Pharos, constructed in Alexandria, Egypt, in 300 BC. In the United States, permanent lighthouses were built starting in the 18th century in order to assist mariners in making safe approaches to our colonial ports beginning with Boston, Massachusetts, in 1716. The federal government, through the Treasury Department, assumed responsibility for navigational aids in 1789 and ordered the construction of new lighthouses in the 1790s at key places such as Montauk Point on Long Island to facilitate safe commerce.

Unlike ocean navigation, sailing on the Hudson did not require night sailing or navigation by dead reckoning, with its inherent errors. Sailing on the river was conducted for the most part by experienced local boatmen with intimate knowledge of the river and its conditions and hazards. At night or in inclement weather, sailors simply dropped anchor to wait until safe sailing conditions returned. Although accidents occurred, particularly through the difficult "World's End" stretch of the Hudson Highlands, the loss of life and property paled in comparison to the shocking wrecks along the coast of Long Island and elsewhere on the Atlantic Ocean.

The need for permanent lighthouses on the Hudson River did not become truly apparent until the age of steam. Inventor Robert Fulton and his financial backer Robert Livingston introduced the world's first commercially successful steamboat on the Hudson in 1807, and the technology improved rapidly. Their monopoly was ended by the US Supreme Court in 1824, and competition led to a new generation of steamboats that ran night and day. At the same time, traffic on the river increased exponentially as New York's Erie, Champlain, and Delaware & Hudson Canals were completed, making the Hudson River the chief connection between New York, the Great Lakes Region, Canada, Vermont, and the coal fields of Pennsylvania. Steamboats were big investments. They carried large numbers of passengers and hauled or towed valuable freight and mail. Competition placed a premium on speed. Unlike the smaller and slower sloops and schooners that preceded them, steamboat owners found it profitable to keep running at night. Lighthouses became indispensable in facilitating the safe and profitable operation of these vessels.

The first lighthouses on the Hudson River included small stone towers with cupolas and adjacent keepers' houses placed on rocky prominences. The lighthouse at Stony Point, built by the US Treasury Department in 1826, has survived and represents the period perfectly. Beginning in the late 1820s, a series of two-story lighthouses were built in the river to mark the entrances to important but tricky landings and river channels. Among them were the first lighthouses at Coxsackie (1828), Stuyvesant (also known as Kinderhook Landing, 1829), Four Mile Point (1831), Saugerties (1835), Rondout (1837), and Esopus Meadows (1839). Little is known about this first generation of Hudson River lighthouses, but all appeared to be built along similar lines—symmetrical structures with hipped roofs and birdcage lanterns or cupolas. Evidence suggests that some lighthouses, including the one at Rondout, were wood-framed. Others, such as the one at Stuyvesant, were purportedly made of stone. Four Mile Point lighthouse was an exception to this architectural rule. Built on a high bluff overlooking the Hudson, it resembled more closely the stone tower at Stony Point, likely because it was located on land. Except for Stony Point, none of these original structures remain, as their simple stone foundations were susceptible to ice damage and all were replaced within a few decades of construction.

First-generation lighthouse lanterns were fueled by whale oil and used brass- or silver-plated copper reflectors with multiple lamps to provide a large diameter beam. A group of reflectors was arranged on a triangular or square framework, rotated by a geared clockwork drive. These early lanterns provided light equaling about 10 candles each and required much maintenance. Wicks had to be trimmed, glass chimneys cleaned of soot, reflectors polished, and lantern room glass kept clean both inside and out. Lamp oil was topped off each night, and spare lamps were filled and kept at the ready.

For the first several decades of the new United States, all lighthouse keepers throughout the country were direct appointments by the president, leading to competition for appointments that some viewed as "cushy" or desirable. By the mid-19th century, most lighthouse keeper positions were professionalizing and the high turnover common in the early days of Hudson River lighthouses had largely stabilized, with dedicated keepers staying on for years and sometimes decades.

In 1852, Congress established the US Lighthouse Board within the Treasury Department and purchased two Fresnel lenses from Europe. Developed by French physicist Augustin Fresnel in 1822, these lenses up to six feet high were widely used along the French coastline and later in England. The barrel-shaped lenses used multiple glass prisms and convex surfaces to direct and concentrate light from a single high-intensity lamp placed in the center of the lens. Clockwork mechanisms were improved to accommodate the increased weight of the glass and brass structure, allowing it to rotate safely. Weights would fall the length of the tower on a cord attached to a drum near the lens. The mechanism would have to be wound every four to six hours, longer for taller towers, to maintain the revolving beam of light. All lighthouses throughout the country, including on the Hudson, were assigned a unique flash caused by the beam or multiple beams. By counting the number of seconds between flashes, boatmen could identify the lighthouses from a distance and know their location on the river.

With the discovery of petroleum and the subsequent availability of kerosene, lighthouses began to phase out the use of whale oil. Although it was preferred by many, whale oil was much more expensive than kerosene. In addition, fog horns and bells began to be adopted in large part due to the proliferation of fog-related boat accidents. In the early days, these signals were horns blown by mouth, or bells rung by hand. Later, fog bells and horns were automated by the same crank-style winding mechanism used to rotate the lanterns.

Following the Civil War, the appointment of lighthouse keepers was switched from the president to the US Lighthouse Board, likely due to the dramatic increase in lighthouses throughout the country. It was difficult for a single person to appoint hundreds of people around the country, and the need for a professional class of keepers was growing with marine traffic. With this professionalization came rules and uniforms, with lighthouse keepers required to keep detailed records, affect rescues, and act as role models in their local communities.

As the first generation of lighthouses from the 1830s succumbed to ice damage and rot, they were replaced in the 1860s and 1870s with a new design of lighthouse. Designed to resist ice, these lighthouses were typically built on stone foundations above wooden platforms and dense fields of pilings below the mud line. In some instances, as many as 400 pilings were driven 50 feet into the sediment in order to support the massive foundation stones. Most of the lighthouse structures from 1865 to 1870 were built from the same plans—a unique Italian Villa–style structure constructed in an L-shape wrapped around a central tower. Stuyvesant, Coxsackie, Saugerties, and the second Rondout lighthouses were all built from these same plans, although they used different local materials for construction. Later plans in the 1870s included a Second Empire style with a mansard roof—both Esopus Meadows and Hudson-Athens are variations on the Second Empire theme. Using the same architectural plans for all lighthouses built within a certain time frame became common throughout the country, and many lighthouses have "sister" lights located hundreds of miles away.

Lighthouses on the Hudson River were built for a variety of reasons, but the most common reason was to warn mariners away from natural obstacles in the navigation channel, such as islands, shallow marshy areas, and hidden shoals. Some, such as Rockland Lake, Rondout, Saugerties, and Hudson, also marked major boat landings or port cities.

Perhaps the most unusual aid to navigation on the Hudson River is the Statue of Liberty. Soon after its completion in 1886, the US Lighthouse Board struggled with its assignment to make the statue serve as an aid to navigation. Several different attempts were made to light the statue at night, until two rows of portholes were cut in the torch itself and lit. In 1892, the torch was further modified as the portholes were replaced with banks of glass windows and a flame-colored skylight installed. The statue served as a lighthouse from its completion in 1886 until 1902, when its use as a lighthouse was discontinued, and the statue and its island were transferred to the War Department and, later, the National Park Service. The statue's iconic torch seemed a natural fit as a lighthouse, but when it was restored in 1986, the existing glass-paned torch was replaced with a windowless gilded copper torch as outlined in Bartholdi's original design.

In addition to the substantial, live-in lighthouses, a number of other beacons were developed throughout the 19th century. The most prevalent was the stake-light (also known as "post light")—a tall wooden pole that allowed a large oil lantern to be raised to the top via a pulley system, much like a flag pole. Similar "portable beacons" were often built on small stone or brick foundations. These beacon lights generally marked hooks, shoals, islands, and artificial dikes near but not within the navigation channel. The majority of these were constructed in the latter half of the 19th century and, by the 1930s, were largely gone.

Starting in the 1860s, the Army Corps of Engineers began what would become a decades-long undertaking to "improve" the navigational channel in the Hudson River and mitigate flooding from spring freshets and damage from ice dams. Starting with dredging and the construction of breakwater jetties at ports like Saugerties and Rondout, by the end of the century, the corps was working to construct dikes to mitigate flooding, deepen the channel, and "shave off" various hooks and other outcroppings in the river. Excess sediment from dredging was used to fill in the narrow channels of islands close to shore, combine smaller islands into larger ones, build up marshy areas, or shore up breakwater jetties. As islands were combined and the navigation channel otherwise reshaped, the need for stake lights and even lighthouses was lessened.

The evidence of these "lost" lights and lighthouses is scant. Very few photographs of stake lights remain. Demolished structures are survived by only a few photographs. For the very earliest generation of lighthouses, most pre-date photography itself, and we must rely upon paintings of the period and a very special document. In 1847, Wade & Croomes published their *Panorama of the Hudson River: From New York to Albany*—a line drawing of the entire shore of the Hudson River, both western and eastern sides. Panoramas were popular with tourists, and the earliest versions were one continuous length of paper rolled onto a scroll with the eastern shore on the top and the western shore (upside down) on the bottom. The user would merely flip the image to change perspective. Later versions, like the 1847 *Panorama*, were published in booklet form. These panoramas depicted ports, steamboat landings, businesses, landmarks of interest, and most importantly for this book, lighthouses. Panoramas continued to be produced into the 1910s, with the first photographic panorama, the Bryant Literary Union's panorama of the Hudson, produced in 1888. The 1847 publication is among the earliest that survives, allowing us a glimpse of what those early lighthouses looked like.

For the stake lights and other lighthouses built in subsequent years, little evidence exists outside of maps. Many structures on navigational maps referred to as "lighthouses" were likely just beacons or stake lights, but without visual evidence, the record is not always clear. Some of the "lost" lighthouses are known to researchers only because they are listed on a map as a "lighthouse," or "L.H." No other references, including newspaper articles, appear to exist. The terminology used in the 19th and even early 20th century also appears to lack consistency, as some structures which we know to be stake lights are referred to as "lighthouses" on maps.

In 1910, the lighthouse branch of the Treasury Department, variously referred to as the Lighthouse Establishment, the Lighthouse Board, and the Lighthouse Service, was reorganized into the Bureau of Lighthouses. In 1939, the Bureau of Lighthouses was subsumed by the US Coast Guard, and by the 1950s, most Hudson River lighthouses were electrified and fully automated. In addition, new tools such as radar, LORAN, and GPS revolutionized safe and accurate navigation and in many ways have made lighthouses nearly obsolete. From the 1930s through the 1950s, many Hudson River lighthouses were torn down and replaced with "skeleton" lights of steel scaffolding, often mounted on the original stone foundations.

In the 1960s, historic preservation became institutionalized in government, and the preservation of lighthouses for their picturesque qualities and rich historical associations became desirable and practical. Of the over two dozen lighthouses and beacons that once lined the shores of the Hudson, just eight remain.

We tend to have a romanticized view of lighthouses and imagine the idyllic lives of the keepers and their families. Life at these stations could, however, be harsh and dangerous. There was significant and continuous labor in maintaining these facilities, trimming lamps, cleaning lenses and windows, hauling oil from the dock to the tower, winding rotating mechanisms, sounding bells and foghorns, maintaining other navigational aids, performing rescues, and keeping records. Provisions arrived by boat and keepers and their families often resorted to small boats to send messages or obtain supplies even in bad weather. Keepers and their families sometimes lost their lives to inclement weather (including floods and ice dams), failed rescue attempts, and the general danger of constantly being around deep and fast-moving water.

The iconography of lighthouses remains compelling today, despite the harsh realities of the past. Whether recalling bygone years of more graceful waterborne transportation or reminding us of the once-teeming industrial shipping on the river, lighthouses evoke a longing for a life bound by wind, time, and tide. We can count ourselves lucky that so many of these fascinating structures remain.

One

New York Harbor

New York Harbor remains today one of the busiest in the world, but throughout the 19th century, it rose in both prominence and traffic. Lighthouses line the shores of Long Island and Northern New Jersey, but only a few exist within the confines of New York Harbor itself. For the purposes of this book, we have defined New York Harbor as existing between the Verrazzano-Narrows and George Washington Bridges. Perhaps the reader wonders why New York Harbor is included in a book of Hudson River lighthouses—it is because the harbor is the mouth of the Hudson, and New York City is the ultimate destination of many of the river's passenger steamboats and freight barges.

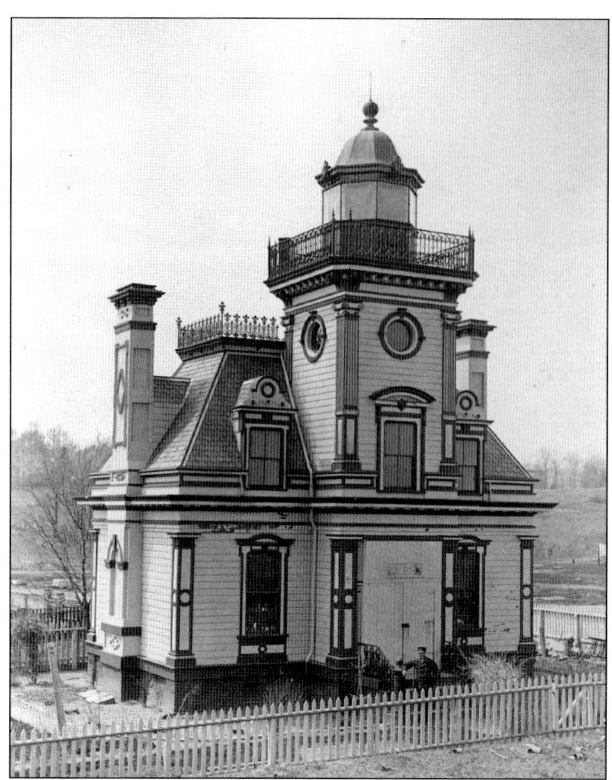

First built in 1828, a 40-foot tower at Fort Tompkins marked the Narrows. It stood in various states of repair until the 1860s, when nearby artillery practice damaged the lantern glass. In 1873, a striking new lighthouse (pictured) was constructed. It served as a lighthouse for the Narrows until 1903, when it was replaced and later destroyed. In 1864, Fort Tompkins and Battery Weed were consolidated as Fort Wadsworth. (NARA.)

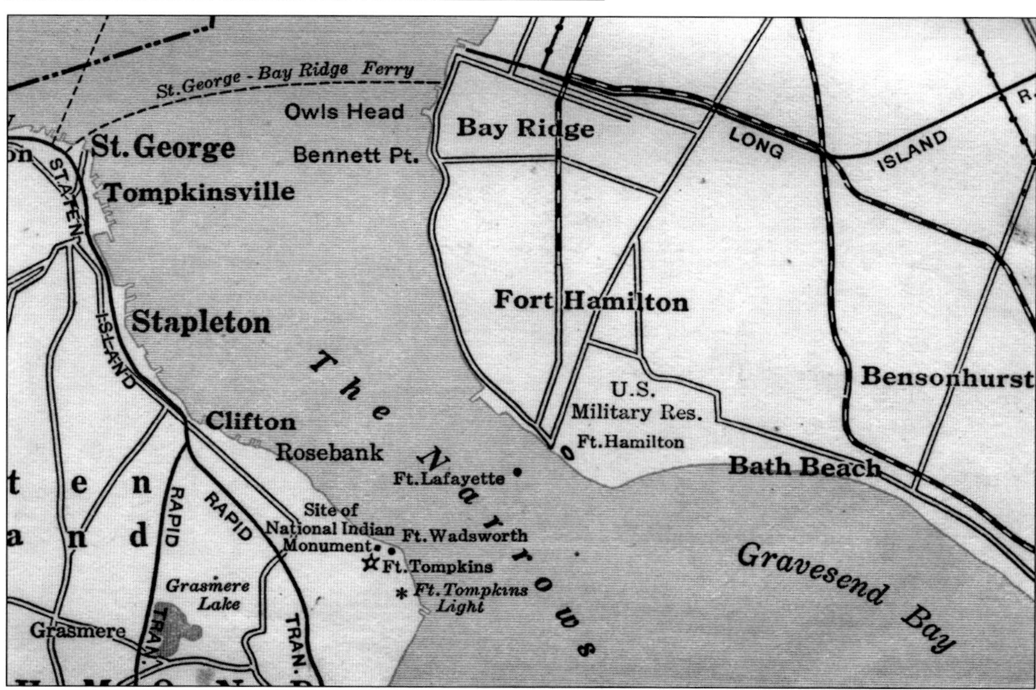

This map is from 1924, before the construction of the Verrazzano-Narrows Bridge. The Fort Tompkins light is shown at the point of the Narrows, entering New York Bay. Fort Wadsworth is just to the north. (HRMM.)

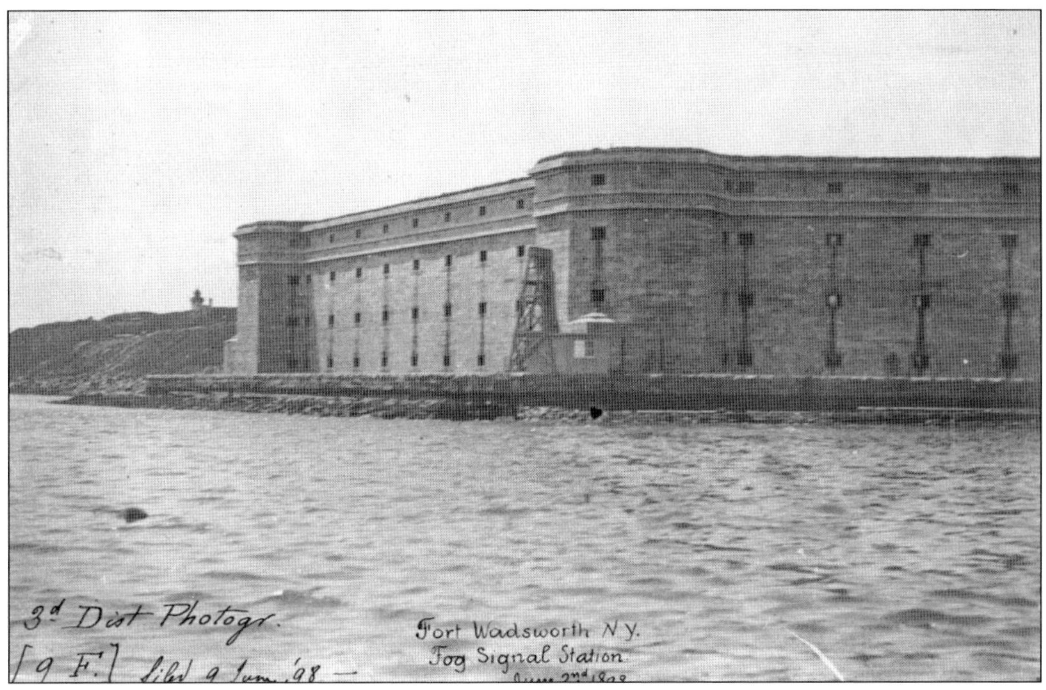

In 1892, the US Lighthouse Board reported that the Fort Tompkins lighthouse was too far back from the shore for adequate navigation. A fog bell (above) was added to Battery Weed in 1898 with William Boyle as its keeper. In 1903, a lighthouse (below) was constructed atop the battery, and the fog bell moved up to the light station. When the Verrazzano-Narrows Bridge was completed in 1964, the light became obsolete and was decommissioned. In 1995, Fort Wadsworth came under the ownership of the National Park Service. In the early 2000s, with NPS approval, the derelict lighthouse was restored and relit by volunteers in 2005. (NARA.)

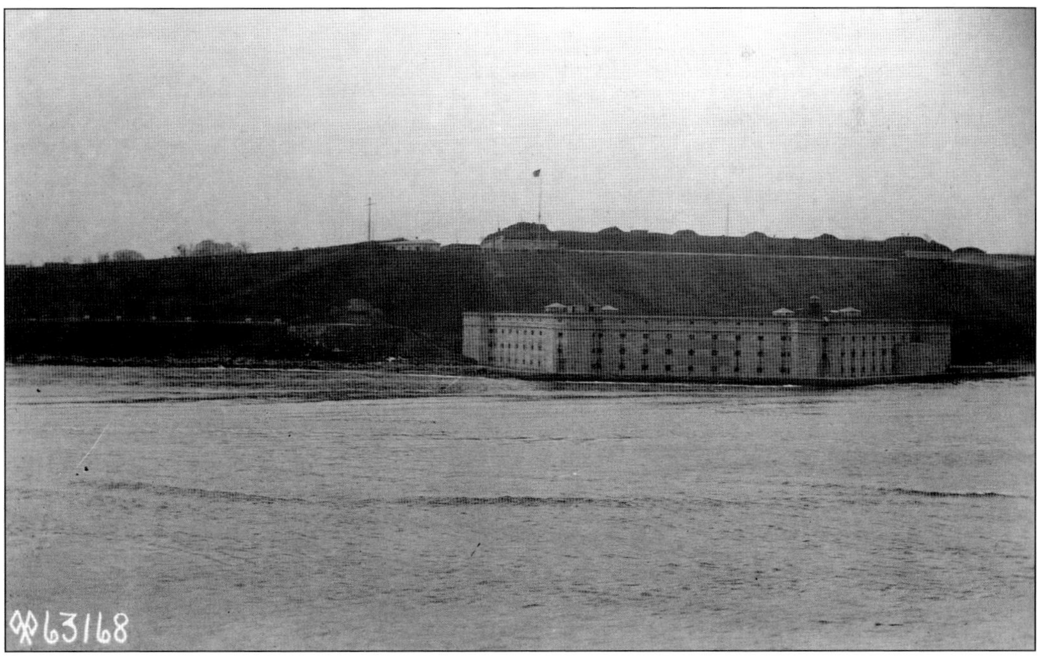

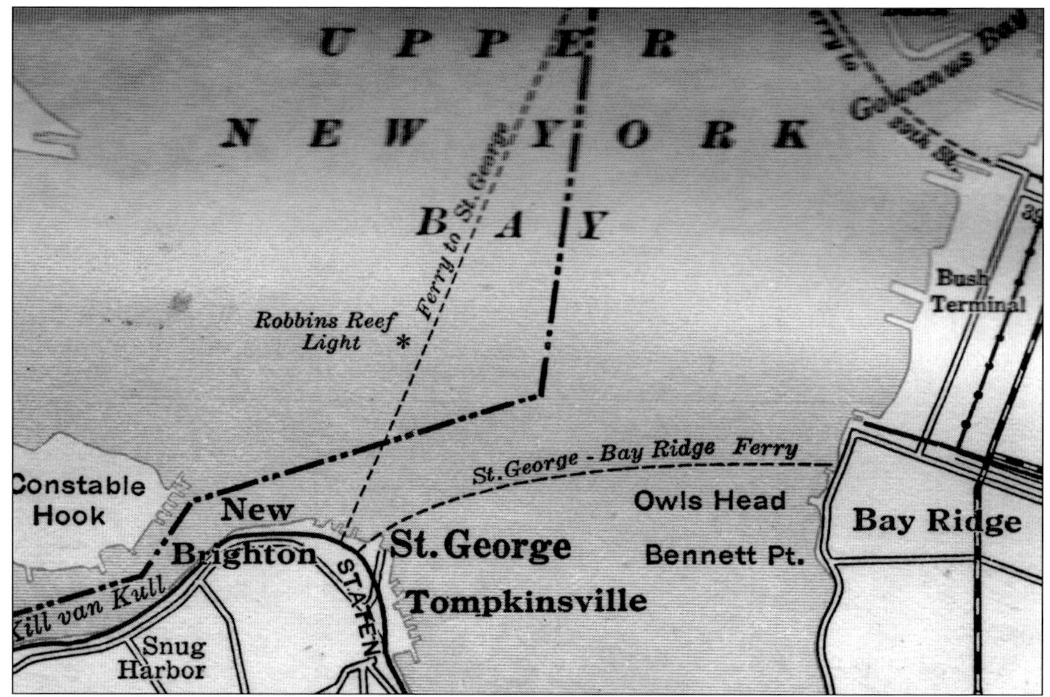

Robbins Reef Lighthouse was built in 1839 to mark the dangerous reef between Staten Island's north shore and Bedloe's Island. Note its proximity to ferry crossings and regular transport through New York Bay. No known images of this early lighthouse survive. It likely resembled other early Hudson River lighthouses. (HRMM.)

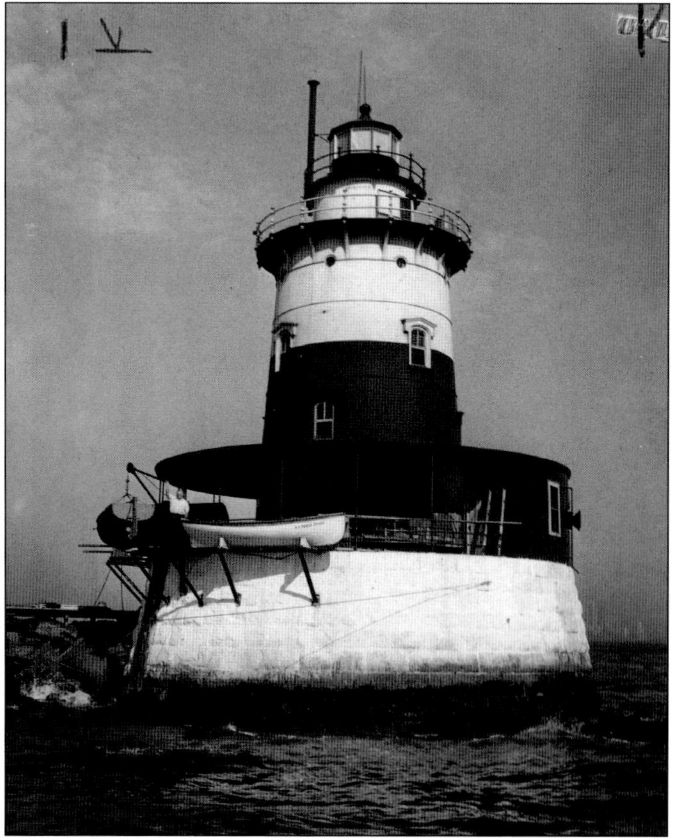

The 1830s Robbins Reef Lighthouse was replaced in 1883 with a cast iron sparkplug. The lighthouse is most famous for its female keeper Katherine Walker, who kept the light from 1890 until 1919, when her son took over as keeper. This image from the 1950s features a US Coast Guardsman on duty. The Robbins Reef Lighthouse remains today. (LOC.)

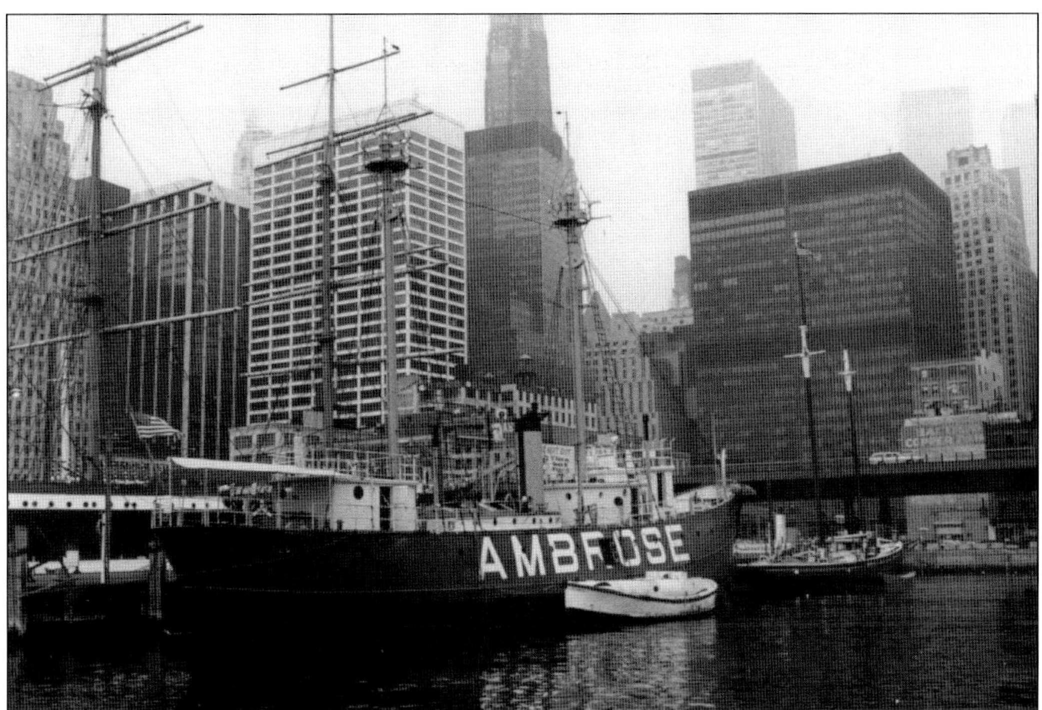

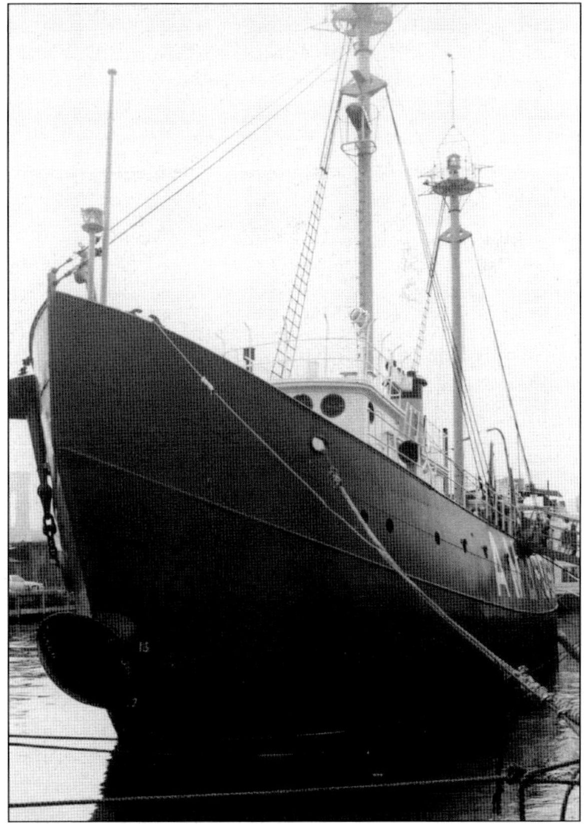

Although not technically a lighthouse, US lightship *Ambrose* (LV-87) was built in 1907 to mark the Ambrose Channel off of Sandy Hook, New Jersey, on the approach to New York Harbor. Lightships are designed to serve as lighthouses in areas where the waters are too deep or treacherous to build a permanent structure. The lights are mounted on their masts and the ships anchored where needed. *Ambrose* was in service from 1908 to 1966. She served in New York's Ambrose Channel until 1932, before being refitted with a diesel engine and sent to other posts. Upon being decommissioned in 1966, she was converted to a museum ship and, in 1989, declared a national historic landmark. These images are from her landmark nomination. She remains open to the public in New York Harbor today. (Both, NARA.)

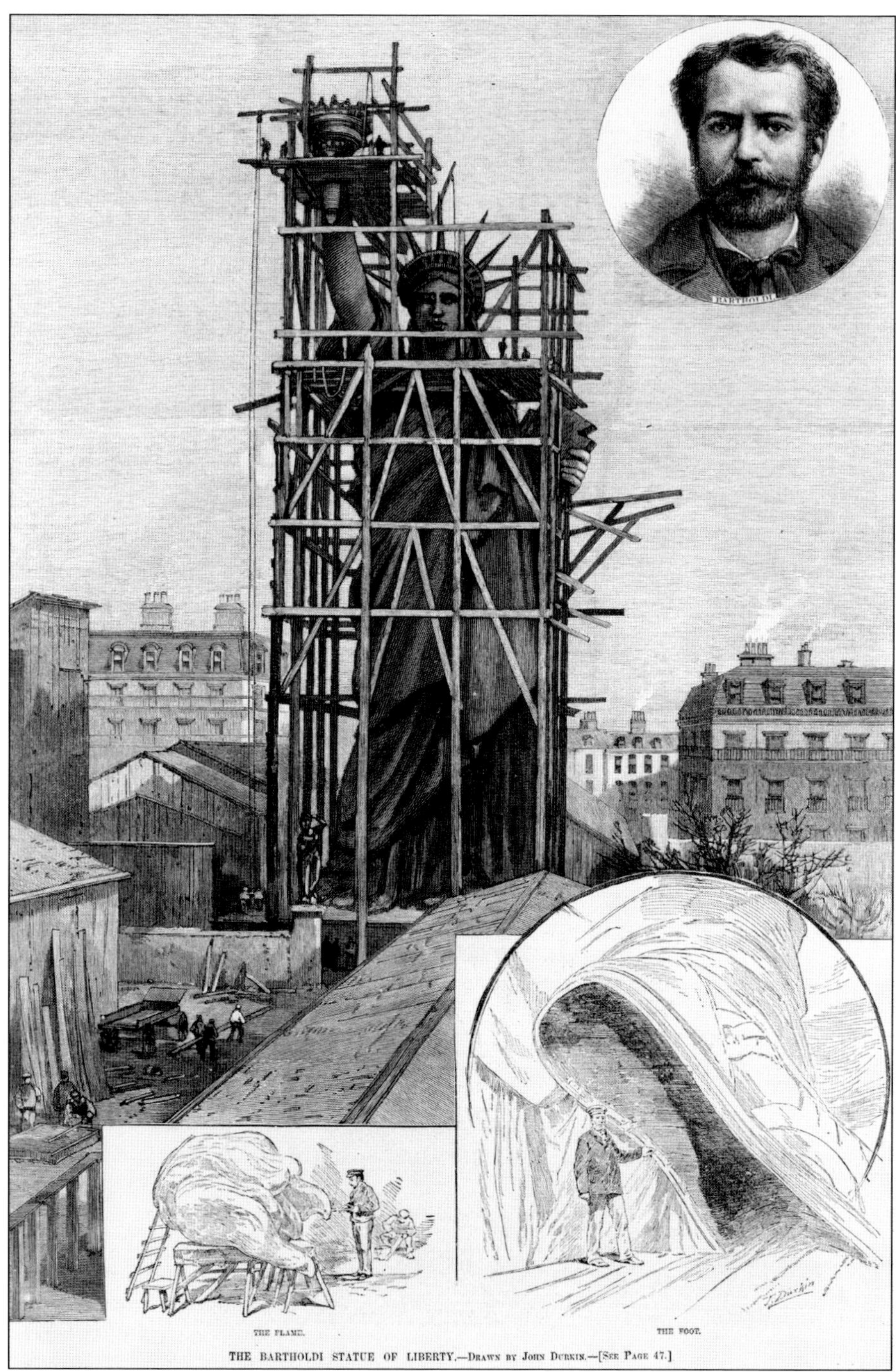

The idea of a monument to the United States from France was first conceived in 1865. By 1875, French sculptor Frederic Auguste Bartholdi had been commissioned to build what would become the Statue of Liberty, called "Colossus" at the time. Intended to be completed for the 1876 American centennial celebrations, the United States was to be responsible for the construction of the pedestal and France for the statue. Unfortunately, the funds for such a huge undertaking were lacking in both countries. This drawing by John Durkin appeared in *Harper's Weekly* in 1884. (LOC.)

By the time the Centennial Exhibition in Philadelphia, Pennsylvania, arrived in 1876, only the hand and torch of the Colossus had been completed, seen here on display at the exhibition. Events like this were used to raise funds. American newspaper magnate Joseph Pulitzer, in particular, railed against those who did not donate in support of the pedestal construction. His critique helped spur donations, and the pedestal, made of Rosendale cement faced in granite, was completed in April 1886. (LOC.)

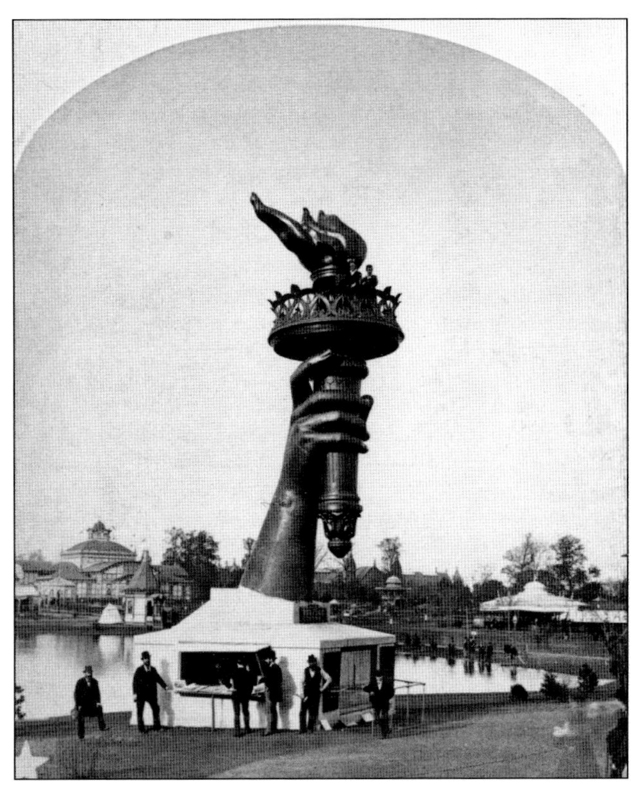

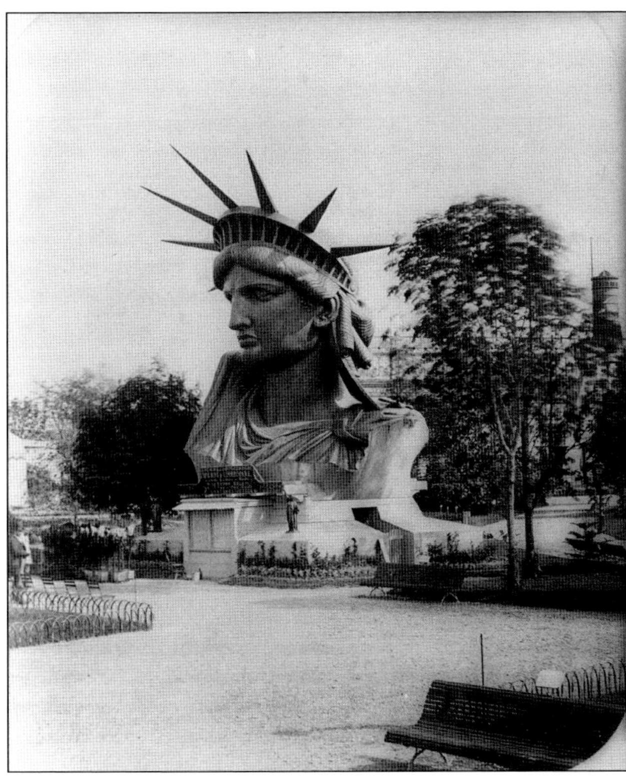

Fundraising efforts were continuing in France as well. Here, the head of the Statue of Liberty is on display in a public park in Paris in 1883. That same year, Emma Lazarus published the poem "The New Colossus" to help with fundraising. The statue was completed in France in 1884 and arrived in New York Harbor in 1885. (LOC.)

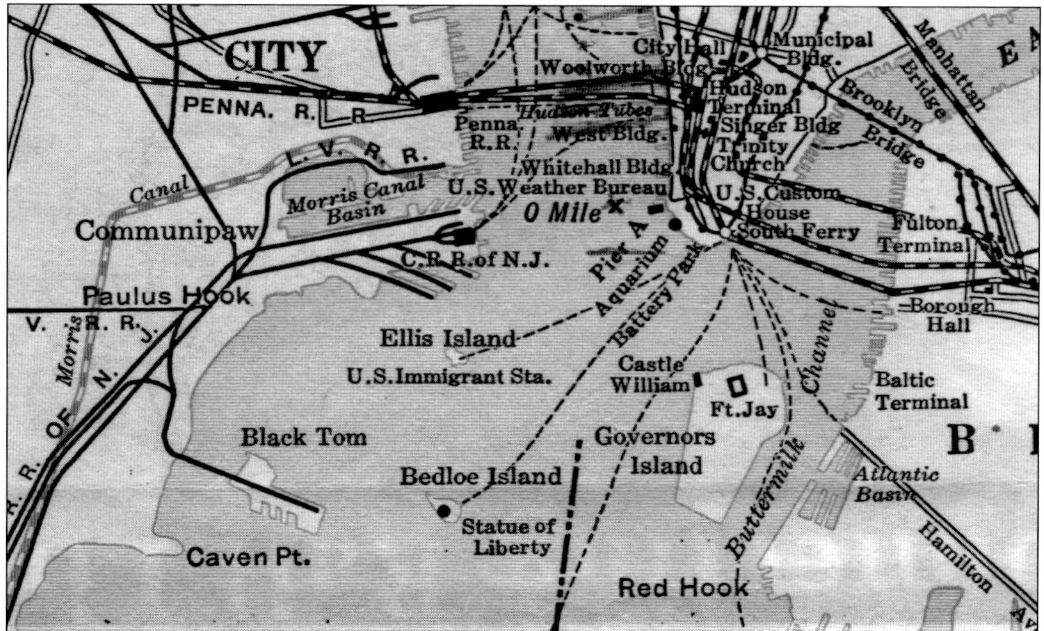

Reassembled in just four months near Fort Wood on Bedloe's Island, near the center of New York Harbor, the statue was dedicated by Pres. Grover Cleveland in 1886, ten years after her original proposed completion date. (HRMM.)

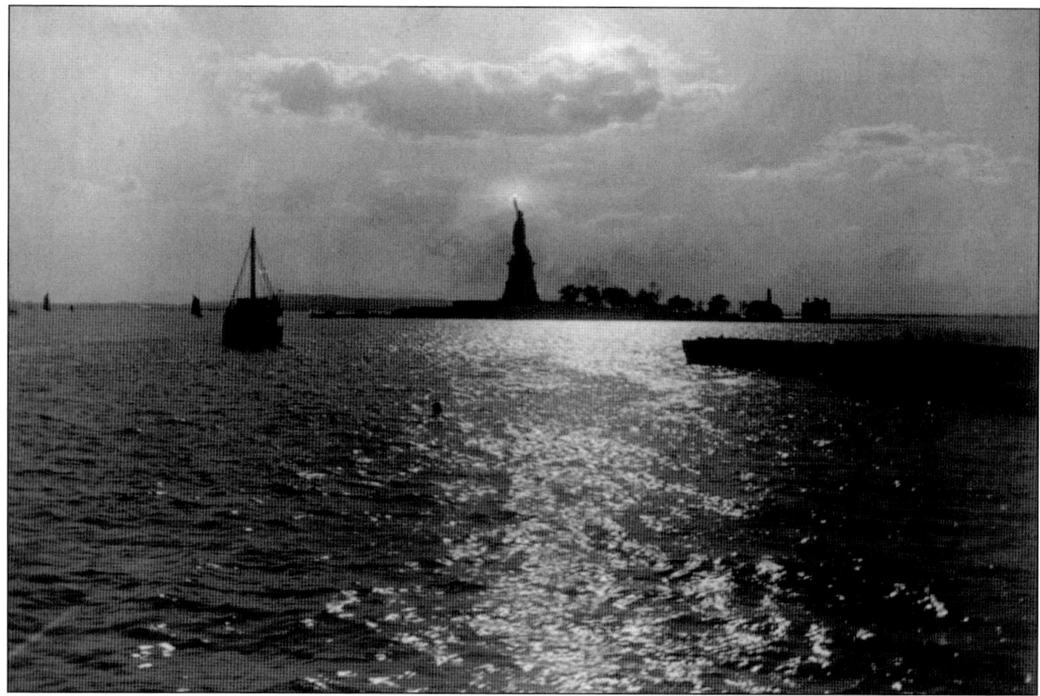

The statue, seen here at night with her torch alight in the 1890s, quickly became an icon of New York City. Although a number of schemes to light the new landmark were under discussion throughout construction, following the October 1886 opening celebrations, portholes were cut in the torch to accommodate electric lights—the first electrically lit lighthouse in the country. (LOC.)

In 1892, a horizontal series of plate glass windows were cut into the torch and a skylight with flame-colored glass installed for a fiery effect. The Statue of Liberty was an official lighthouse under the operation of the US Lighthouse Board (with upwards of four keepers and assistant keepers at a time) until 1901, when she was turned over to the War Department. Lighthouse operations ceased in 1902. (LOC.)

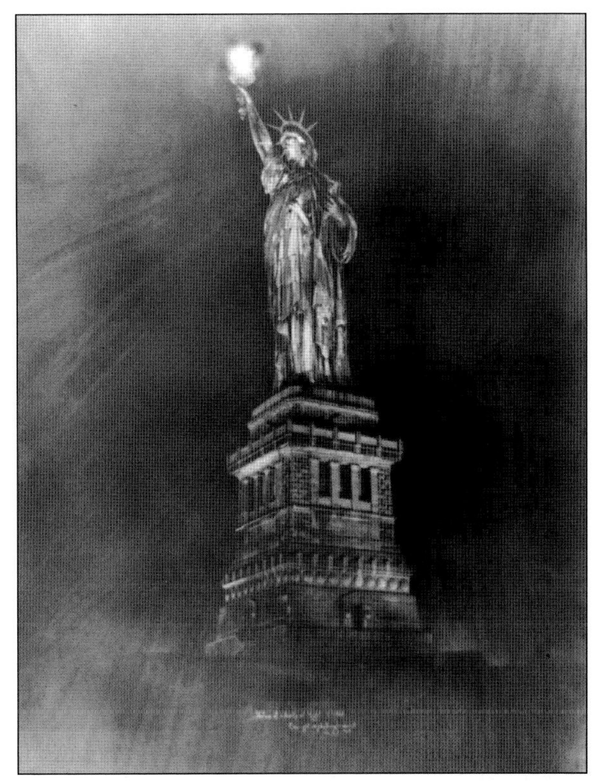

In 1903, Emma Lazarus's poem was added to the pedestal, and in 1924, the Statue of Liberty, and the fort she stood on, became a national monument. In 1933, she was transferred to the National Park Service. In this remarkable photograph from 1905, the Statue of Liberty faces the entrance to the harbor, looking east toward France, welcoming all to one of the greatest ports in the world. (LOC.)

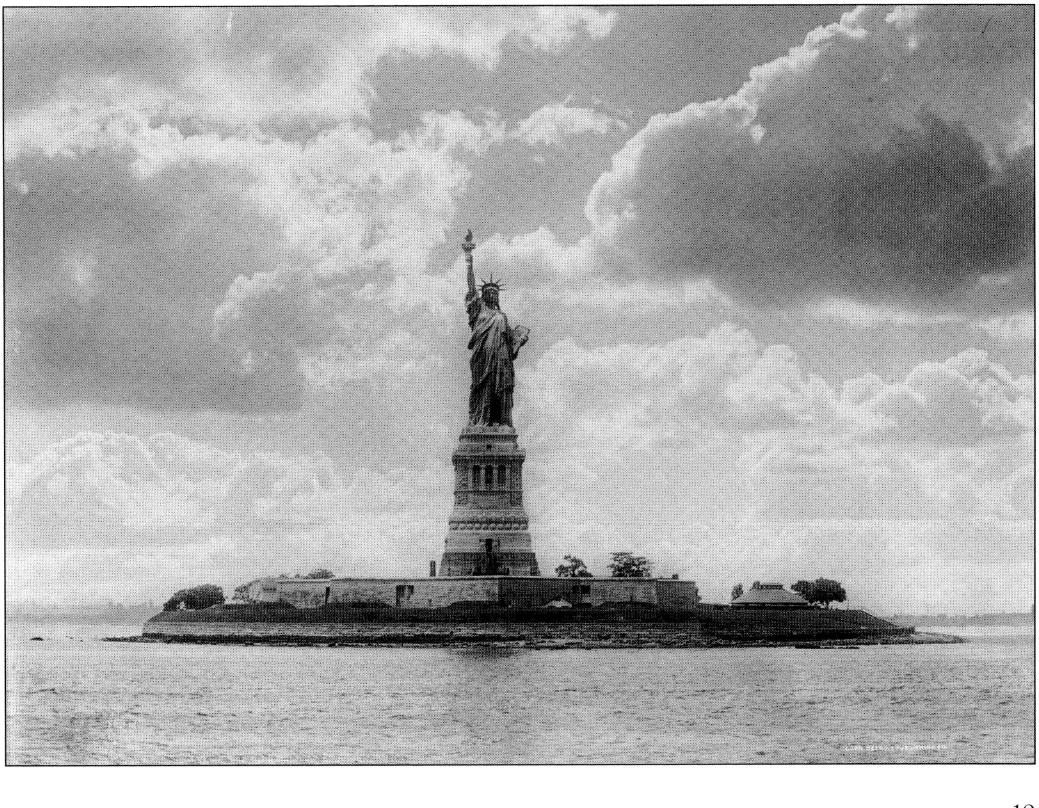

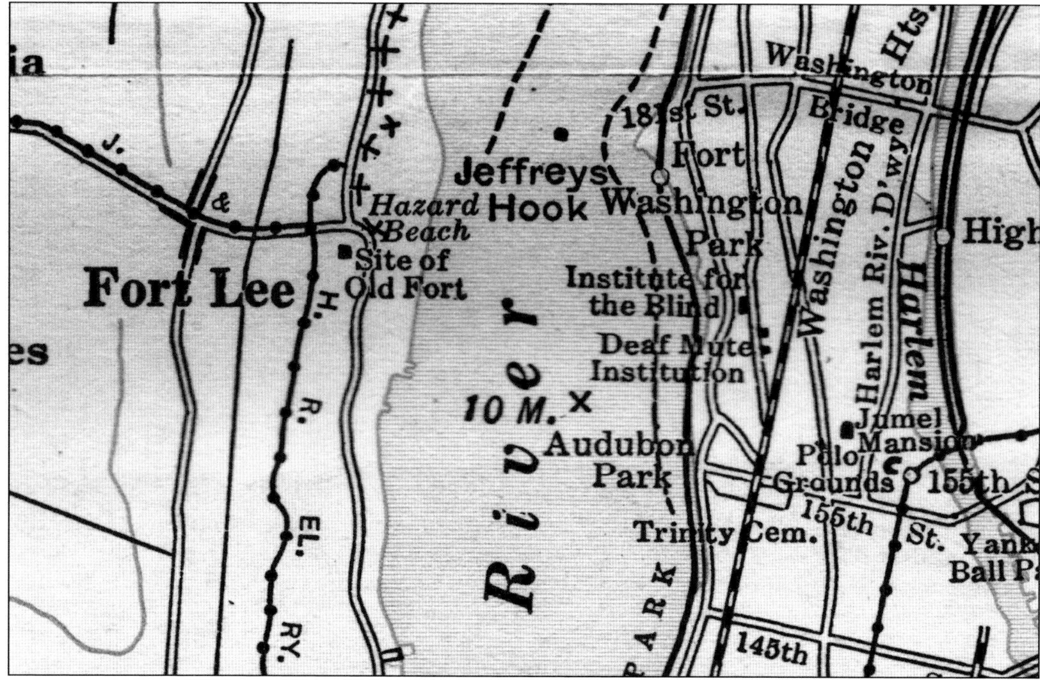

The navigation channel up the Hudson River shore of Manhattan is relatively obstruction-free, with one exception. Jeffrey's Hook is a spit of land that juts out into the river where Fort Washington once stood. In 1889, a fixed red light on a black post was installed there to warn mariners away from the hook, which was close to the navigation channel. (HRMM.)

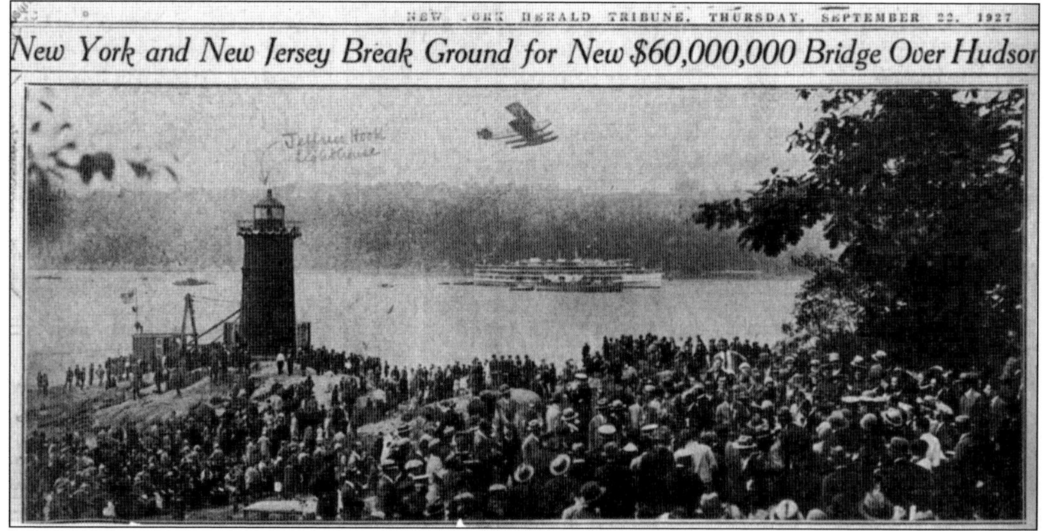

THURSDAY, SEPTEMBER 22, 1927

New York and New Jersey Break Ground for New $60,000,000 Bridge Over Hudson

In 1921, a red spark-plug lighthouse was installed at Jeffrey's Hook. Interestingly, the lighthouse itself had previously been in use since 1880 at Sandy Hook, but was disassembled in 1917 and placed in storage until it was installed at Jeffrey's Hook. In 1927, a new bridge connecting Fort Lee, New Jersey, to Washington Heights in New York City was proposed. This newspaper clipping features the Jeffrey's Hook lighthouse. (NARA.)

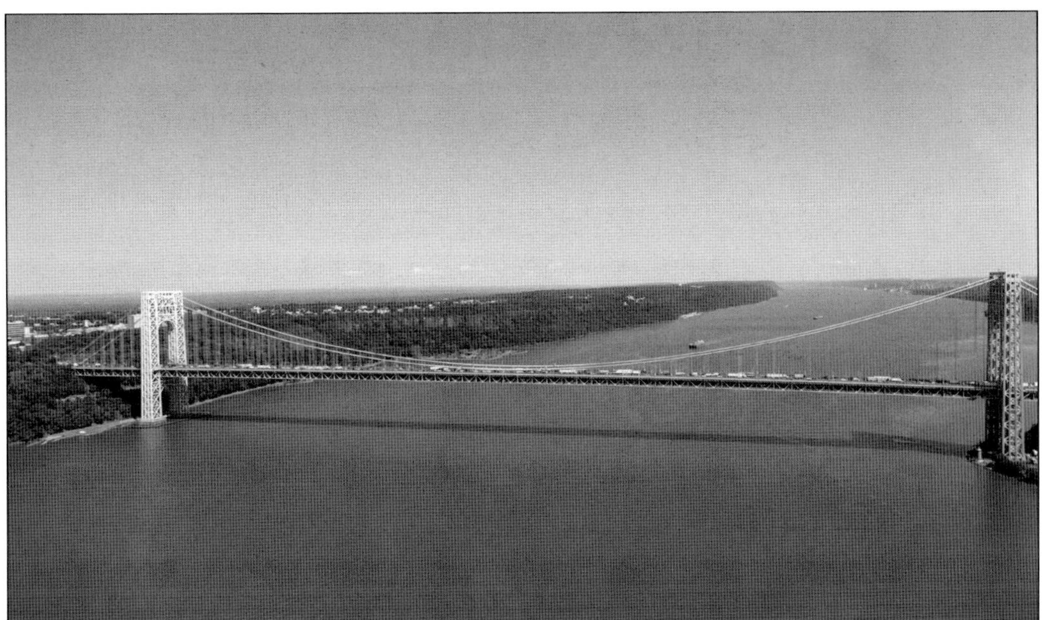

Completed in 1931, the George Washington Bridge both dwarfed the Jeffrey's Hook lighthouse and made it obsolete. In this image from 2017, the Jeffrey's Hook lighthouse can barely be seen under the bridge at right. Although the light was designed as a family light, the keeper did not live onsite as the lights were battery-powered electric. In 1948, the US Coast Guard decommissioned the light, and the lantern went dark. (LOC.)

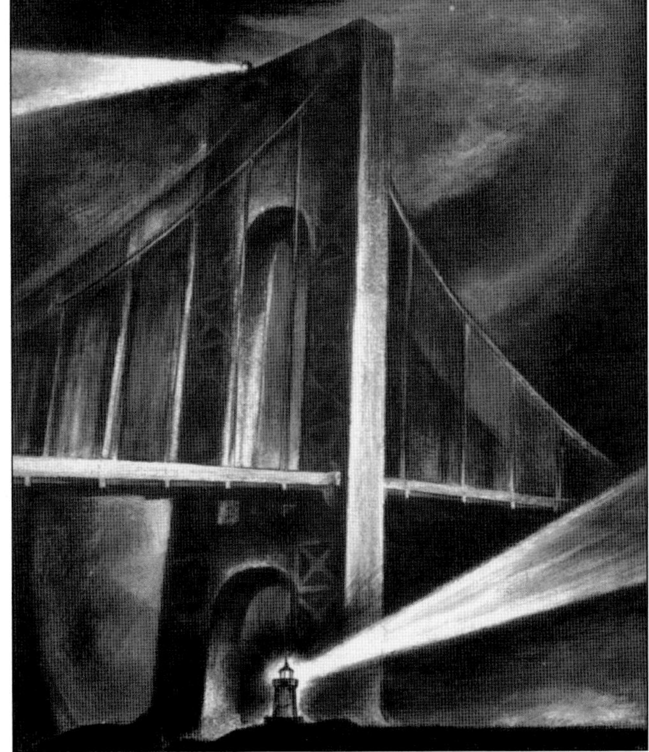

Just a few years earlier, in 1942, a children's book entitled *The Little Red Lighthouse and the Great Gray Bridge* was published by Hildegarde Swift, with illustrations by Lynd Ward. Telling the tale of the intrepid lighthouse that thought it was useless in the shadow of the bridge but ends up saving the day, the book won the hearts of countless children. When the Coast Guard proposed selling the lighthouse, children and adults alike wrote letters and sent money to help save the beloved "Little Red." This illustration is by Lynd Ward. (LOC.)

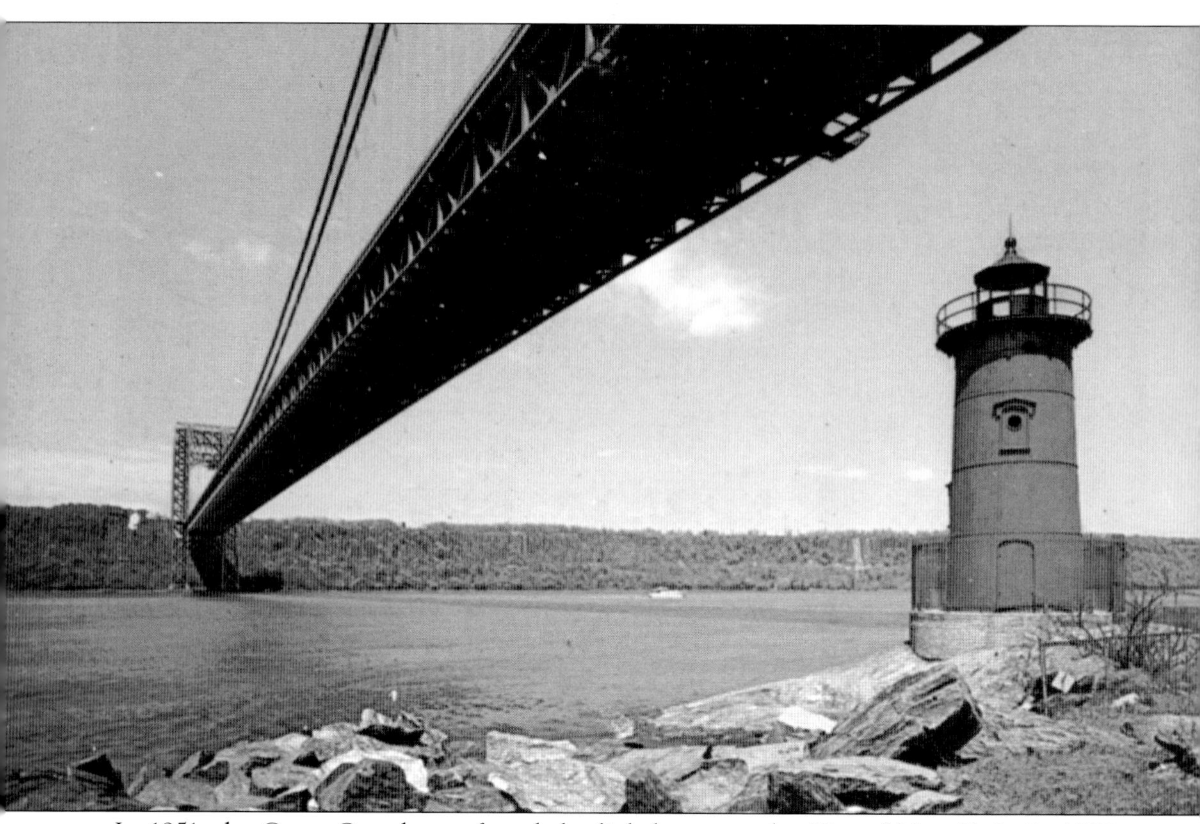

In 1951, the Coast Guard transferred the lighthouse to the City of New York. In 1979, it was listed in the National Register of Historic Places and is a part of Fort Washington Park today. (HRMM.)

Two

TAPPAN ZEE

The Tappan Zee is the widest part of the Hudson River, located north of New York City. The name comes from the Dutch, who named the "sea" after the indigenous Tappan tribe who lived along its banks. When Henry Hudson reached this stretch of the river, nearly three miles across, he thought he had found the Northwest Passage. Just a few miles north, however, the river narrows considerably through the Hudson Highlands. Flanked by the cliffs of the Palisades to the west, the Tappan Zee is relatively free of natural obstructions. The three lighthouses listed in this chapter were all constructed in the late 19th century as steamboat traffic increased. As steamboats got bigger, their drafts also got deeper, making shoals and other formerly passed-over underwater obstacles more of a problem. Only the Sleepy Hollow Lighthouse (formerly the Tarrytown Lighthouse) remains today.

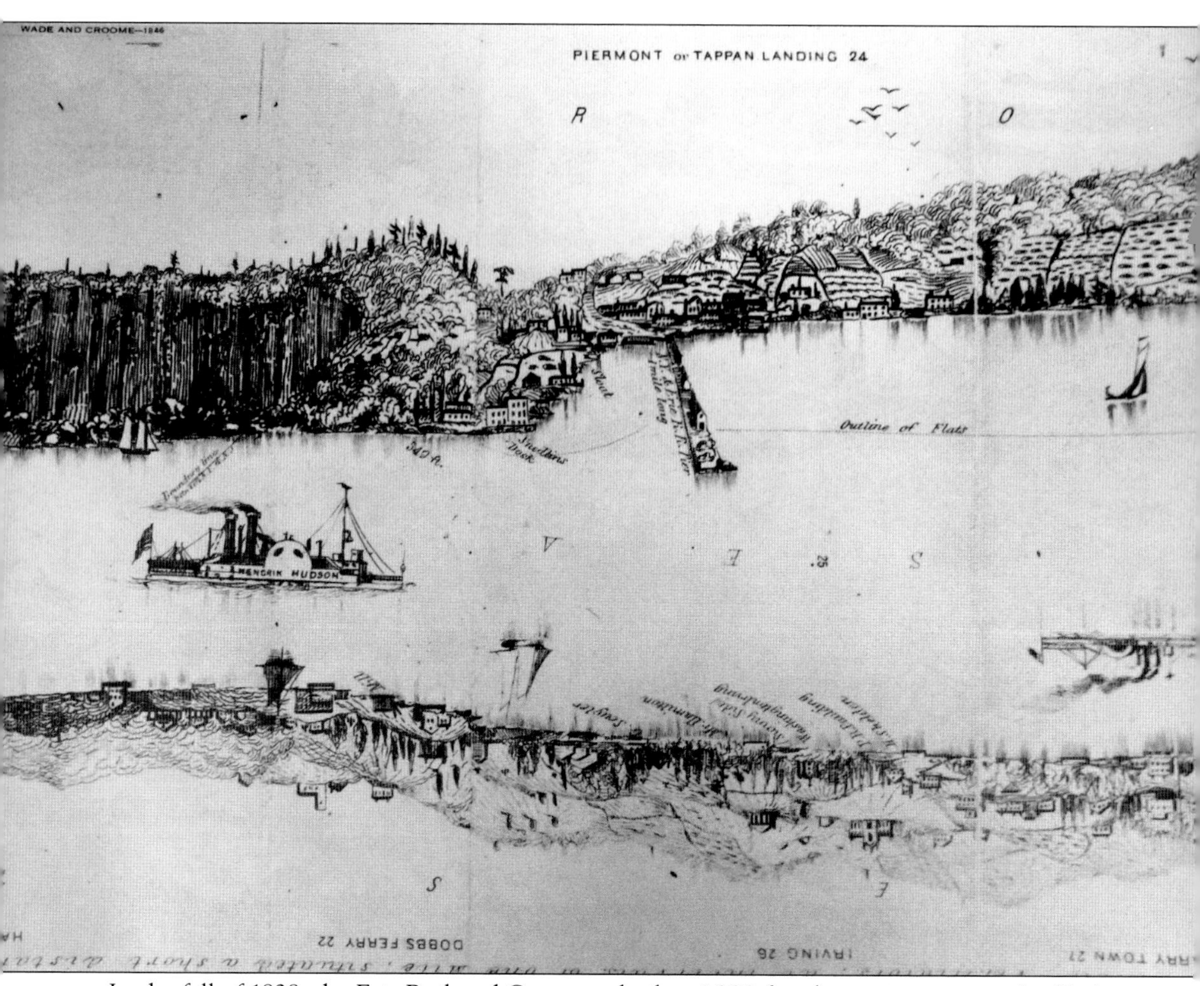

In the fall of 1838, the Erie Railroad Company built a 4,000-foot-long pier out into the Hudson at what would become known as Piermont. The railroad had failed to receive permission from the State of New Jersey to continue the railroad across state lines, and so the pier was built for passengers to complete the last leg of the journey to New York City by steamboat. The long pier bypassed the shallow shoreline, allowing steamboats to approach even at low tide. (NPL.)

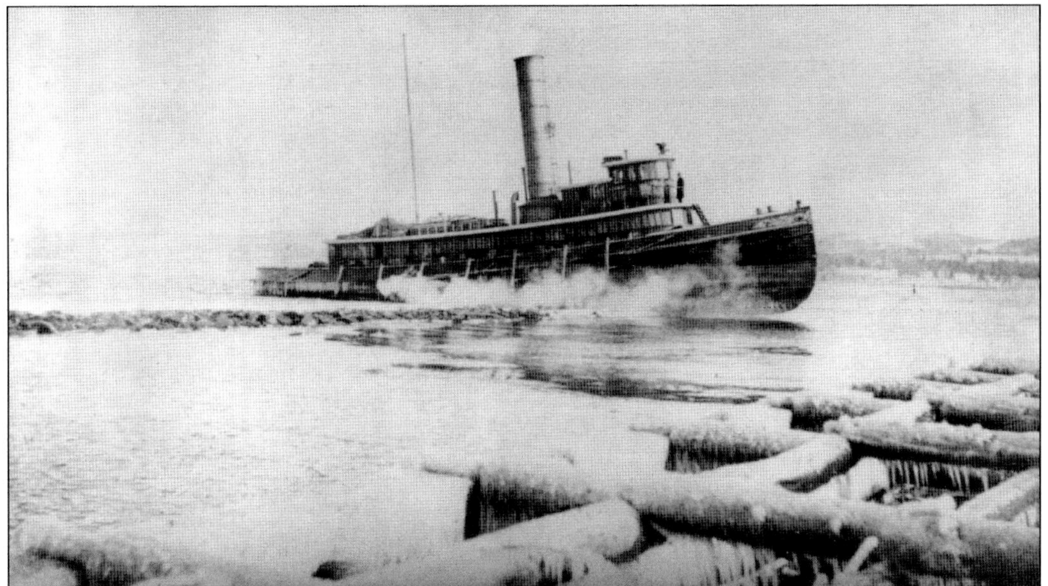

In 1903, the Cornell Steamboat Company tug *Osceola* was heading up the Hudson when, off of Yonkers, a heavy snowstorm with high winds set in. Feeling their way through the storm by listening for echoes of their steam whistle, the captain and pilot started to round the bend near what they thought was Irvington. A slight jolt and a list to port told them otherwise, and they could not back off of what they had hit. By morning, the snow cleared, and they found themselves hung up on the old Erie Railroad pier at Piermont. (HRMM.)

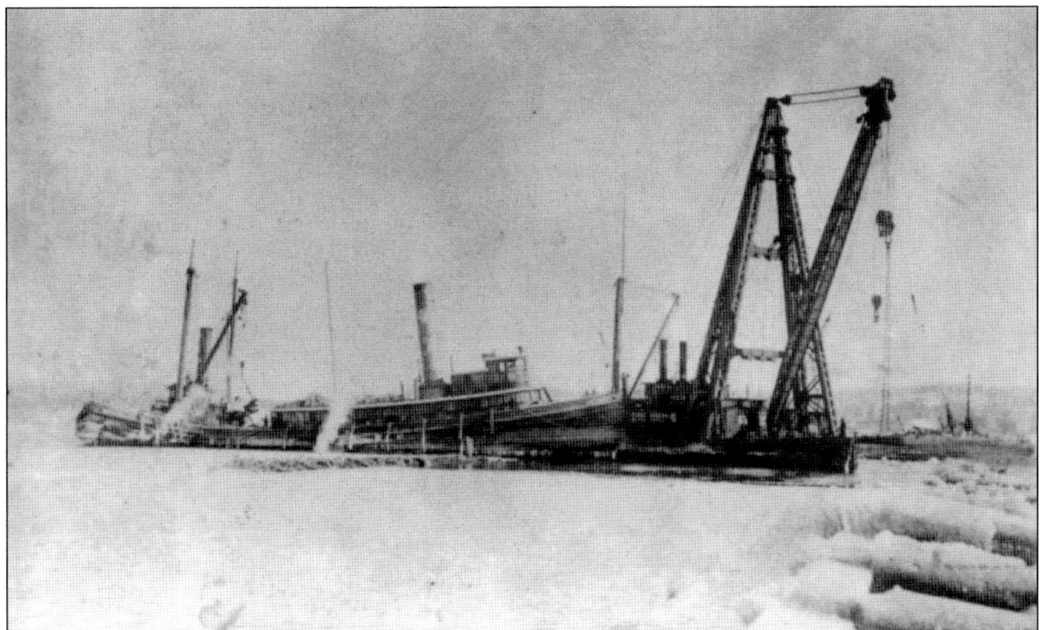

Osceola was hung up on the pier for two weeks until a crane barge from the Merrit & Chapman Derrick & Wrecking Company could be brought in to lift her off. The damage was minimal, and the *Osceola* continued towing until 1929. (HRMM.)

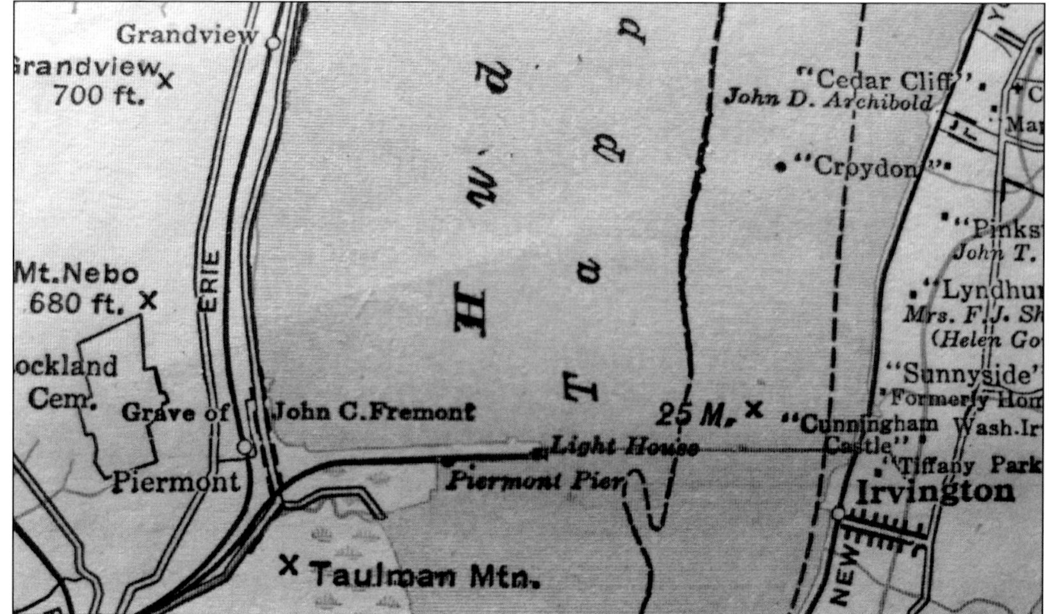

Although a new Erie Railroad line was installed in the 1860s to Jersey City, Piermont Pier continued to be used for local freight access. On a number of maps, including this one from 1923, a "Light House" is marked at the end of the pier. Whether this was an actual lighthouse or a simple beacon is unclear, but it is likely that the *Osceola* played a role in the installation of some kind of aid to navigation on the pier. (HRMM.)

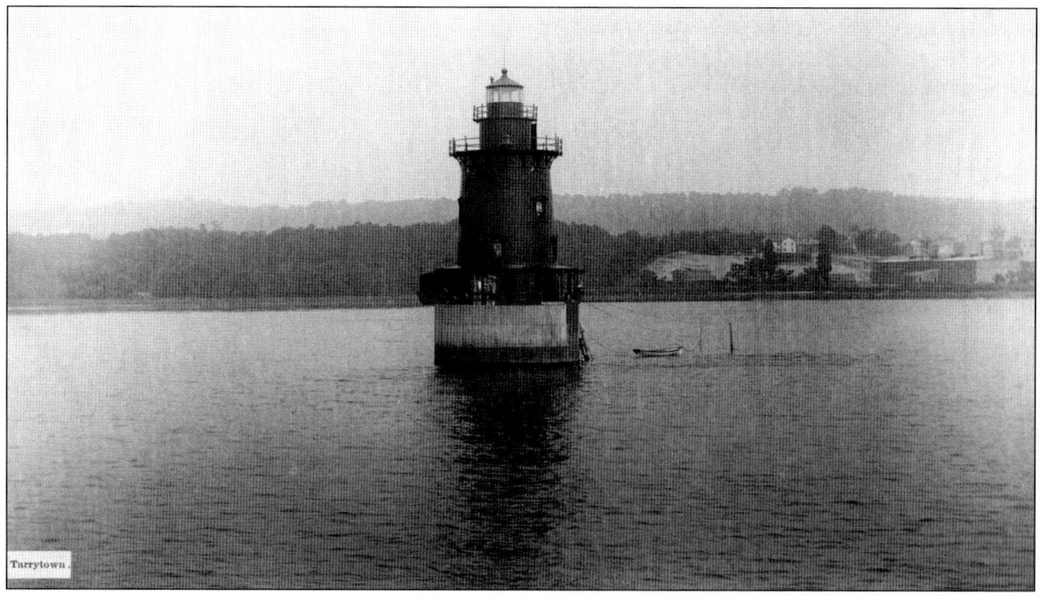

In 1881, a cast-iron sparkplug lighthouse was placed off of Kingsland Point to mark the point, which juts out into the Hudson very close to the navigational channel. Called alternately the Kingsland Point, Tarrytown, and Sleepy Hollow Lighthouse, it is seen here directly after it was installed. Built in sections in a factory and stacked on site, the original brown paint was likely a factory-applied primer. Note the exposed iron caisson foundation; protective stone riprap was installed later. (NARA.)

The Sleepy Hollow Lighthouse was painted white with a red pier and black lantern sometime before 1883, when the first keeper, Jacob Ackerman, began service. Note the installation of stone riprap to protect the lighthouse from ice floes and the fog bell on the secondary deck. The fog bell was operated by clockwork, much like the light. This photograph was taken in October 1893. (NARA.)

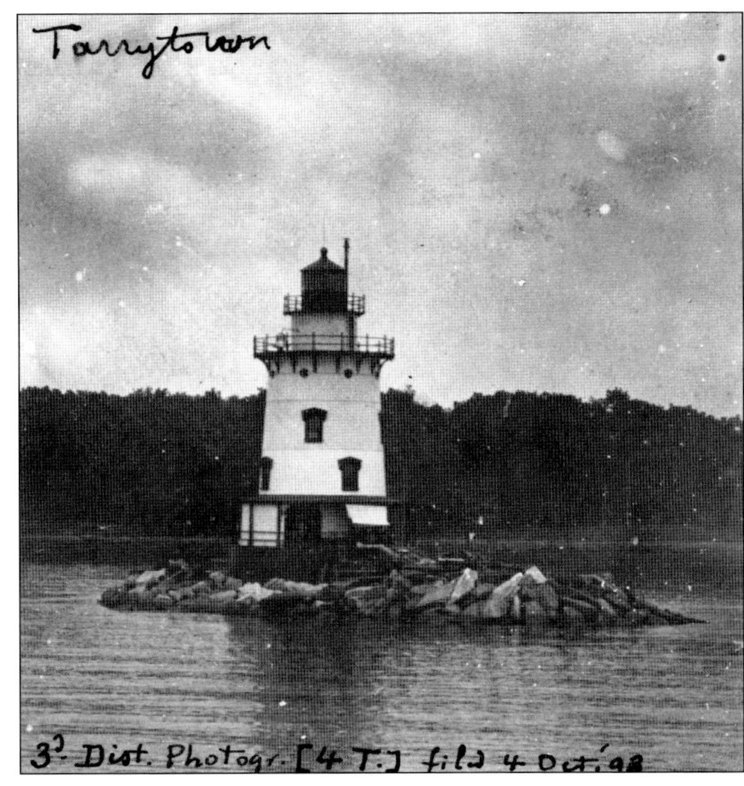

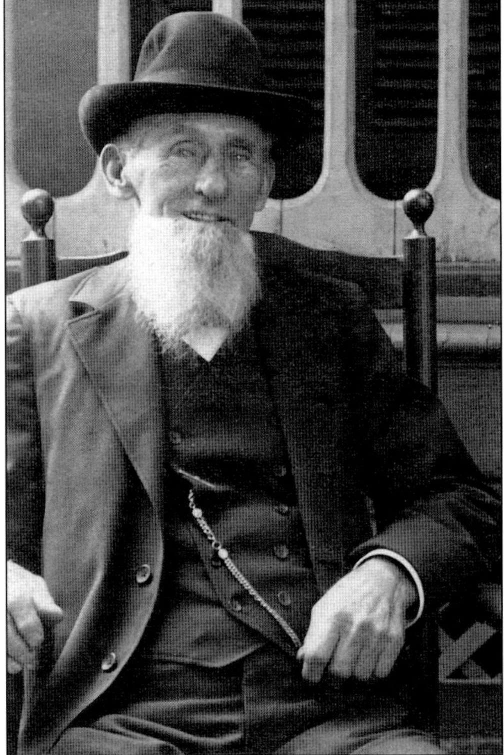

Jacob Ackerman served as keeper of the Sleepy Hollow light from 1883 to 1904, when he retired. At age 78, the duties had become too heavy for him. He was credited with rescuing 19 people from drowning and was very fond of pets, keeping three cats, a dog, and two dozen chickens at the lighthouse year-round. One cat was aged 13 at the time of Ackerman's retirement and had spent her entire life at the lighthouse. (HSISHT.)

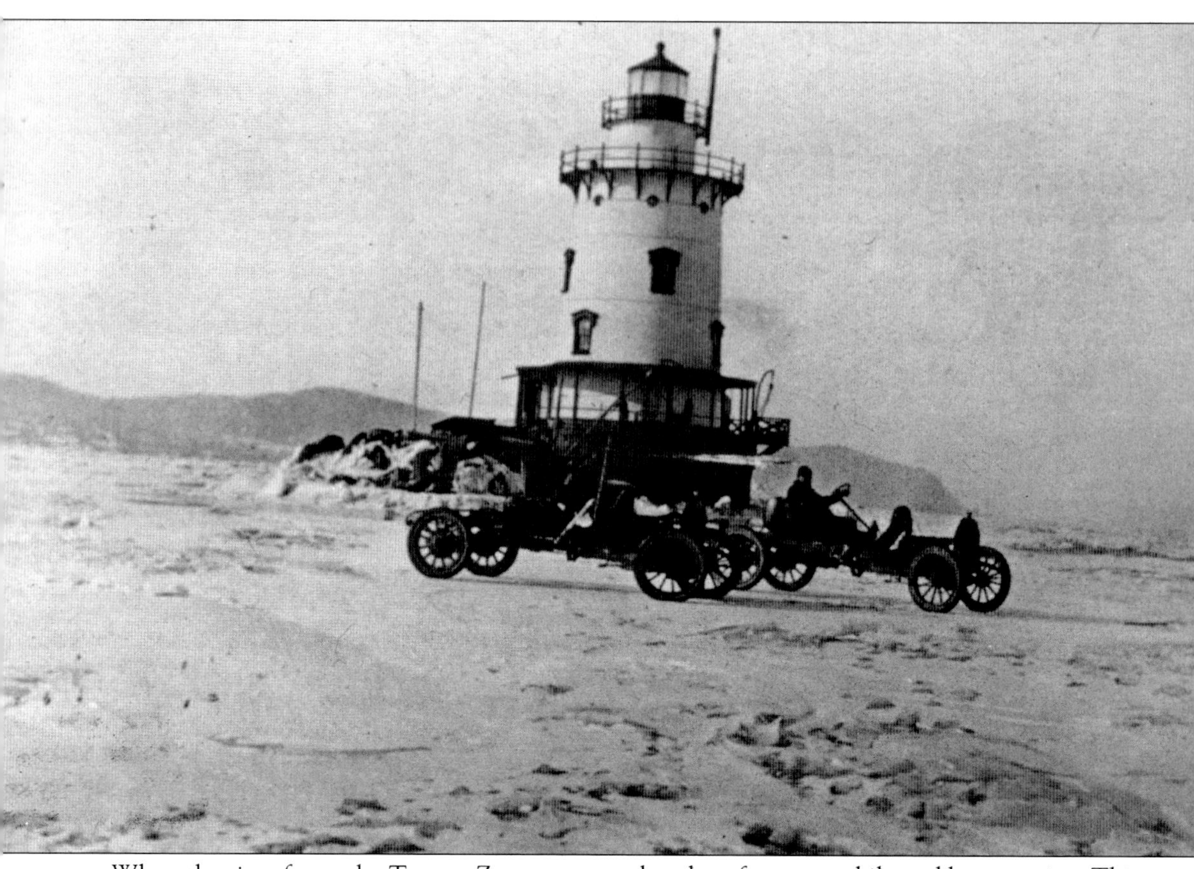

When the river froze, the Tappan Zee was a popular place for automobile and horse racing. This image features automobiles that raced on February 3, 1912. Fred Koenig raced his Mercedes against M.R. Beltzhoover's Mercer 25 miles from Tarrytown to Newburgh, New York, where the ferry channel had been kept open. Koenig won the longer race, but on a three-mile straightaway from the Tarrytown lighthouse to the Tarrytown Boat Club, Beltzhoover won. (NPL.)

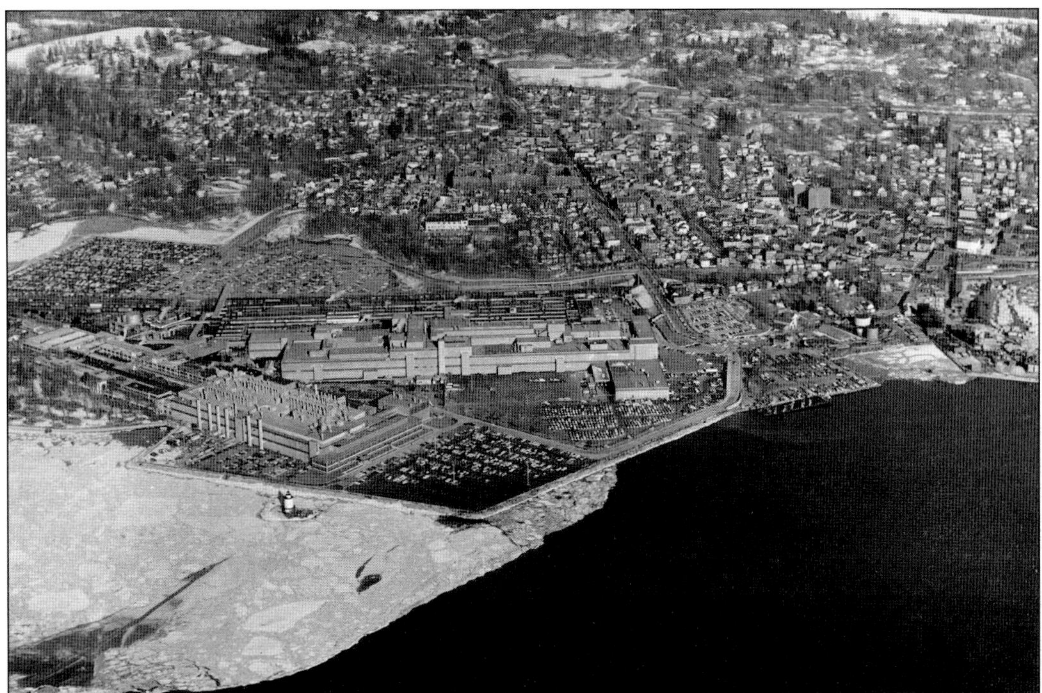

The Stanley Steamer car company was an automobile plant located in North Tarrytown (now Sleepy Hollow). Chevrolet bought portions of the plant, but the company was acquired by General Motors in 1918. The plant expanded through the 1920s, and at some point, the water stretching between the point and the lighthouse was deemed surplus property by the federal government and sold to General Motors—all but a distance of 100 yards from the lighthouse. These aerial photographs show the plant coming very close to the lighthouse. (Both, HSISHT.)

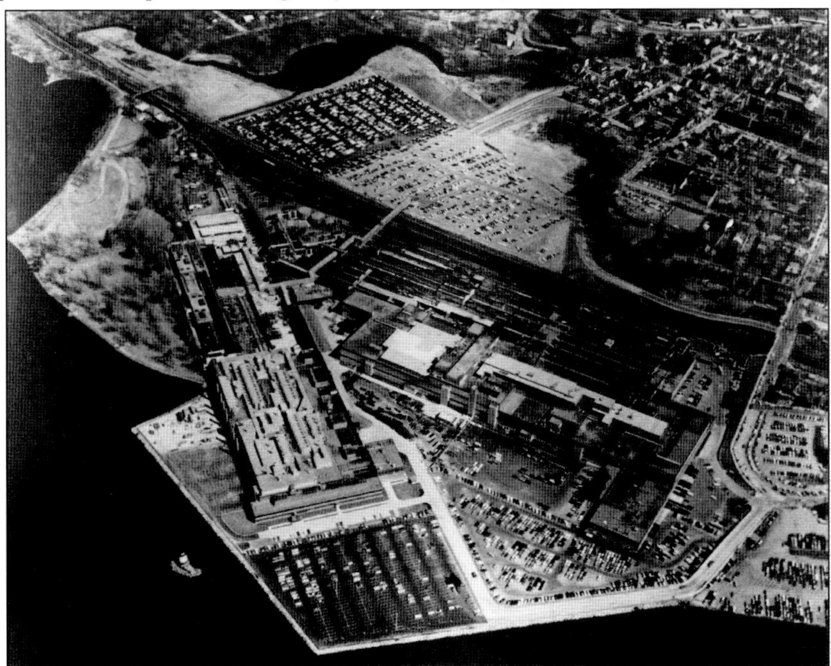

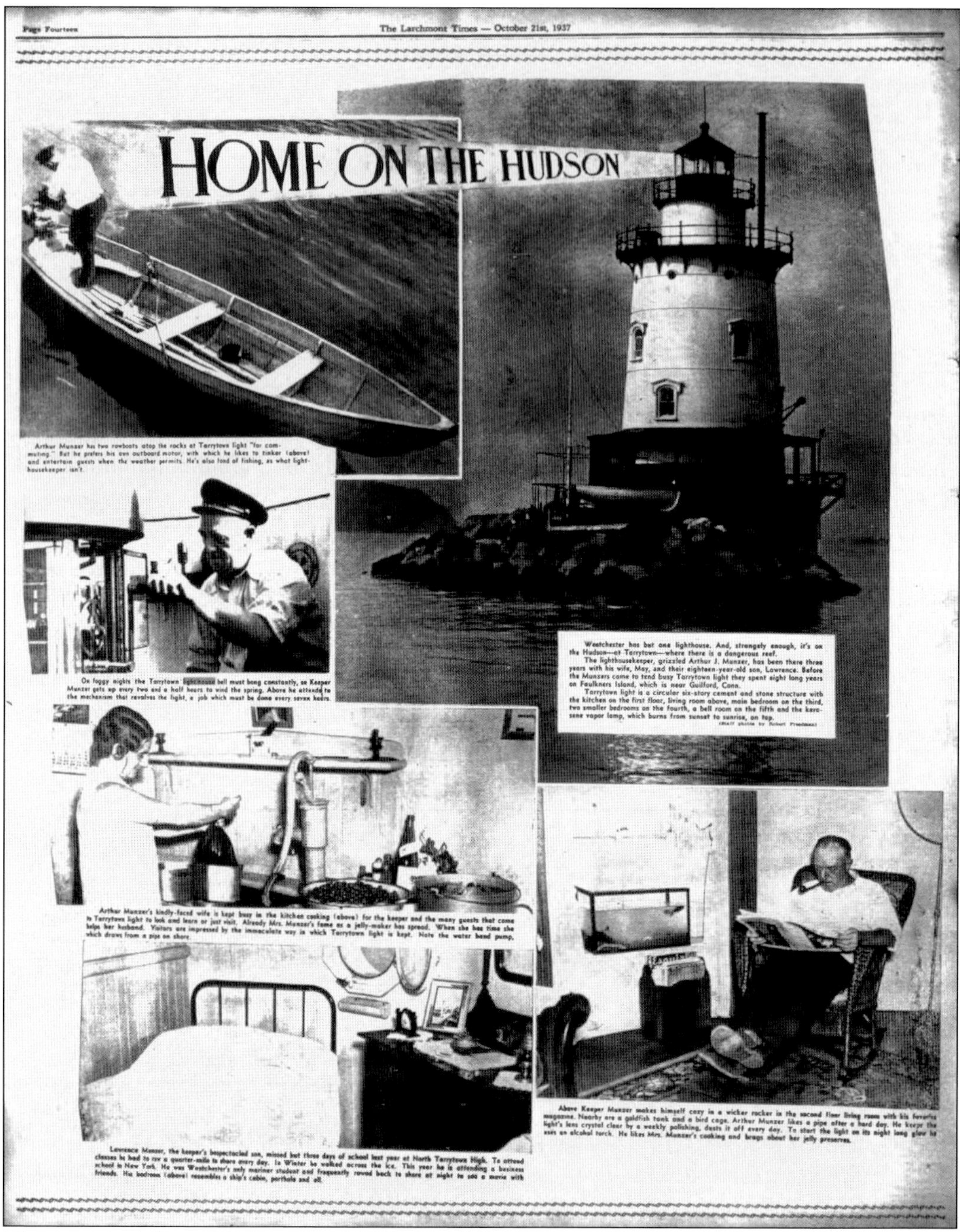

Page Fourteen — The Larchmont Times — October 21st, 1937

HOME ON THE HUDSON

Arthur Munzer has two rowboats atop the rocks at Tarrytown light "for commuting." But he prefers his own outboard motor, with which he likes to tinker (above) and entertain guests when the weather permits. He's also fond of fishing, as what lighthousekeeper isn't.

Westchester has but one lighthouse. And, strangely enough, it's on the Hudson—at Tarrytown—where there is a dangerous reef.

The lighthousekeeper, grizzled Arthur J. Munzer, has been there three years with his wife, May, and their eighteen-year-old son, Lawrence. Before the Munzers came to tend busy Tarrytown light they spent eight long years on Faulkners Island, which is near Guilford, Conn.

Tarrytown light is a circular six-story cement and stone structure with the kitchen on the first floor, living room above, main bedroom on the third, two smaller bedrooms on the fourth, a bell room on the fifth and the kerosene vapor lamp, which burns from sunset to sunrise, on top.

On foggy nights the Tarrytown lighthouse bell must bong constantly, so Keeper Munzer gets up every two and a half hours to wind the spring. Above he attends to the mechanism that revolves the light, a job which must be done every seven hours.

Arthur Munzer's kindly-faced wife is kept busy in the kitchen cooking (above) for the keeper and the many guests that come to Tarrytown light to look and learn or just visit. Already Mrs. Munzer's fame as a jelly-maker has spread. When she has time she helps her husband. Visitors are impressed by the immaculate way in which Tarrytown light is kept. Note the water hand pump, which draws from a pipe on shore.

Above Keeper Munzer makes himself cozy in a wicker rocker in the second floor living room with his favorite magazine. Nearby are a goldfish tank and a bird cage. Arthur Munzer likes a pipe after a hard day. He keeps the light's lens crystal clear by a weekly polishing, dusts it off every day. To start the light on its night long glow he uses an alcohol torch. He likes Mrs. Munzer's cooking and brags about her jelly preserves.

Lawrence Munzer, the keeper's bespectacled son, missed but three days of school last year at North Tarrytown High. To attend classes he had to row a quarter-mile to shore every day. In Winter he walked across the ice. This year he is attending a business school in New York. He was Westchester's only mariner student and frequently rowed back to shore at night to see a movie with friends. His bedroom (above) resembles a ship's cabin, porthole and all.

This wonderful page from the October 21, 1937, issue of the *Larchmont Times* showcases the lives of the Munzer family—keeper Arthur, wife May, and 18-year-old son Lawrence. Of note are the kitchen hand pump (purportedly fed by a pipe from the mainland), the goldfish tank, and May's jelly-making prowess. Lawrence rowed or walked the ice to get ashore for high school. (www.fultonhistory.com.)

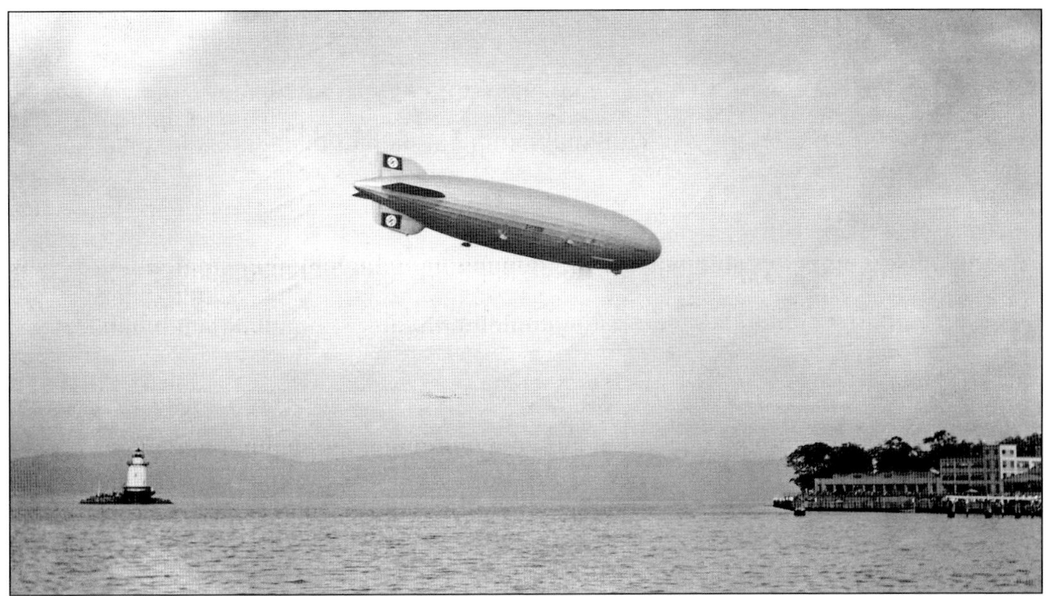

In October 1936, the German dirigible *Hindenburg* flew over the lighthouse and Chevrolet plant, sending a radiogram, "Very new and young Hindenburg salutes very old and storied Tarrytown, extending felicitations to Irving School on 100th anniversary." Launched in March 1936, the *Hindenburg* had made several trips across the Atlantic. On its first flight of the following year, on May 6, 1937, it tragically burst into flames over Lakehurst, New Jersey, killing a third of the people onboard. Note the Nazi emblems on the tailfins of the dirigible; Germany was under Nazi control at the time. (HSISHT.)

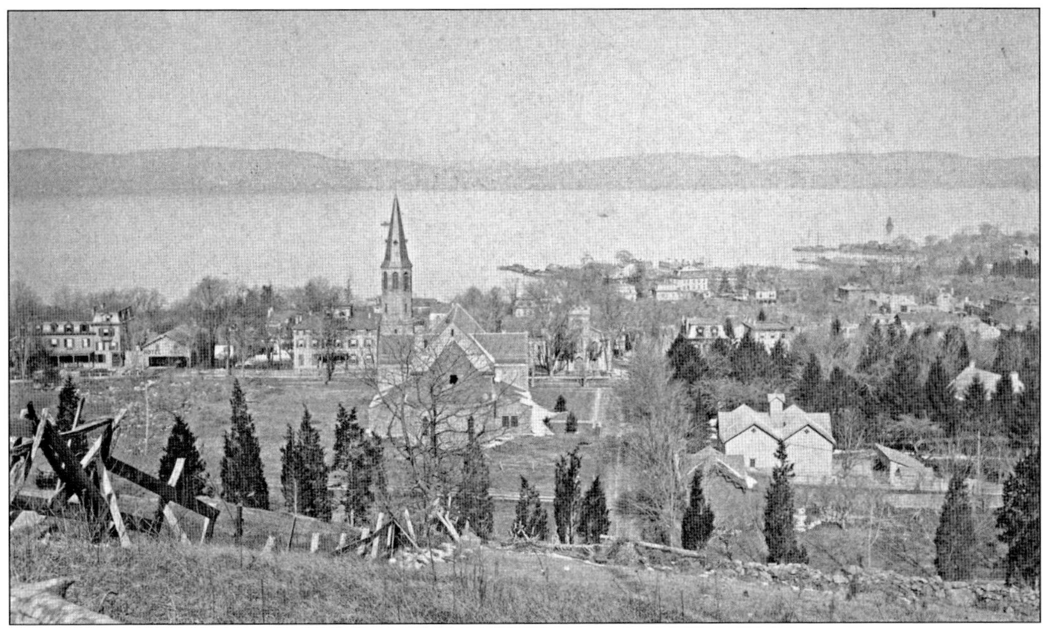

This image gives a clearer view of the Sleepy Hollow lighthouse (center right), and its position in the village of Sleepy Hollow (formerly North Tarrytown) in the 1930s and 1940s. (HSISHT.)

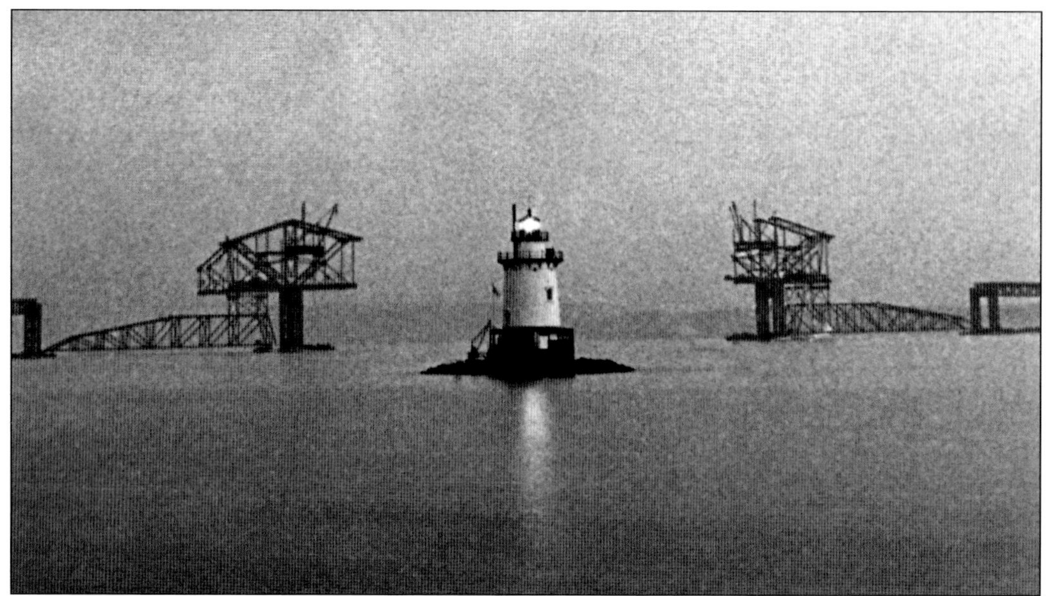

In 1952, construction began on a cantilevered bridge to span the Tappan Zee. Constructed at one of the widest points on the Hudson River—nearly three miles across—it was completed in 1955. Here, the bridge construction can be seen in the background of the lighthouse. The bridge was built quite close to the lighthouse and essentially rendered it obsolete. Several more families lived in the lighthouse, including the Morelands, Leclers, and Flecks, before it was shut down in 1965. (HSISHT.)

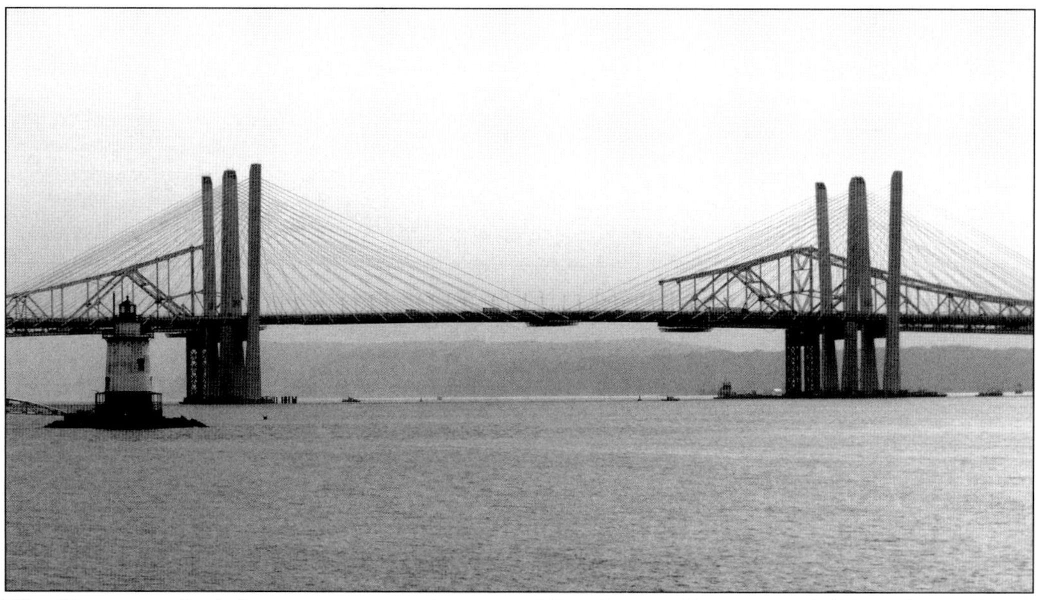

The Tarrytown Lighthouse was turned over to Westchester County in 1974, and in 1979, it was listed in the National Register of Historic Places. In 1996, the village name changed from North Tarrytown to Sleepy Hollow, and the lighthouse was renamed Sleepy Hollow Lighthouse to match. In 2017–2019, the old Tappan Zee bridge was removed as the new one was completed, as seen here. Now as before, the lighthouse can be seen from the westbound lane of the bridge. (Joan Mayer.)

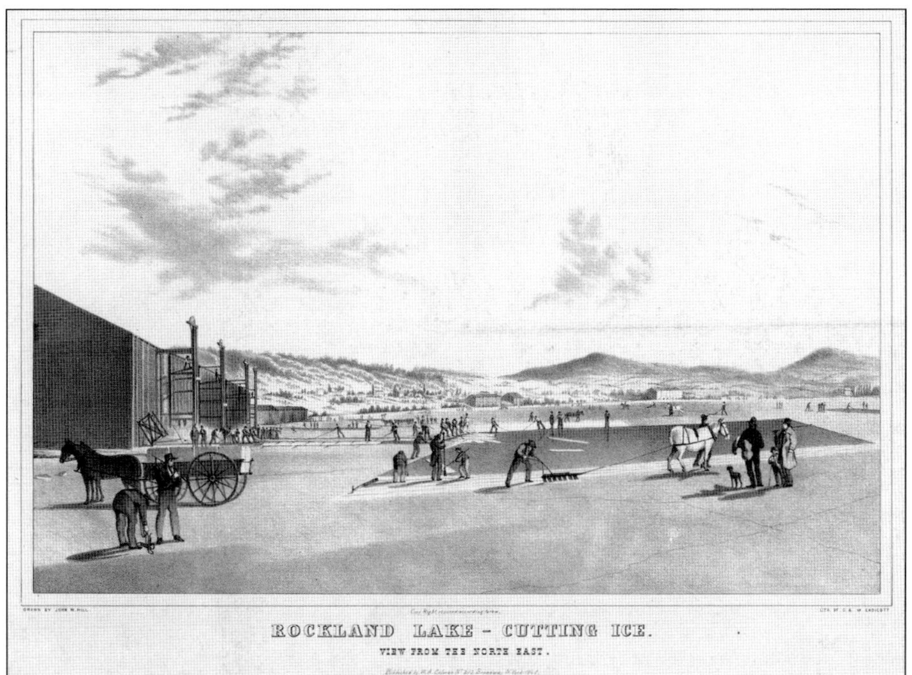

Rockland Lake, the largest body of fresh water in close proximity to New York City, was the major source of natural ice for the city until the early 20th century. It was also fairly close to the shores of the Hudson River, where ice could not be harvested due to the salt content. The Knickerbocker ice docks were a major freight destination for steamboats and barges. In this pair of images from the 1840s, ice is being harvested in large blocks. The warehouses on the banks of Rockland Lake were used to pack and store the ice for summer use. (Both, LOC.)

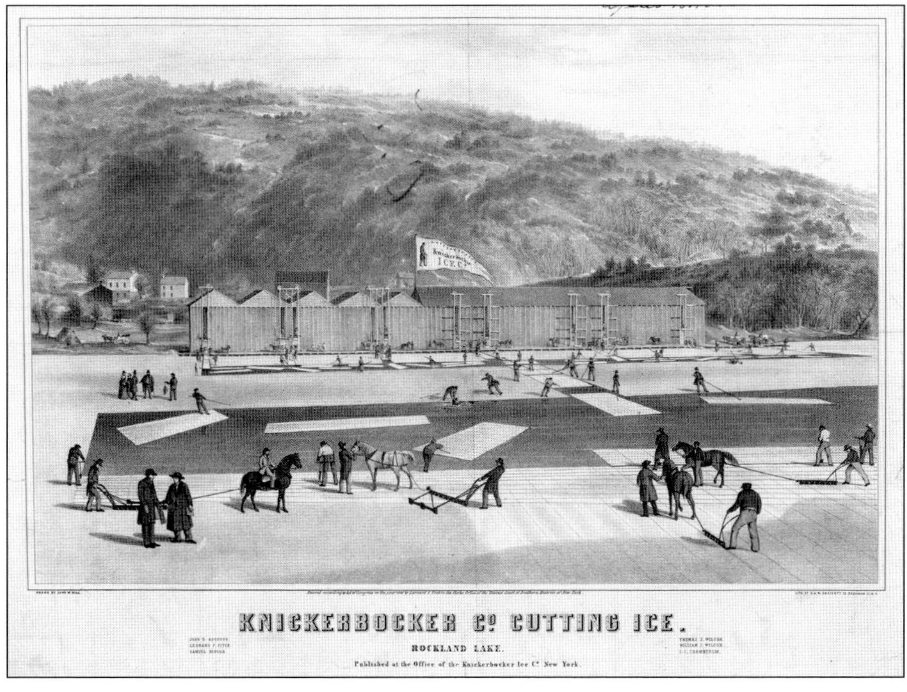

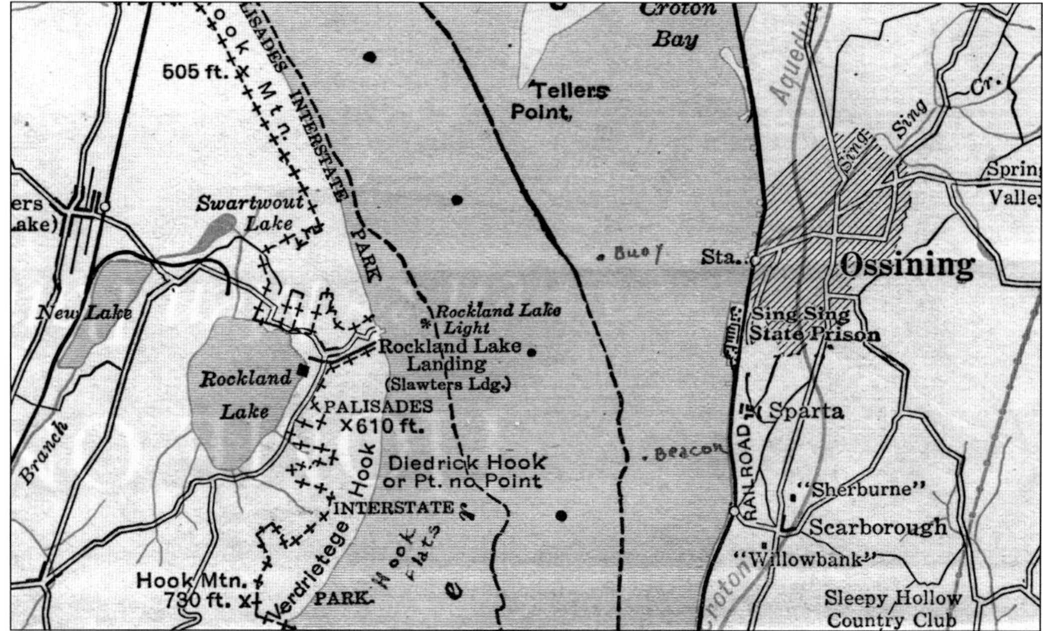

This map shows Rockland Lake's close proximity to the Hudson. The navigation channel passes close to the western shore, and Rockland Lake Lighthouse is marked on this map just north of the landing. (HRMM.)

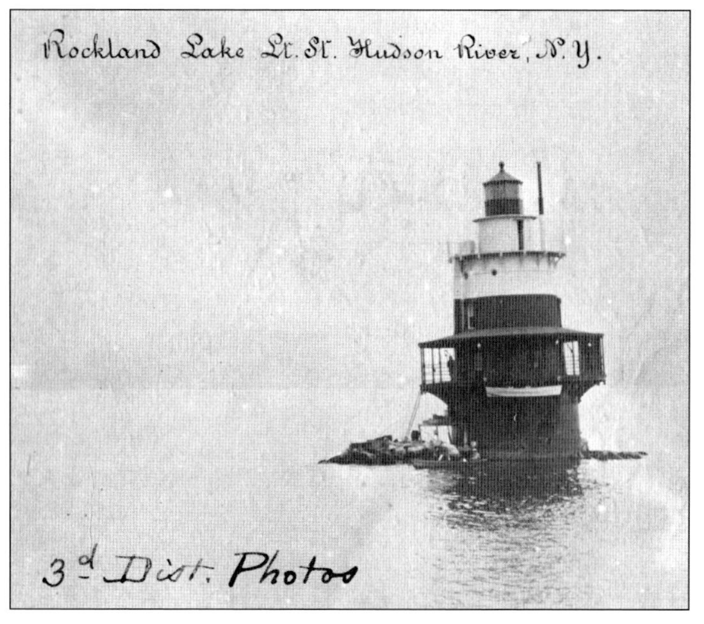

Rockland Lake Lighthouse was installed in 1894, just one year after Tarrytown. During construction, in August 1894, the half-built lighthouse was struck by the steam canal-boat *Richard K. Fox* of Buffalo, with a tow of four canal barges. The collision destroyed the dock as well as a number of temporary buildings, including workmen's housing. Several workmen narrowly escaped drowning. The boatmen blamed the tide for crowding them into the lighthouse, but the pilot may have been asleep at the wheel. (NARA.)

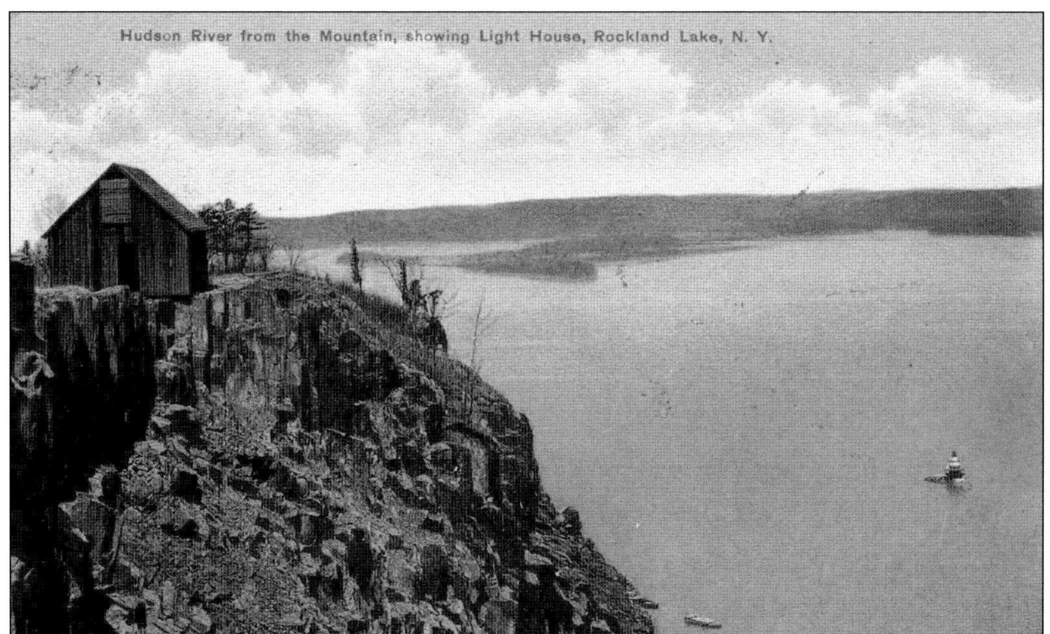

Rockland Lake Lighthouse was installed to mark the oyster bed flats it partially rested upon as well as the entrance to Rockland Lake Landing. Boatmen were at odds about its usefulness; some complained that it got in the way, but others said it helped them keep their bearings on the unmarked stretch between Tarrytown and Stony Point. (NPL.)

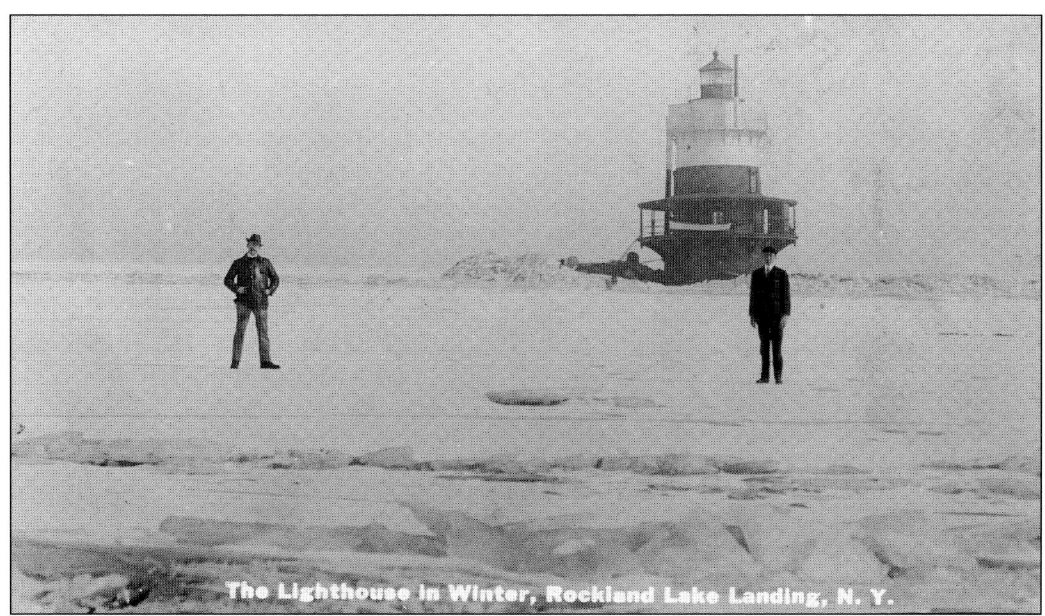

Several keepers were stationed at Rockland Lake over the years. Stephen Collyer, formerly employed at Sing Sing Prison, took over in 1894. W.H. Spanburgh, originally of Hudson, New York, retired in 1903 after several years of service. Here, two men, probably not keepers because they lack the official uniform, pose on the ice near the lighthouse. (NPL.)

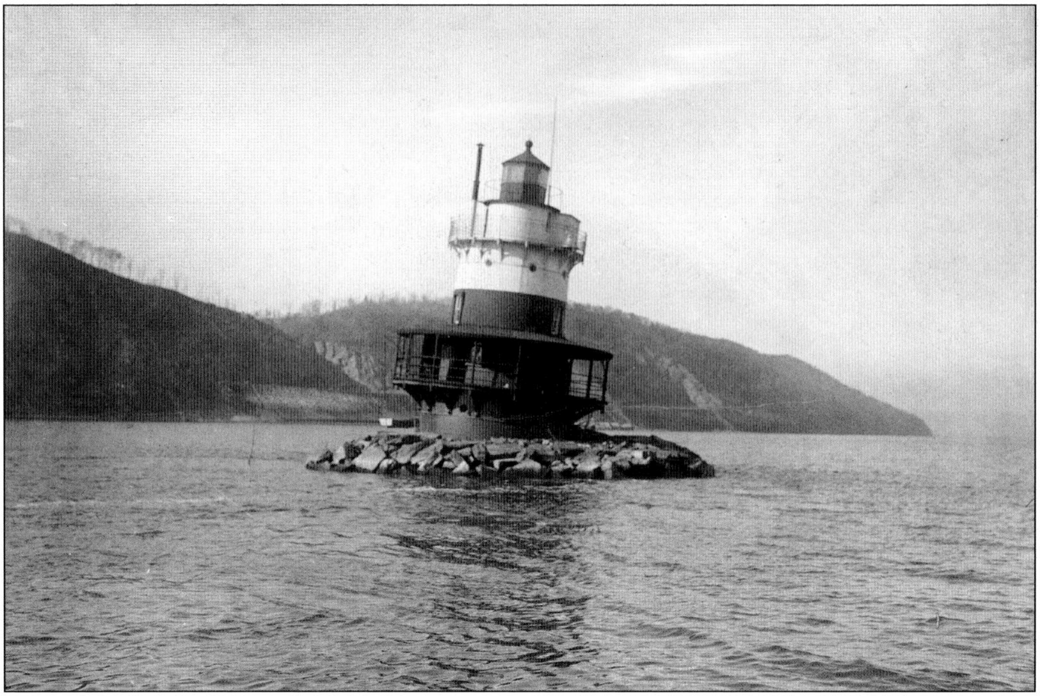

By the 1910s, the lighthouse had acquired a significant tilt, as shown in this photograph from 1915. Historians speculate that the addition of thousands of tons of riprap to mitigate ice damage was crushing the oyster beds beneath, causing the lean. Given the high costs of repair, the lean was left uncorrected, and the clockwork and other lighting machinery were adjusted to ensure the light still functioned. (NARA.)

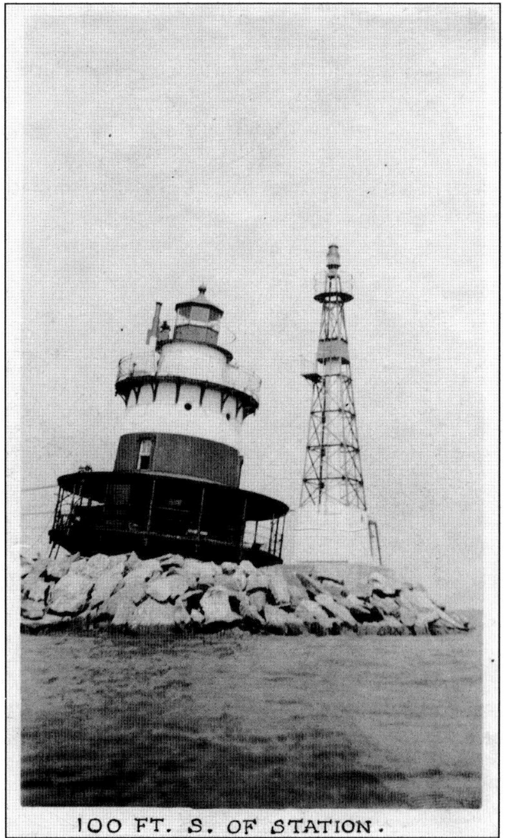

The brown and white lighthouse was in operation for not quite 20 years. In 1923, Rockland Lake Lighthouse was decommissioned and a steel tower installed just adjacent. The lighthouse structure was torn down in 1924. (NARA.)

Three

Hudson Highlands

The Hudson Highlands are a mountain range flanking both sides of the Hudson River from Stony Point to Newburgh. As the river makes its way through these mountains, it has some of the sharpest bends and deepest waters. The area between West Point and Constitution Island, in particular, was known to sailors as "World's End" because of the depths of the water (over 200 feet deep). Throughout the Hudson Highlands, the unpredictability of the winds that blew through the mountains made this section of the river dangerous for sailors. This area was an important defense point during the American Revolution, with Continental forces stationed at Fort Putnam (West Point) and Fort Montgomery. The great chains across the Hudson were stretched here, and important battles took place at Stony Point, West Point, and Fort Montgomery. Toward the end of the war, troops were stationed at West Point and around Cornwall Bay. In the 19th century, the picturesque nature of the Hudson Highlands caused the Hudson River to be favorably compared to the Rhine River in Germany—a major tourist destination.

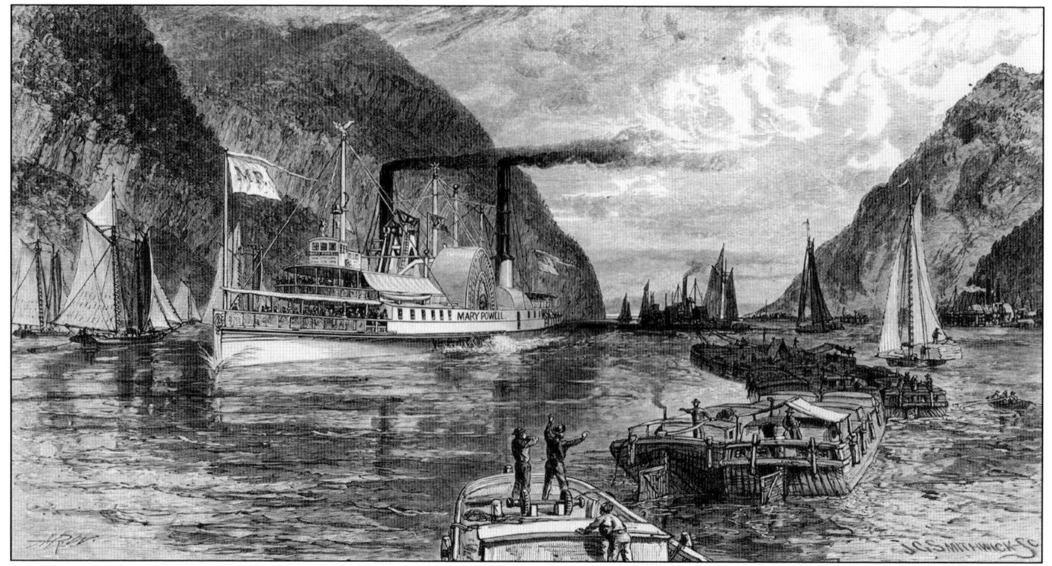

Here, the famous steamboat *Mary Powell* (center left), which served passengers for nearly 60 years, is seen steaming through the Hudson Highlands. Note the schooners, sloops, and steam towboat with long strings of barges. By 1828, New York's three major canals—the Champlain, Erie, and Delaware & Hudson—had opened, considerably increasing traffic of goods and people on the river. This lithograph by A.R. Ward from the 1875 *Ulster County Atlas* illustrates the traffic that traveled through the Highlands on a daily basis. (HRMM.)

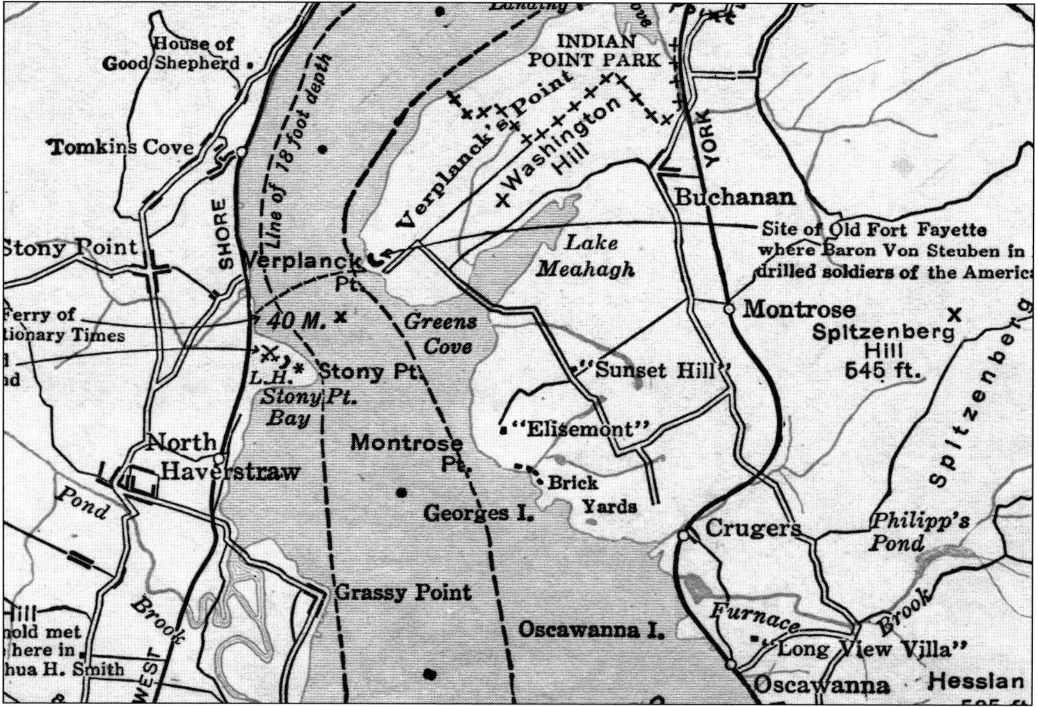

Stony Point is, in fact, a stony point that juts out into the Hudson, and the deepest part of the navigation channel passes very close to it. On this map, the beginning twists and turns of the Hudson Highlands that eventually made a lighthouse necessary can be seen. (HRMM.)

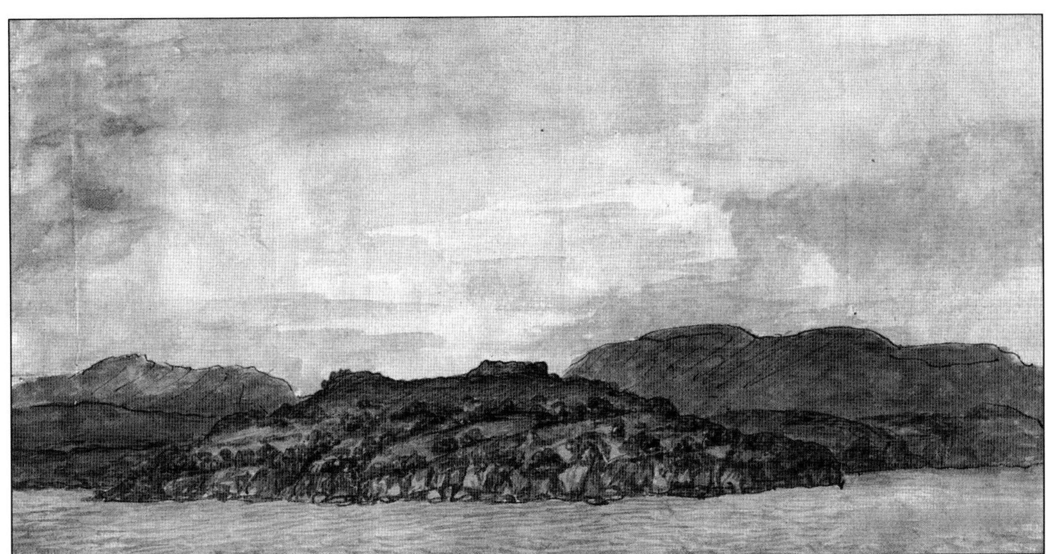

This watercolor and ink sketch of Stony Point by Charles Wilson Peale was done swiftly as he cruised past in a boat on his way to Newburgh in 1802. The painting shows the raised earthworks remaining on the island's summit from the fortifications built there during the Revolutionary War. The island was still largely denuded of trees from the military occupation, and the earthworks made the perfect foundation on which to construct the Stony Point Lighthouse in 1826. (SPB.)

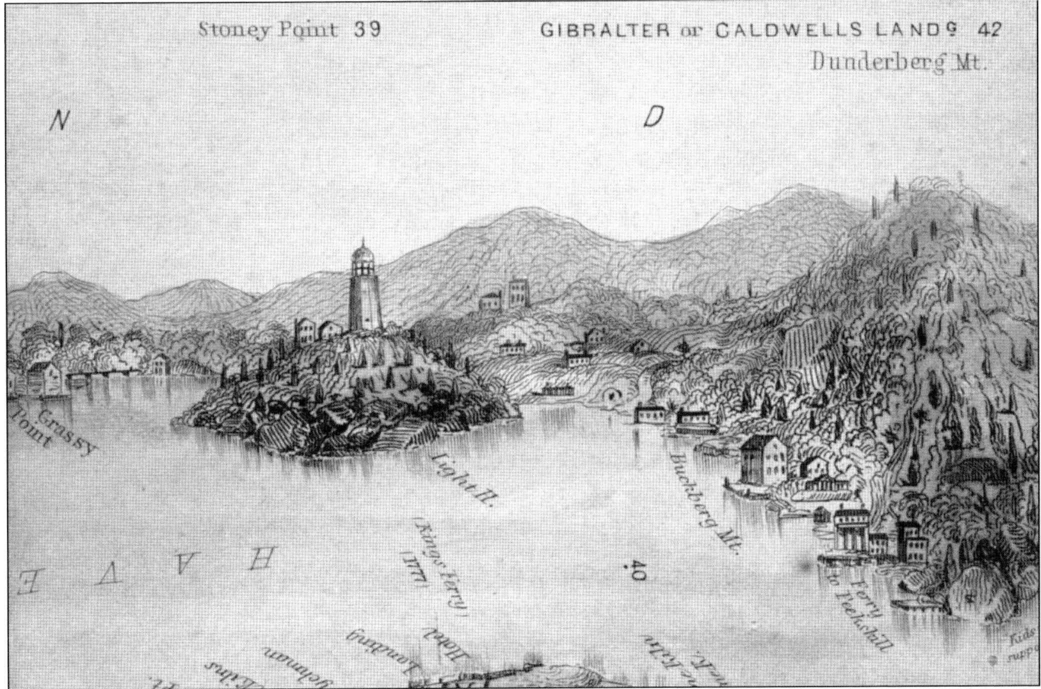

The Stony Point Lighthouse is the oldest lighthouse on the Hudson River (1826) and the only survivor of the first class of lighthouses installed in the 1820s and 1830s. Using the added height of the old military earthworks, the lighthouse base sat 150 feet above the river's high tide mark, allowing for a simple three-story tower. In this 1847 image from a panorama of the river, the tower appears much larger than it actually was. (ARC.)

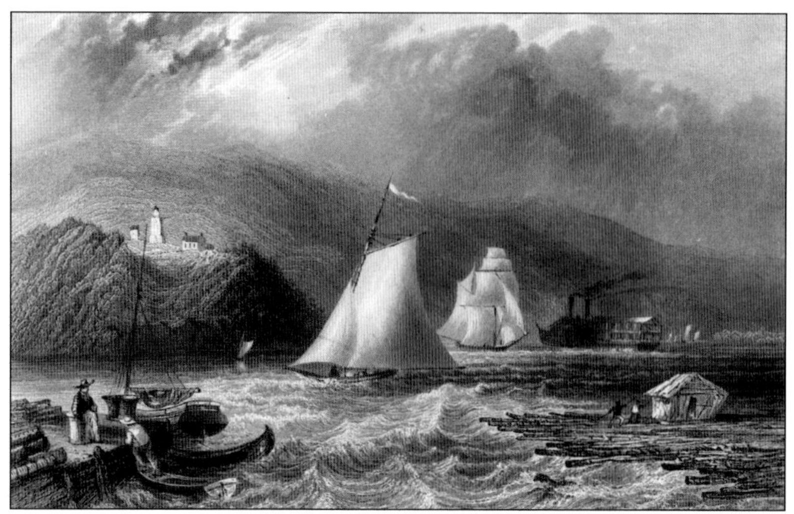

In this c. 1840 lithograph by William Bartlett, the lighthouse is viewed from Caldwell's Landing toward the eastern shore. Although the height of the tower is exaggerated, the traffic of sloops, schooners, steamboats, and canal barges reflects the busy nature of marine traffic at that time. (NARA.)

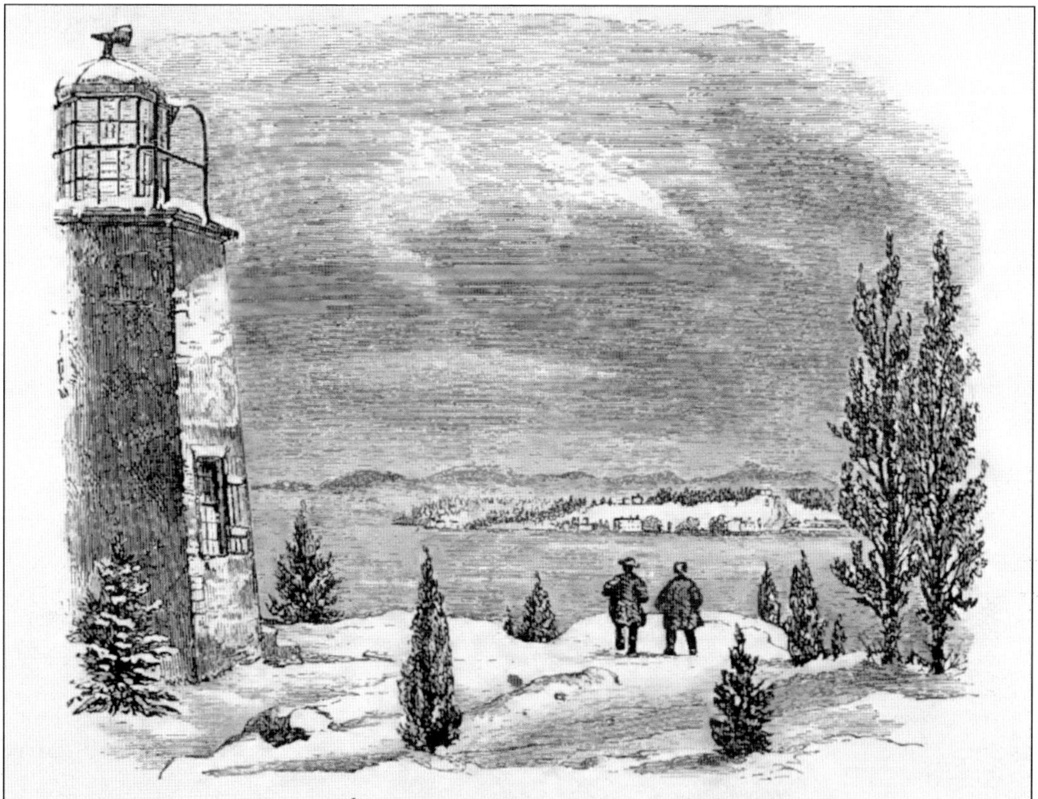

VERPLANCK'S POINT, FROM STONY POINT LIGHTHOUSE.

Stony Point Lighthouse and its keeper's cottage were built for $3,350 by architect Thomas Phillips of New York City. Superintendent of lighthouses for the Department of the Treasury at the time, Jonathan Thompson gave specifications for "an octagonal pyramid of blue split stone and the best quick lime and sand mortar," two stories tall with a wrought iron and glass lantern on top, and a deep stone cellar to store the whale oil to fuel the lamps. This drawing of the lighthouse from Benjamin Lossing's *The Hudson: From the Wilderness to the Sea* (1866) is a more realistic depiction of the true size of the lighthouse. (SPB.)

The six-room keeper's cottage was built of the same materials as the lighthouse and was the first of three successive houses built for keepers and their families to live in. It sat on the terraced land below the light and had an extensive vegetable garden and a shed for the cow, which supplemented the keeper's food supply. (SPB.)

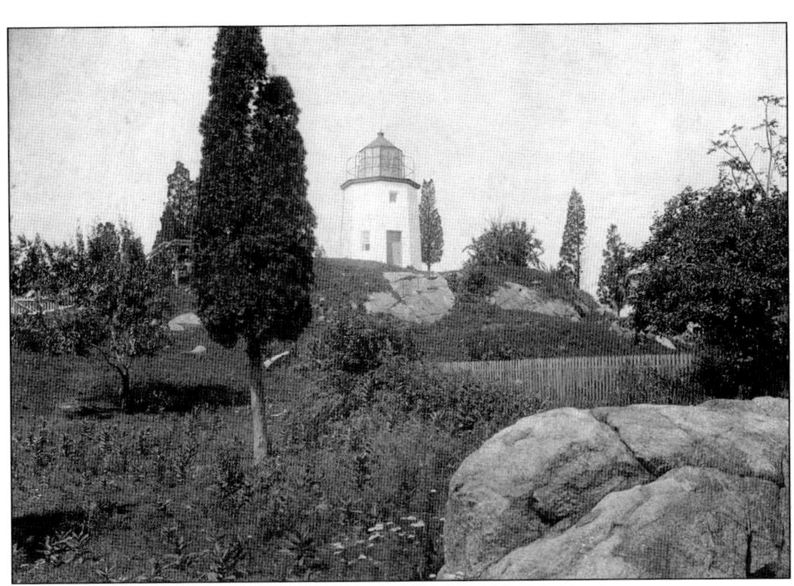

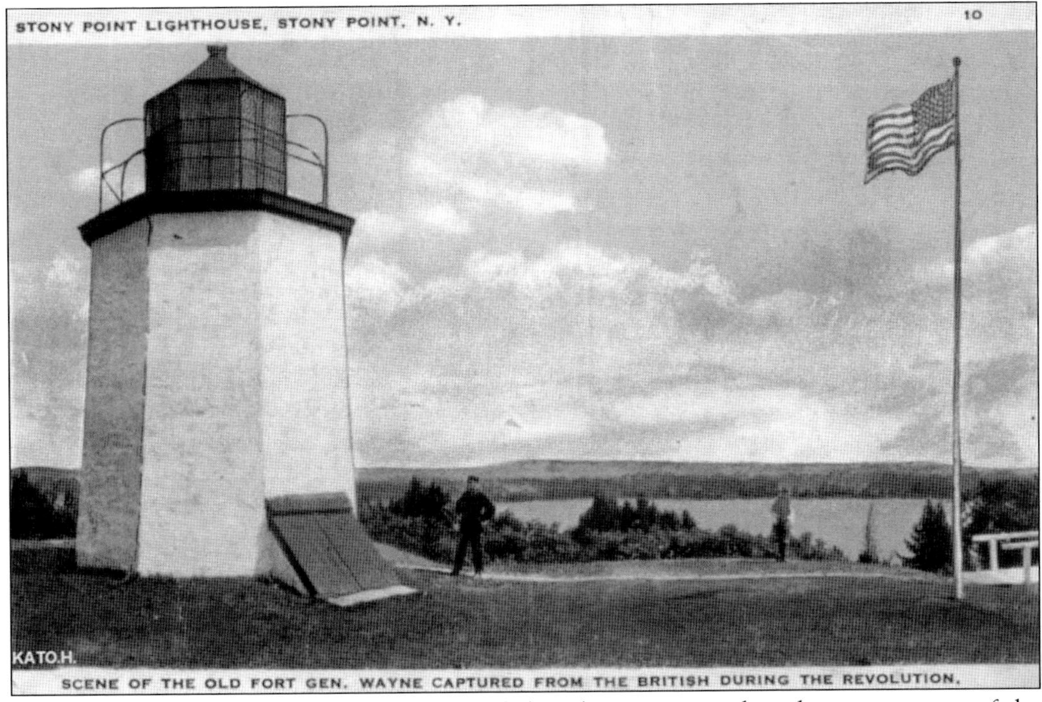

In 1838, Navy Lt. George M. Bache reported that the mortar used in the construction of the 12-year-old stone tower had not hardened, the stone lintel over the door and the masonry over the cellar window were cracked, and the wood timbers, beams, and rafters were quite decayed. The lighthouse and the six-room stone dwelling house required repairs. (SPB.)

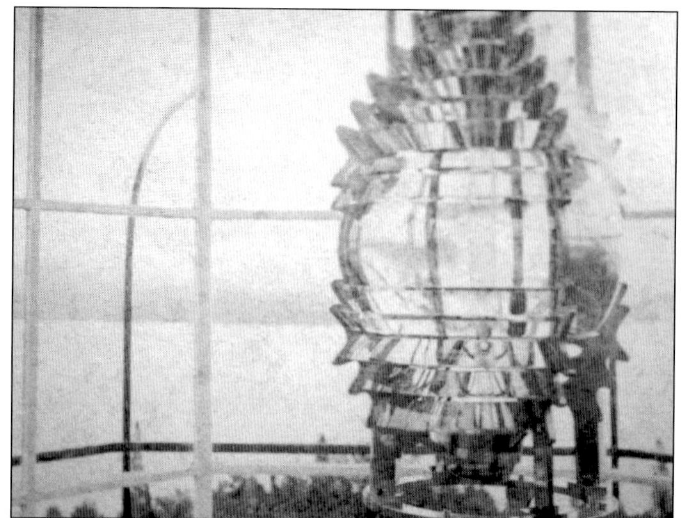

In 1856, a fifth-order Fresnel lens was installed in the lighthouse, which was a huge improvement for visibility and maintenance over the earlier lamps. This rare photograph of the first Fresnel lens shows it was "in the round" with a fixed white light emanating from a lamp placed in the center of the lens. This lens was in use for 46 years until 1902, when a larger and even more powerful fourth-order Fresnel lens was installed and used until the tower was decommissioned in 1925. (SPB.)

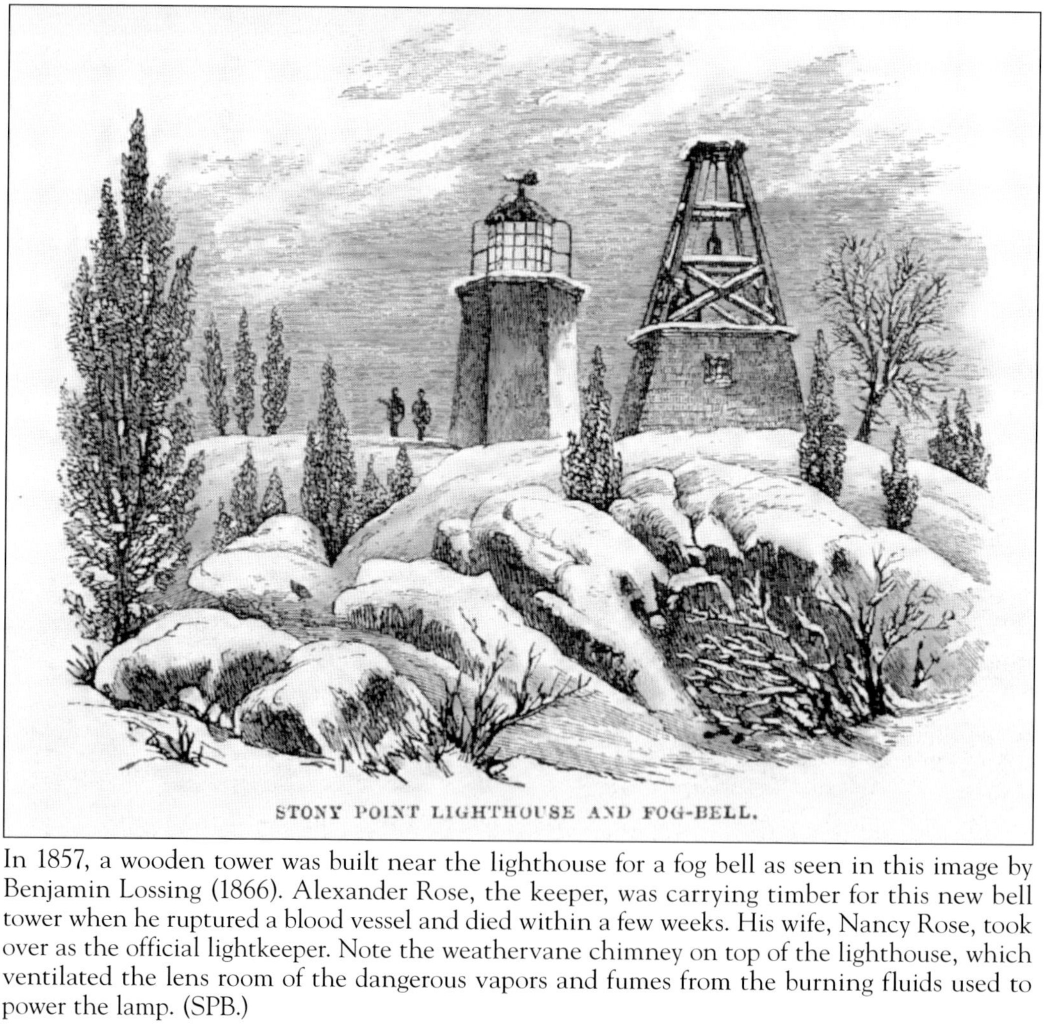

STONY POINT LIGHTHOUSE AND FOG-BELL.

In 1857, a wooden tower was built near the lighthouse for a fog bell as seen in this image by Benjamin Lossing (1866). Alexander Rose, the keeper, was carrying timber for this new bell tower when he ruptured a blood vessel and died within a few weeks. His wife, Nancy Rose, took over as the official lightkeeper. Note the weathervane chimney on top of the lighthouse, which ventilated the lens room of the dangerous vapors and fumes from the burning fluids used to power the lamp. (SPB.)

This architectural drawing from 1866 served as the plan for work being done to restore the building. Newer, more volatile lamp fuels were introduced after whale oil became increasingly difficult to procure. These fuels could not be stored in the cellar as they were highly flammable and would damage the building if they caught fire. A separate outbuilding was constructed for storage of the fuel supply. (SPB.)

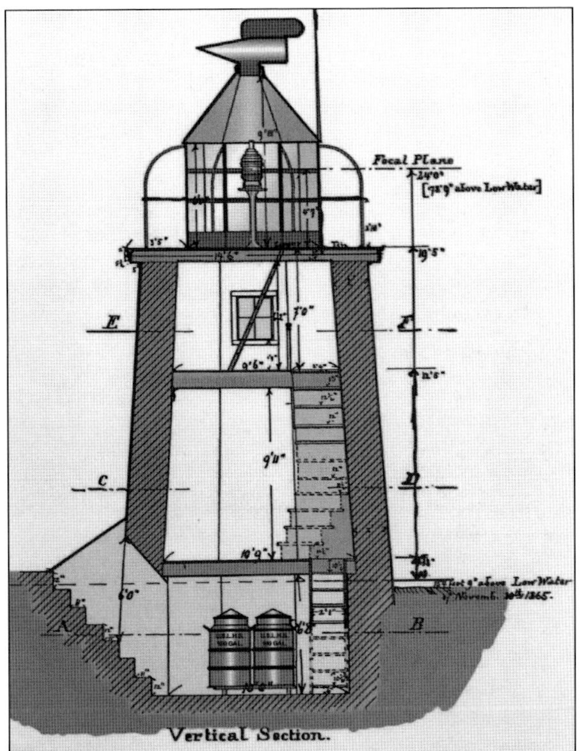

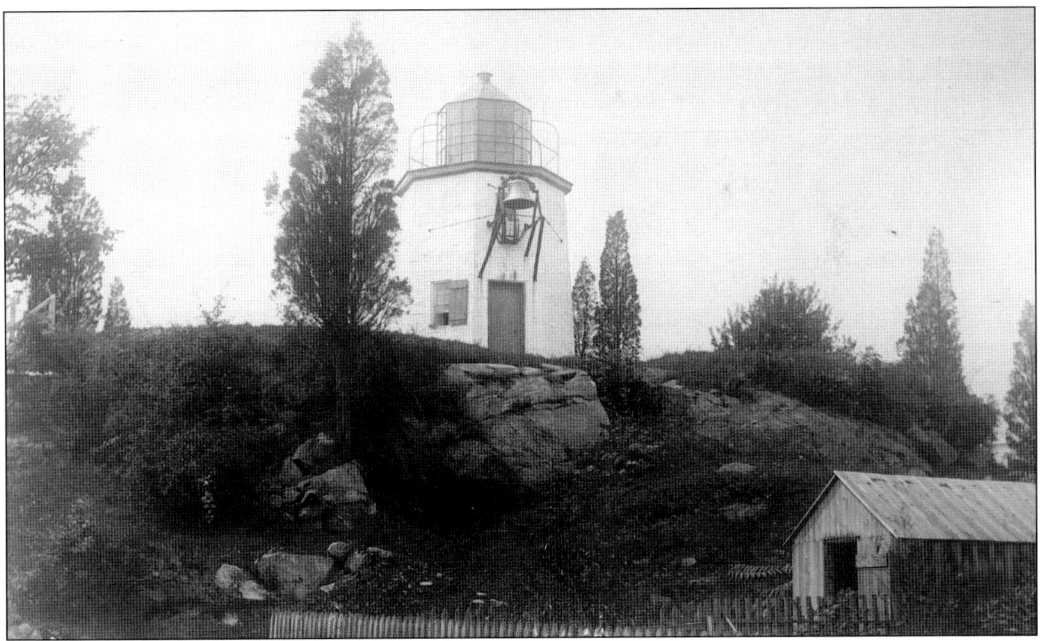

In 1876, the rotting wooden fog bell tower was torn down and the fog bell attached to the lighthouse, as seen here. Today, the two anchor bolts that held the ends of the cables are still visible in the lighthouse's stone walls. Note that the required day curtains are in place in the lantern room to help keep the lantern cool. The floor of the lantern rooms was covered with sheets of copper, soldered together with lead, minimizing the risk of fire from spilled lamp oil. (NARA.)

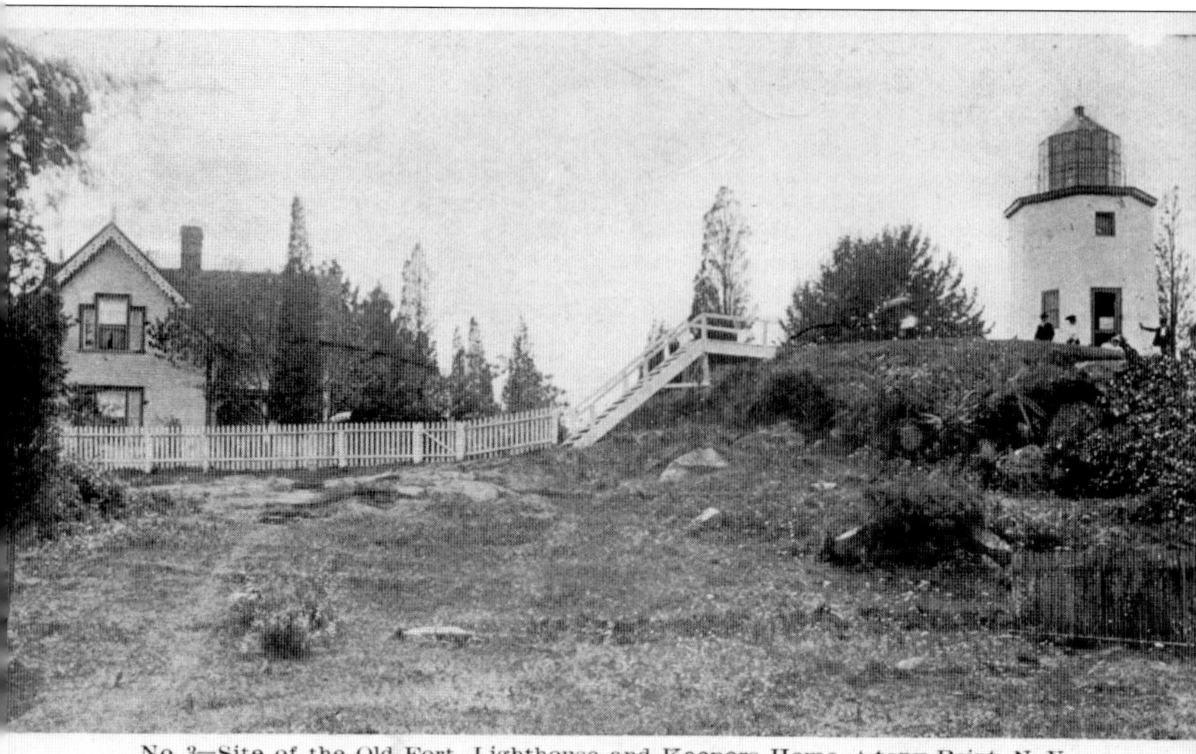

Around 1880, the original stone keeper's residence was torn down and replaced with the six-room Gothic Revival–style house on the flat area below the lighthouse to the south. This photograph was taken from the foundation of the first cottage. An improved wooden staircase was built for Nancy Rose to safely access the lighthouse when she moved into her new home with her children. (NPL.)

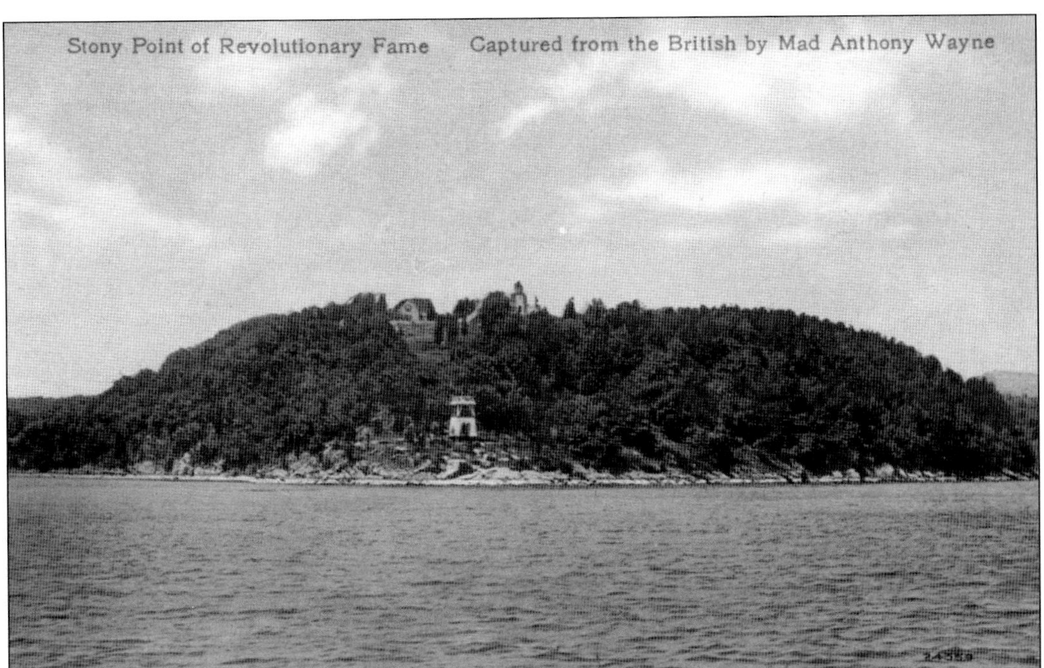

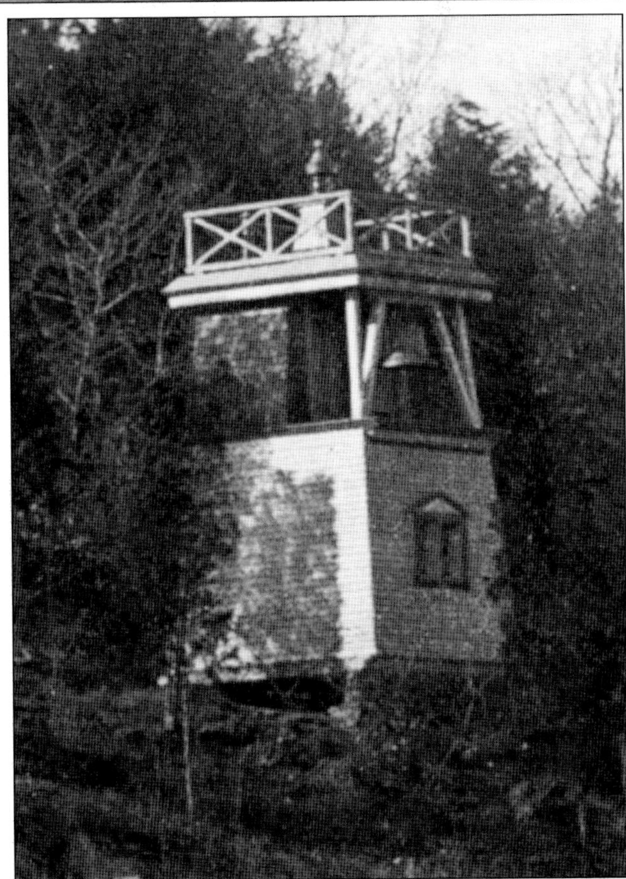

In 1889, a new fog bell tower was constructed closer to the shipping lane. Nancy Rose hiked about one-eighth of a mile each way down and back up this steep hill to wind the mechanism every three and three-quarter hours whenever fog closed in. In 1895, the fog bell mechanism malfunctioned, and Rose had to ring the bell by hand. Some accounts indicate she rang the bell for as many as 56 hours straight. In 1902, the white light on top of this bell tower was replaced with a red lens lantern, which also had to be tended nightly. Nancy Rose received no additional pay for these new duties. (Above, NPL; right, NARA.)

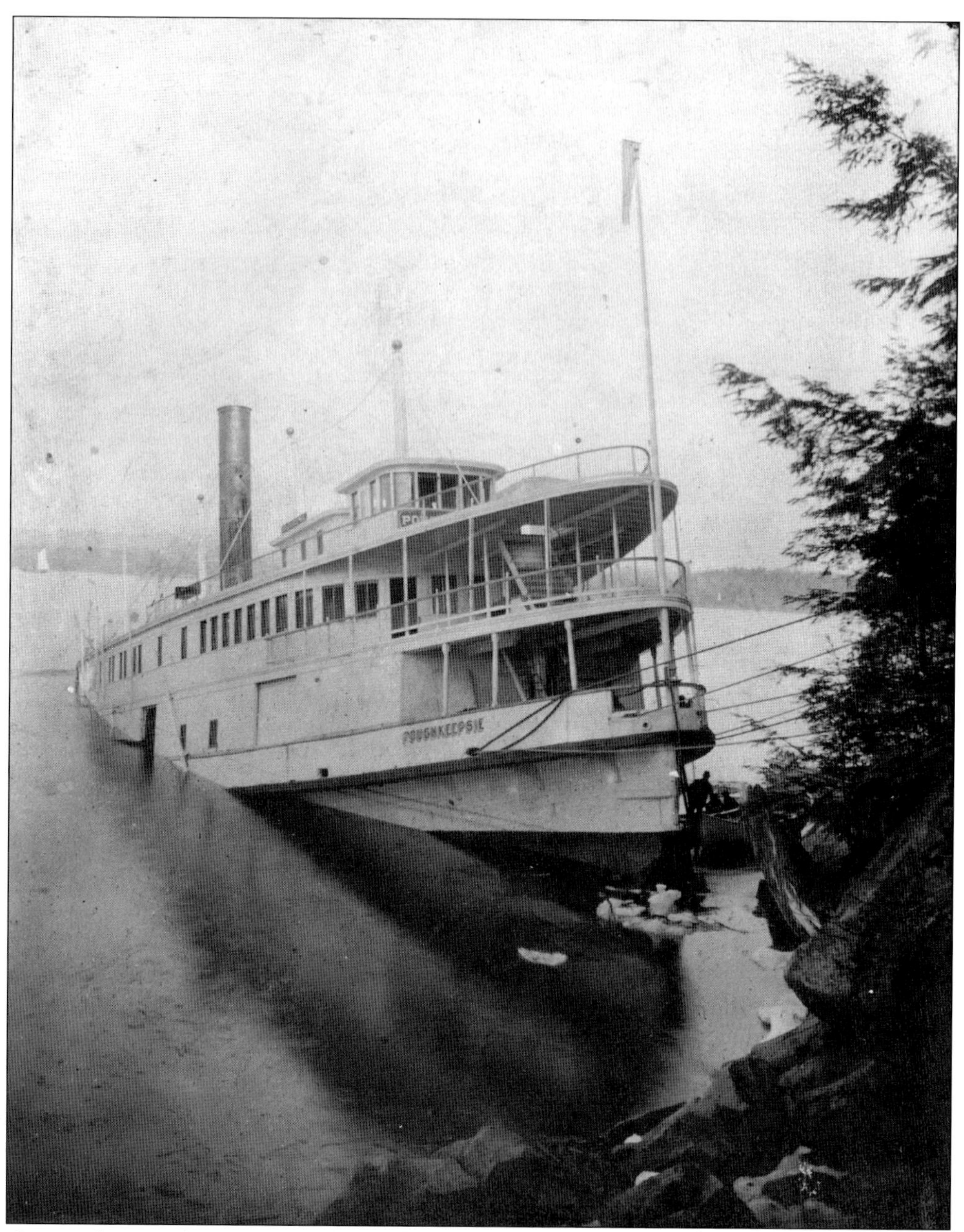

Only one shipwreck was ever recorded at Stony Point Lighthouse: the wreck of the steamer *Poughkeepsie*. Run aground in a fog in March 1901, the captain admitted that he had failed to listen for the bell and turned too early, running aground at the point instead of maneuvering around it. Rescued passengers spent the night with Nancy Rose and were sent to New York City on the morning train. The owner of the boat, however, insisted Rose had been remiss in her duties and had not kept the bell ringing. Newspapers and public outcry leapt to her defense, many insisting that they had heard the bell that night and seen the light burning. The *Poughkeepsie* was recovered, including a shipment of horses that stood in the water for four days before rescue, but other cargoes of printing paper and agricultural goods were a total loss. One year later, in 1902, the Stony Point Lighthouse received a more powerful fourth-order Fresnel lens. (SPB.)

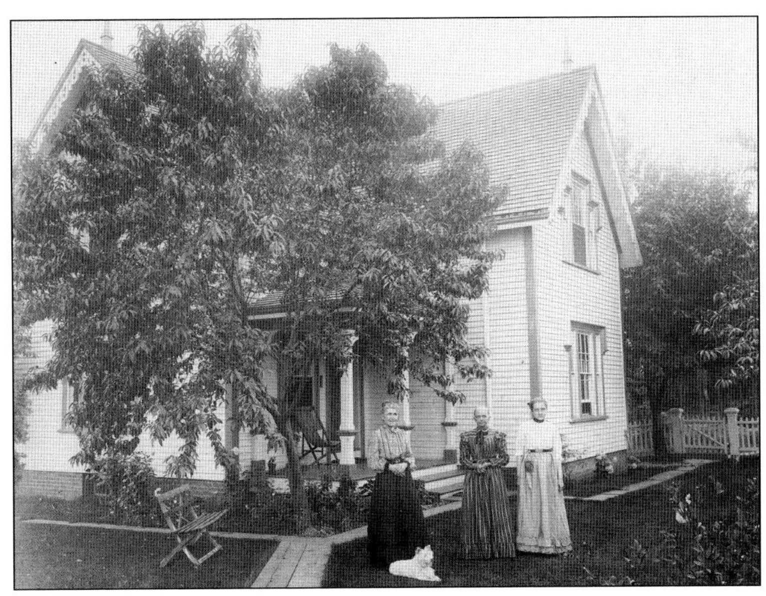

Nancy Rose (center) kept the Stony Point Lighthouse for 47 years. She retired in 1903 and passed away in 1904. Her daughter Melinda Rose (left) took over as keeper but served for just one year. Nancy was a well-known figure both in the Stony Point community and on the river. (SPB.)

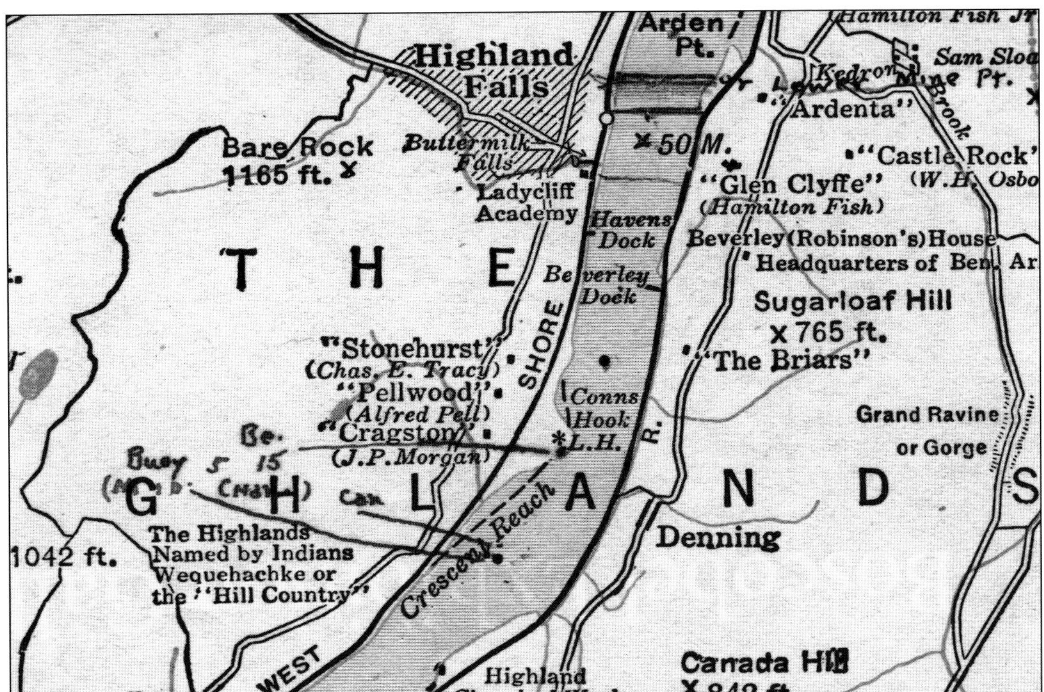

North of Stony Point, halfway between Fort Montgomery and West Point, another point or "hook" juts out near the navigation channel, and the river narrows considerably. Marked on this map is "Conns Hook L.H." or "lighthouse." In fact, the beacon marking Con Hook was not actually a lighthouse, but a stake light. (HRMM.)

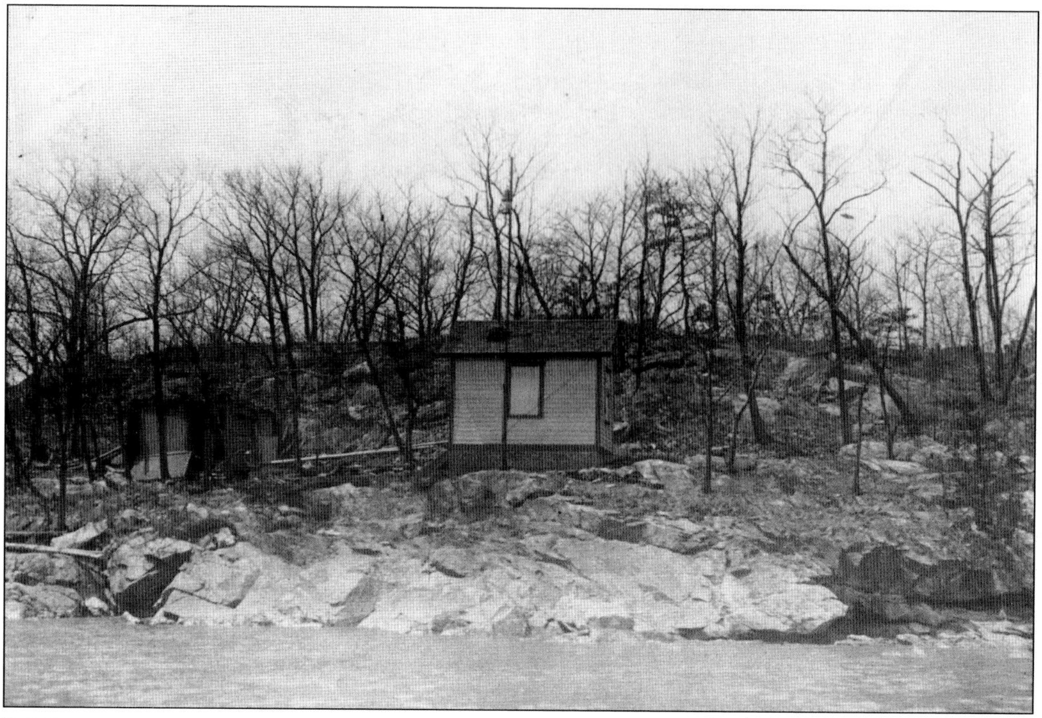

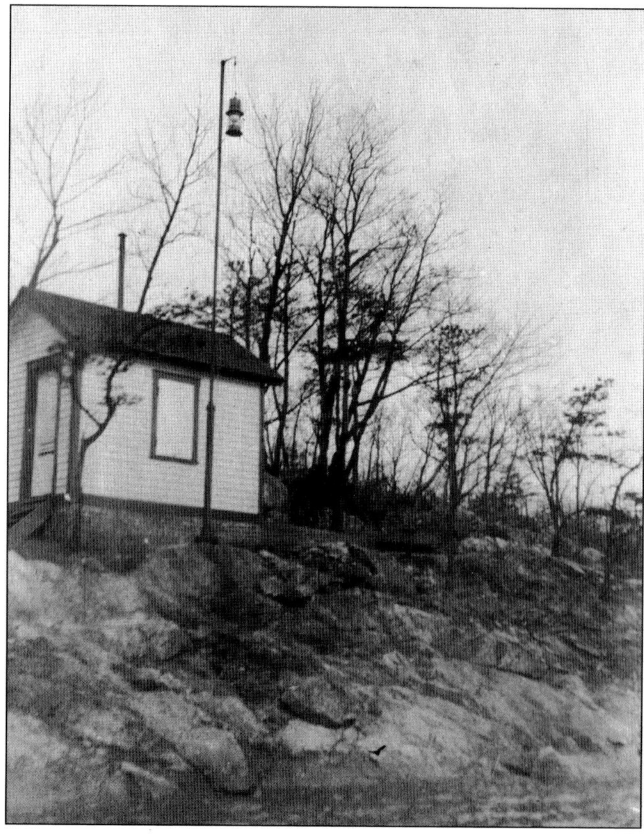

Stake lights were placed on Con Hook and on nearby Iona Island in 1889. These two photographs of the Con Hook Light are some of the only known images of Hudson River stake lights. A tall pole with a pulley system to raise and lower lanterns was located near a small shed for storing kerosene and other supplies. Most keepers of stake lights did not live on-site. In 1894, Con Hook keeper Joseph Elsen took over as keeper of the West Point Lighthouse. In 1897, the Con Hook keeper was John Boyle, who had a "very intelligent" dog named Bounce, who accompanied his owner to and from the light each day. The light was updated in 1916, but the date of its removal is unknown. (Both, NARA.)

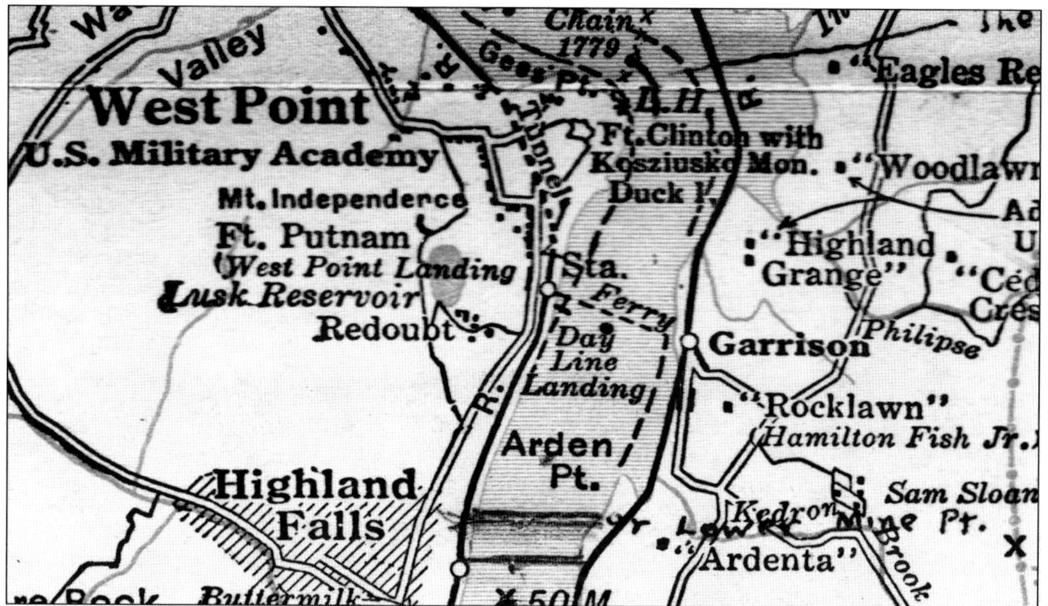

West Point was another, much larger point jutting out into the navigation channel and also the location of the historic US Military Academy, founded in 1802. The US Army Corps of Engineers was stationed at West Point the same year and went on to have significant impact on the navigation of the Hudson River. (HRMM.)

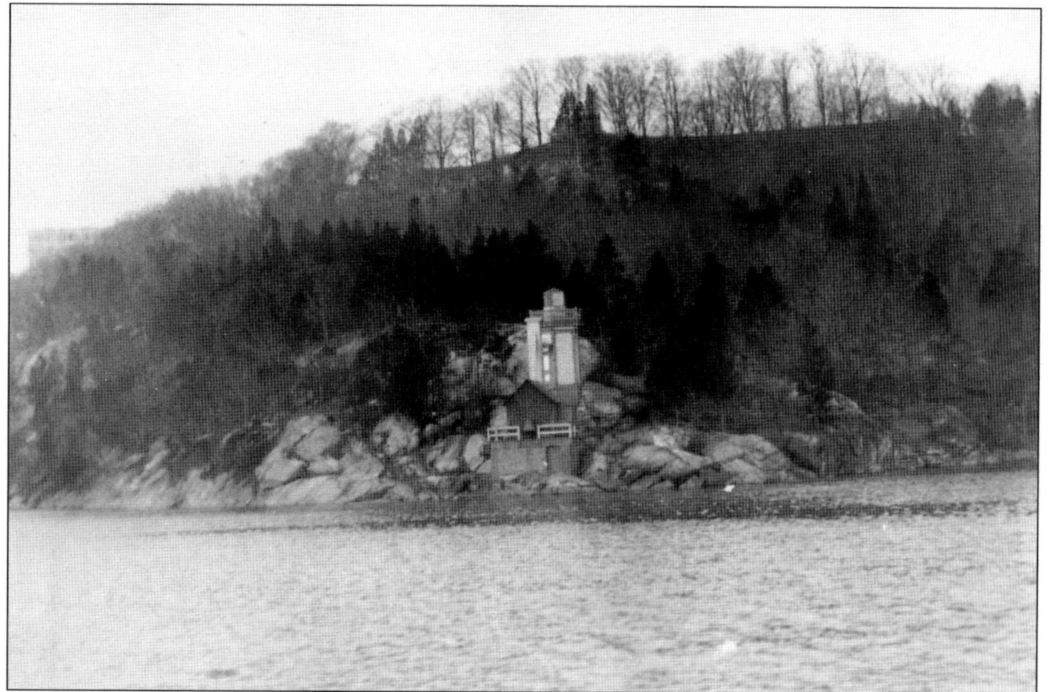
Built in 1853, the West Point Lighthouse, also called Gee's Point or Old Cro' Nest Lighthouse, was originally a stake light. In 1870, construction began on a more permanent structure, and the wooden tower light was lit in 1872. In 1888, a fog bell tower and house were added in front of the lighthouse. (NARA.)

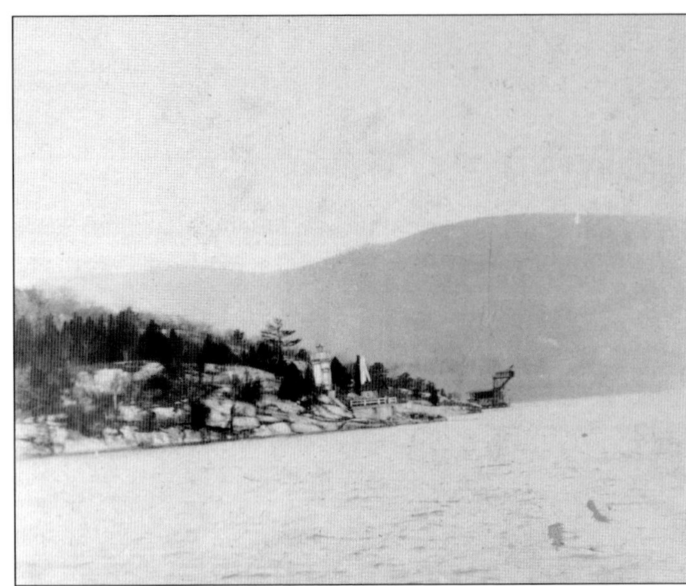

In February 1894, West Point keeper Joseph C. Miller was removed from office for electioneering and neglect of duty for wearing his uniform while leading a political parade, and for "disrespect to the president." The midterm election of 1894 resulted in a Republican landslide and a repudiation of Democratic president Grover Cleveland's failure to address the Panic of 1893. Miller was replaced by Con Hook keeper Joseph Elsen in March 1894. (NARA.)

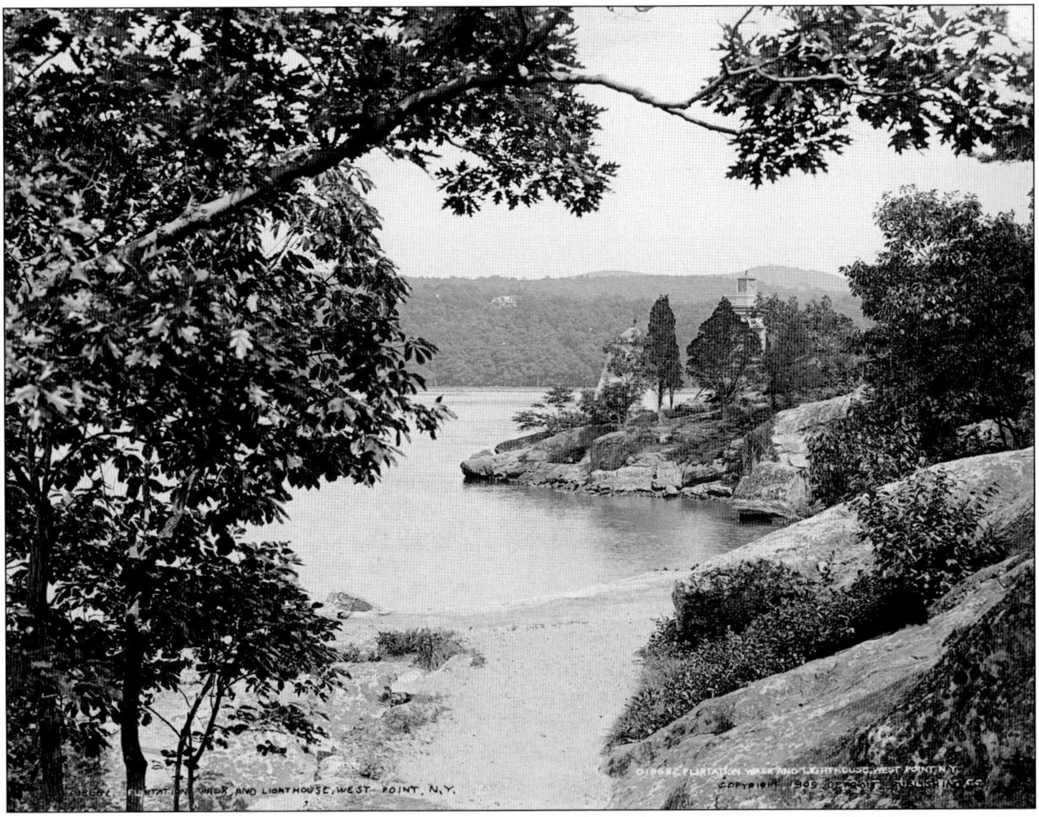

The West Point fog bell tower and lighthouse is seen here from "Flirtation Walk." In December 1908, the original bell tower burned to the ground, and the lighthouse was only saved by bucket brigade. The bell tower, visible behind the pine trees, was rebuilt. The West Point Lighthouse was decommissioned sometime after World War II and later torn down and replaced with a skeleton light. It remains a navigational light today. (LOC.)

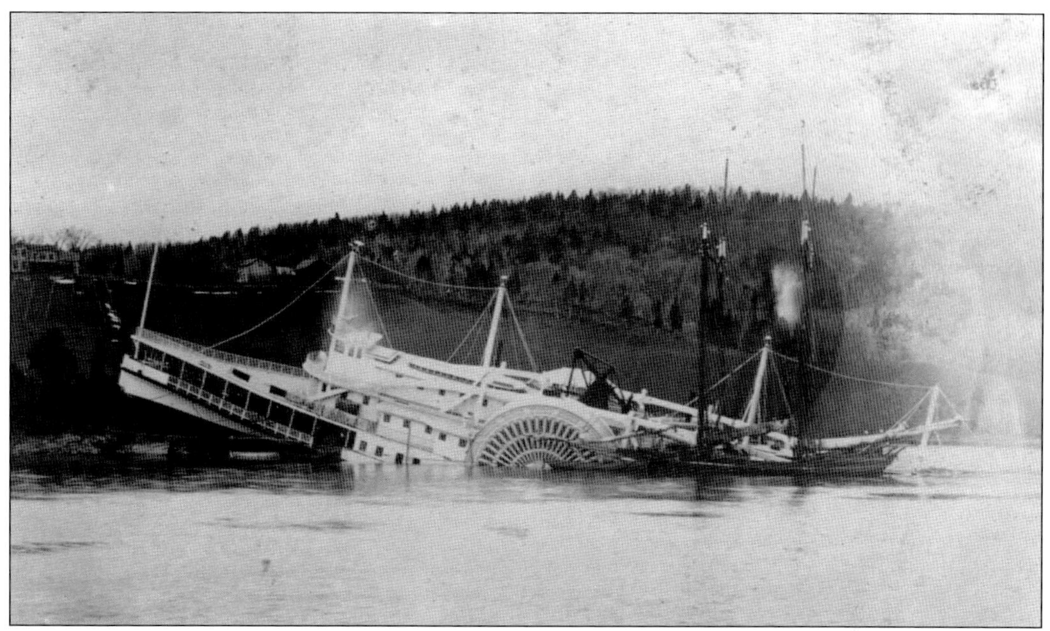

Danskammer Point is a rocky outcropping on the west side of the Hudson north of Newburgh. In 1882, the passenger steamboat *Thomas Cornell* ran up on the point and was wrecked beyond salvage. This incident brought calls for a lighthouse and fog bell to be placed there to prevent further accidents. (HRMM.)

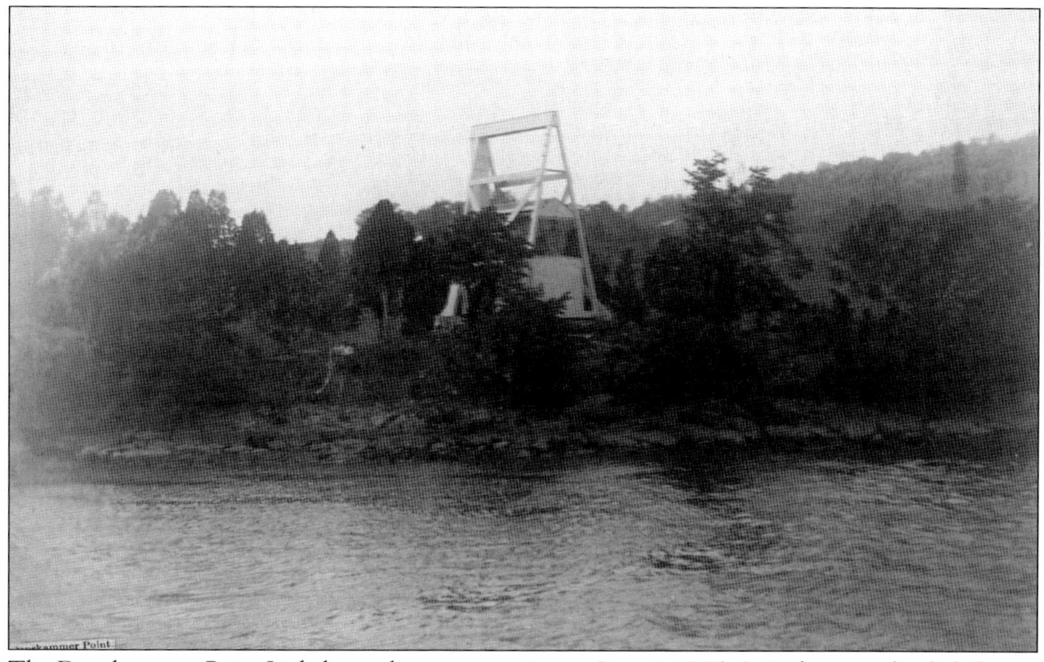

The Danskammer Point Lighthouse began operation on June 1, 1885. A 30-foot wooden lighthouse was built at Danskammer Point to a height of 44 feet. The light was a tubular lantern suspended from the front of the tower. The Danskammer Point Lighthouse was discontinued in 1925. It was replaced by a pyramidal steel skeleton tower (pictured) 53 feet high above high water with a flashing acetylene light and a fog bell. (NARA.)

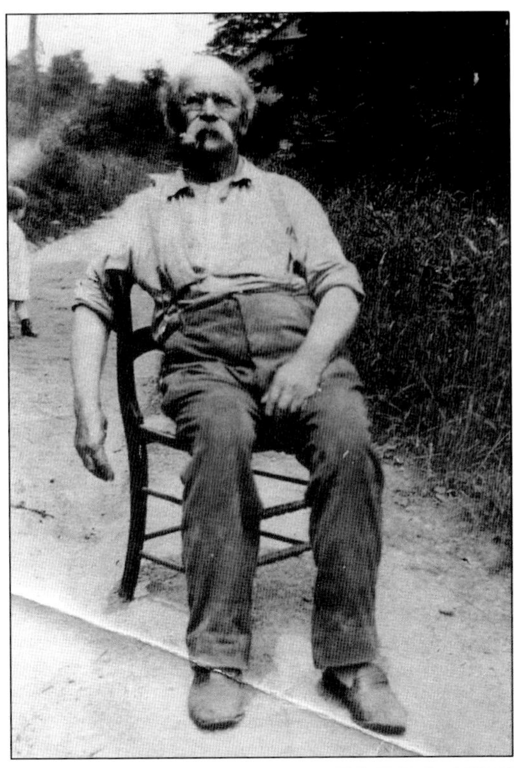

A number of keepers manned the Danskammer Point Light, including in the 20th century. James Wiest, pictured here, was among the longest-serving. He kept the light from 1886 to 1919. Noel and Nancy Armstrong, whose family lived in the Danskammer House near the point for many years, were keepers until 1939. (Warren Mumford.)

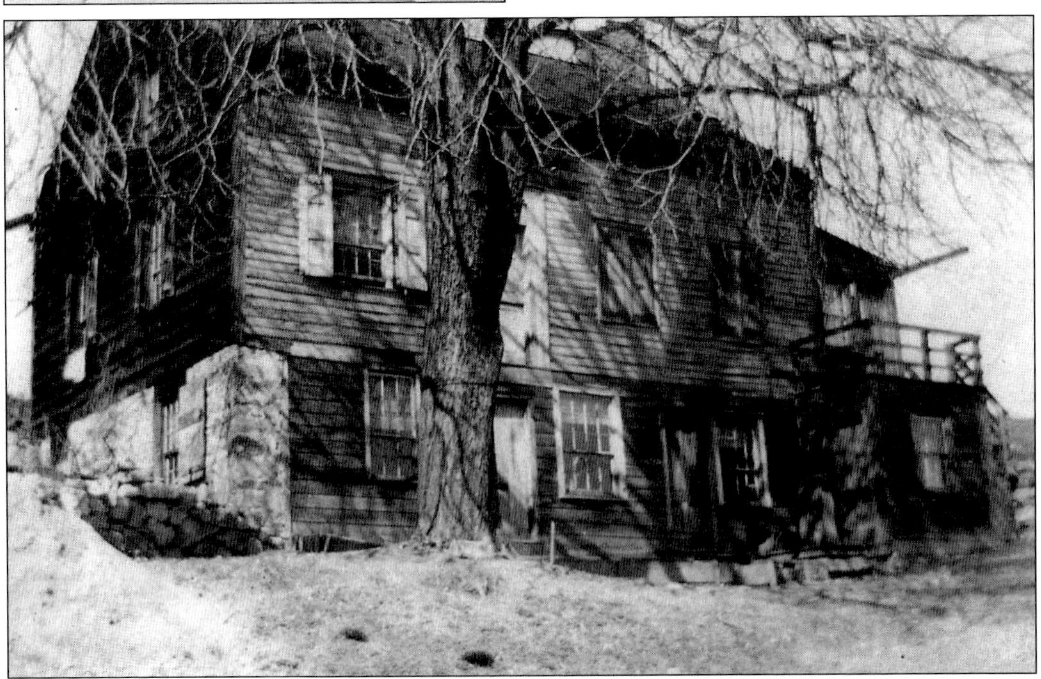

A separate keeper's house, seen here, was necessary as the wooden tower did not include family quarters. The lighthouse was decommissioned in 1925 and later demolished. Today, Danskammer Point is home to the Danskammer Generating Station, operated by Central Hudson Gas & Electric Company. (Warren Mumford.)

Four

Poughkeepsie to Kingston

Between Danskammer and Esopus Island, no lighthouses were ever necessary on the Hudson—the River is largely straight and easily navigable. Esopus Island is a narrow strip of land in the river south of Norrie Point, creating the only hazard on that straight stretch. So named because of its location just off the village of Esopus, it also marks the mouth of Black Creek. A few miles north of Esopus Island the river bends considerably at a location called the Middle Hudson River. Along the west shore of this bend lies the Esopus Meadows, a treacherous bit of wetland off the coast of Ulster Park. These mud flats stretch nearly to the center of the river. The navigation channel hugs the east shore, avoiding the shallow flats, but to the layman's eye, the flats are undetectable, even at low tide when they are only a few feet deep.

Although the Esopus Island light has since been removed, the Esopus Meadows Lighthouse is one of the few lighthouses to remain on the Hudson River and the only surviving wooden lighthouse.

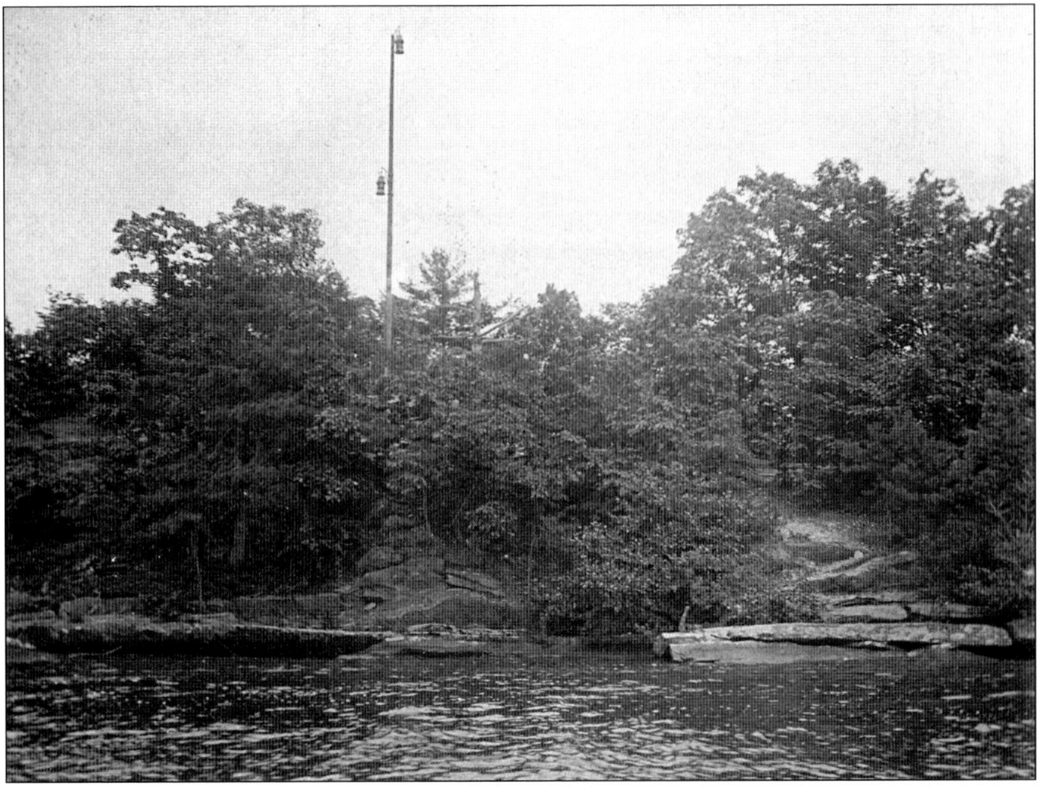

The Esopus Island Light was a post or stake light, and these two photographs account for some of the only surviving images of this style of light on the Hudson River. A tall pole with fixed lanterns raised and lowered by pulley, it was designed to mark the hazard of the island in the center of the river. Very little is known about this light, but it was updated in 1916 with a brighter light. This photograph was taken in June 1901. (NARA.)

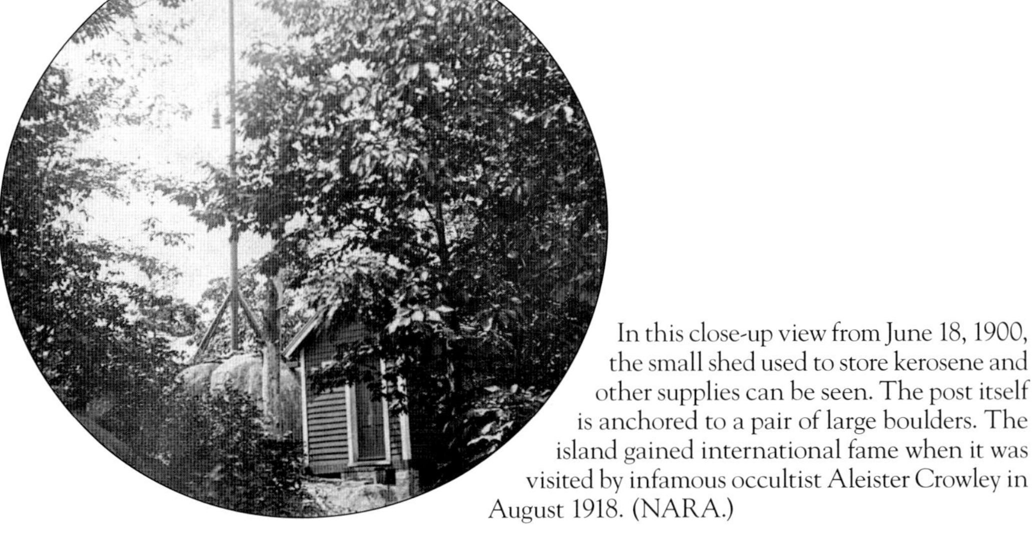

In this close-up view from June 18, 1900, the small shed used to store kerosene and other supplies can be seen. The post itself is anchored to a pair of large boulders. The island gained international fame when it was visited by infamous occultist Aleister Crowley in August 1918. (NARA.)

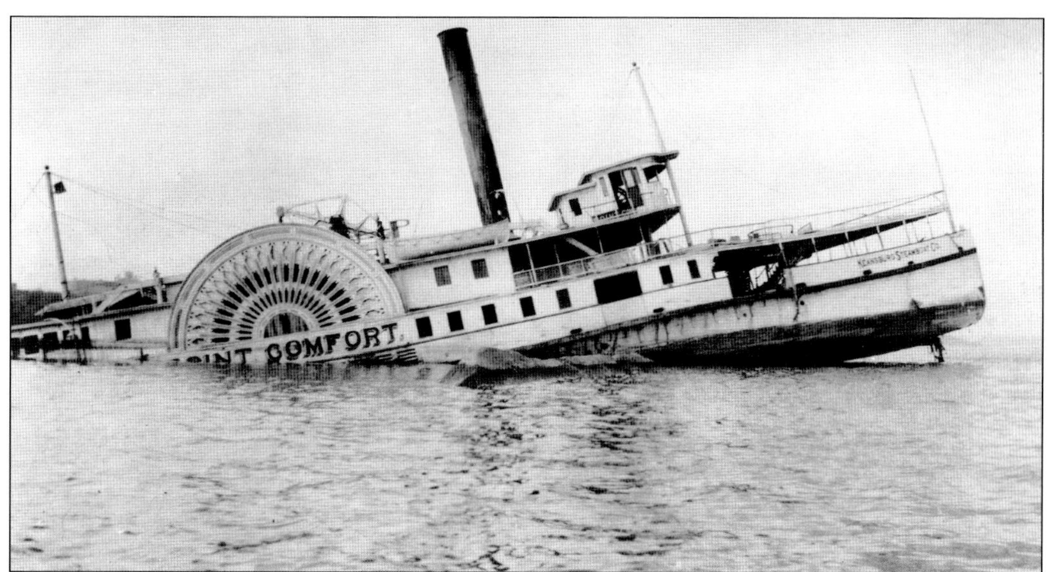

In the fall of 1919, the steamer *Point Comfort*, newly assigned to night boat service from New York City to Catskill, encountered several banks of heavy fog on her way north to Catskill. Upon nearing the Esopus Meadows Lighthouse, the captain decided to turn around in the third bank of fog, which was not clearing as the others had. On heading south, they decided to pass Esopus Island along the west side but miscalculated how far to the east and south they already were. They struck a large rock on the north side of the island, with the force turning the boat perpendicular to the banks of the Hudson. Although no one was injured, her cargo of sugar was a total loss, and the wreck was left to rot until the 1930s, when her remains were mostly removed. Pieces of the *Point Comfort* remain underwater just offshore and on the banks of Esopus Island today. (Both, HRMM.)

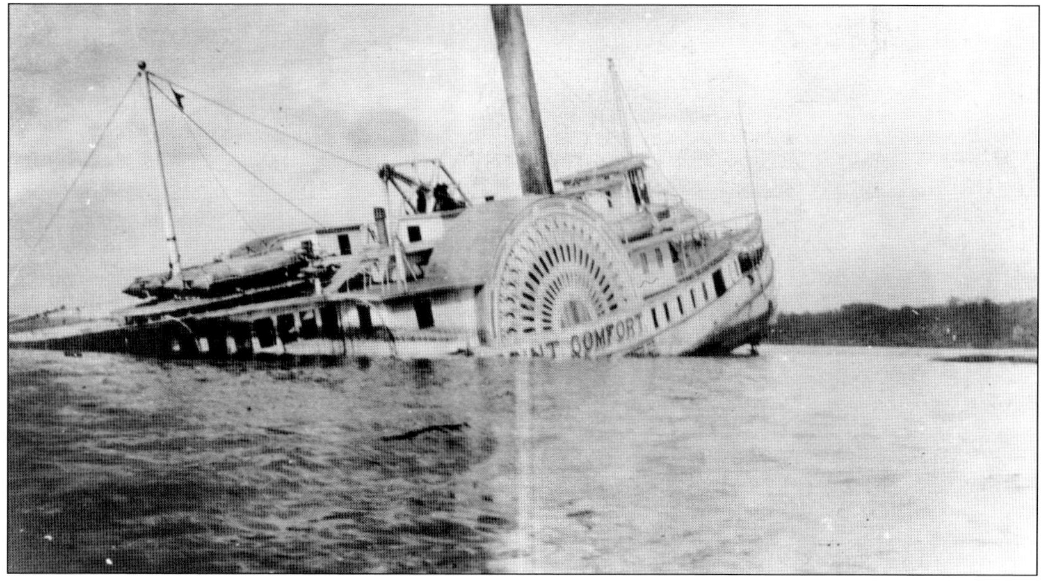

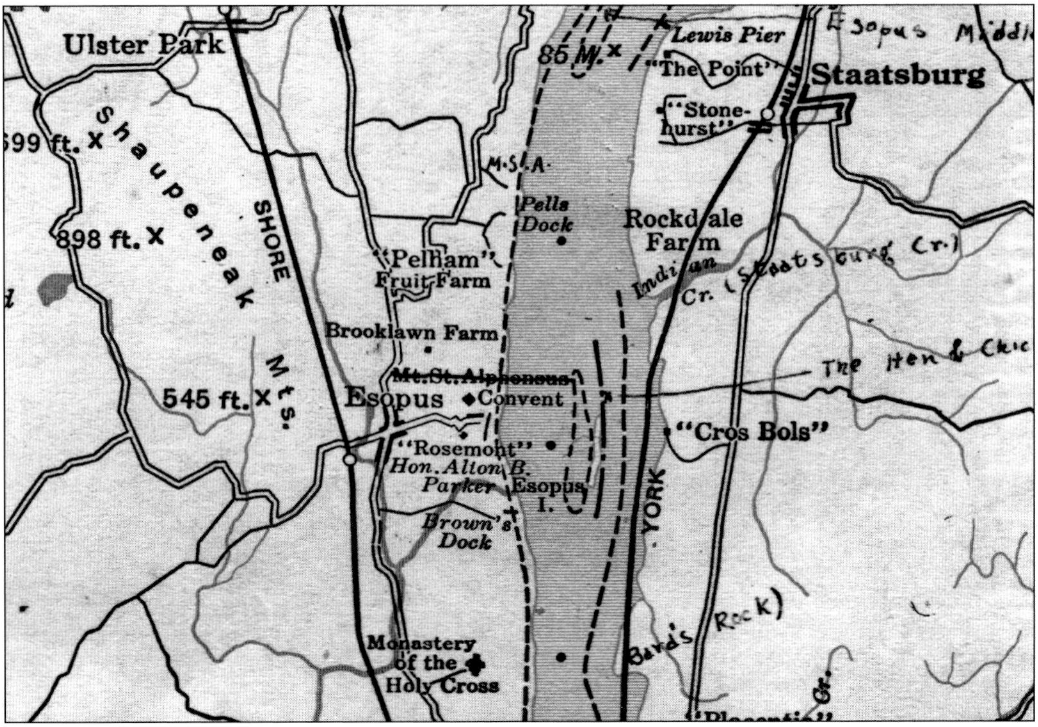

Esopus Island, seen here, is located off the mouth of Black Creek near the town of Esopus. Esopus Meadows is several miles to the north. (HRMM.)

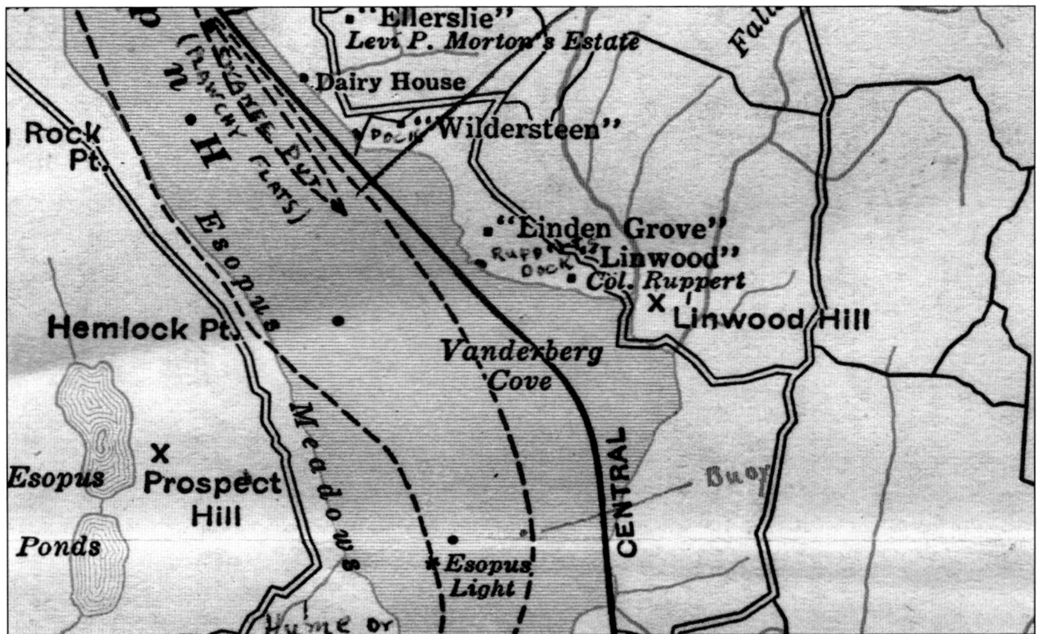

The Esopus Meadows are mud flats so named because in the 19th century, when water levels were lower, cows could graze on the marsh grasses. Today at low tide, the water is only about knee deep. The dotted line near "Esopus Light" on this map marks how far out into the river the flats extended. (HRMM.)

The Esopus Meadows Lighthouse was constructed in 1837 on land deeded by George Terpenning for the sum of $1. The land consisted of a very small island to be used for the construction of what is believed to be a bluestone house. The house was officially occupied in 1839, but by 1869–1870, it had taken too many blows from freshets and ice floes and was deemed unsafe. This drawing from the 1847 *Panorama* is one of only two images of the original lighthouse. (ARC.)

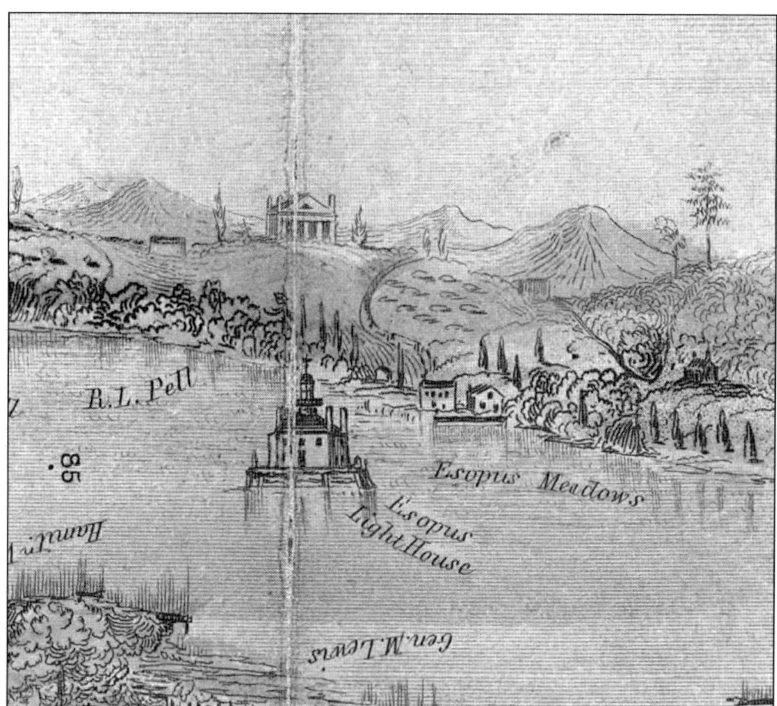

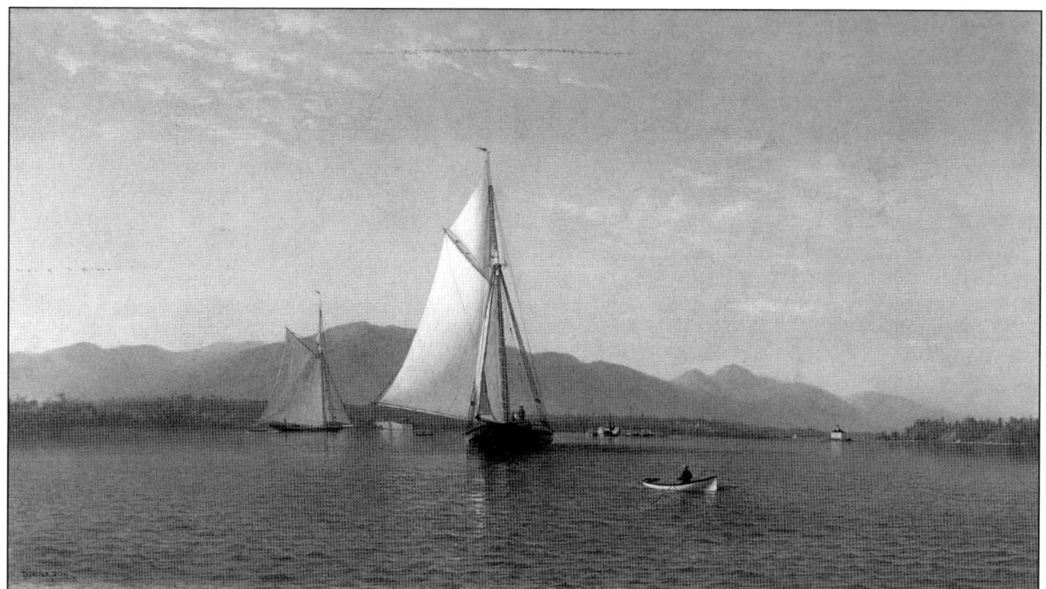

This 1876 oil painting by Francis Augustus Silva, *The Hudson at the Tappan Zee*, is the only other known image of the original Esopus Meadows lighthouse. The accuracy of Silva's painting leads historians to believe that this is close to what the 1830s lighthouses looked like. Although the painting is misattributed as the Tappan Zee, the mountains in the background match the ridge line behind today's Esopus Meadows Lighthouse. (Brooklyn Museum, Dick S. Ramsay Fund, 65.10.)

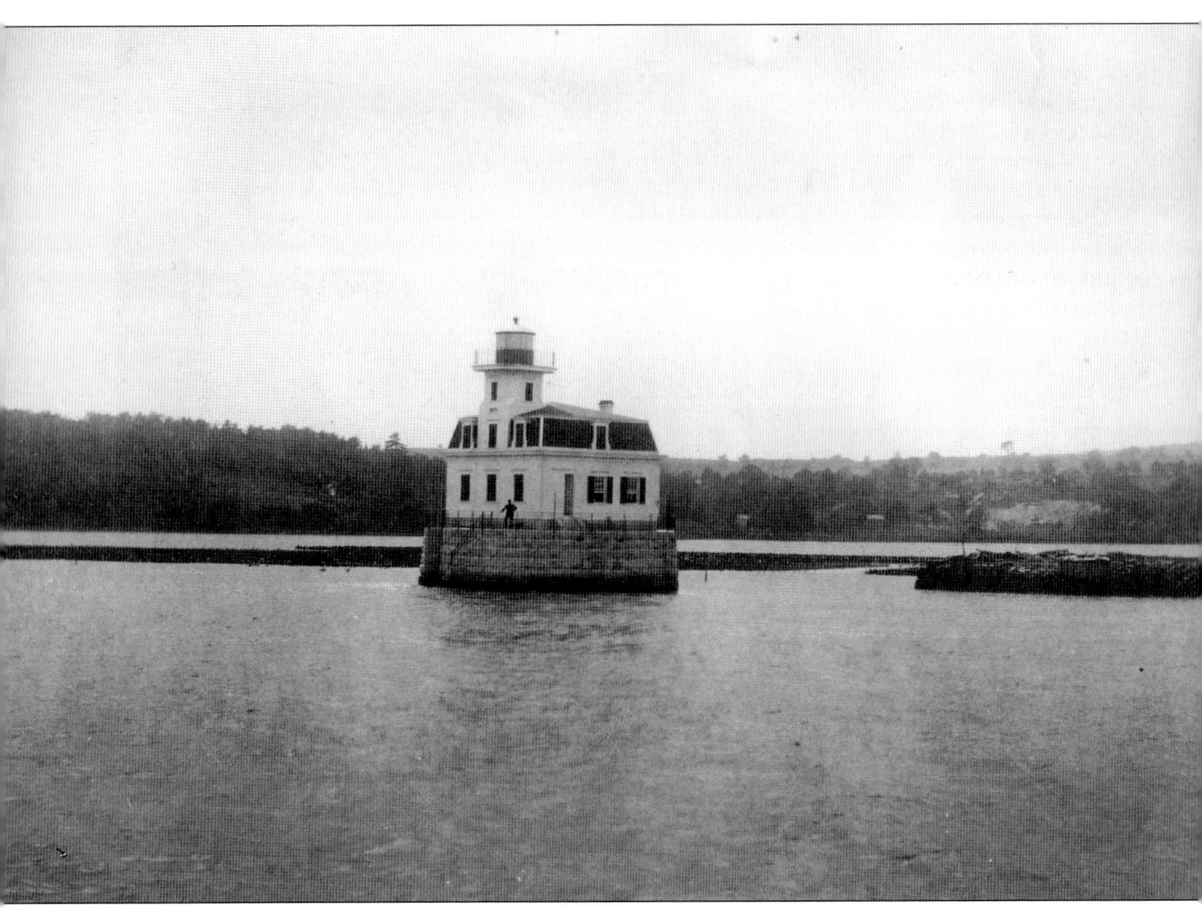

Esopus Meadows Lighthouse as we know it today was started in 1870. It was designed by Albert R. Dow, who designed several other houses throughout the United States (see Rose Island, Colchester Reef, and Pomham Rocks). Unusually, the 1870 mansard-roofed lighthouse was built of wood; it remains the last wooden lighthouse on the Hudson River. Jonathan Cole, the keeper who agreed to man the new lighthouse, helped with the construction of the new building over the winter of 1870. He was not paid until it was finished. (HRMM.)

The lighthouse was designed as a keeper's home for Cole and his family. There was a first-floor parlor, kitchen, a supply storeroom, and pantry. The second floor contained two bedrooms and two other rooms that served various functions over the years from children's playroom to fog bell room. In these original plans, note the presence of closets in every room. This is very unusual for the period, as homes on shore often did not have this luxury yet and relied on cupboards for storage of personal effects. Note the sink with a hand pump in the corner of the kitchen. (Both, EML.)

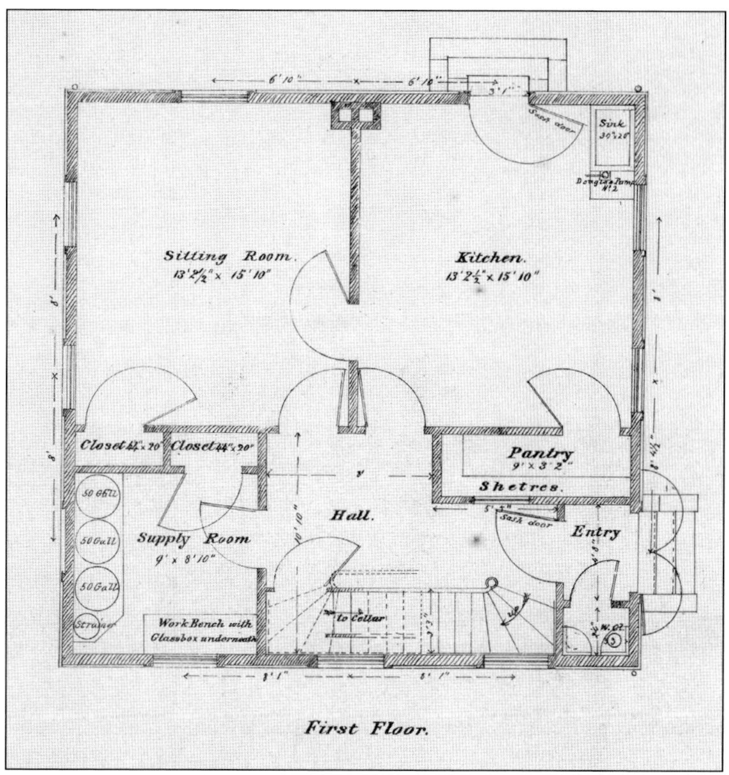

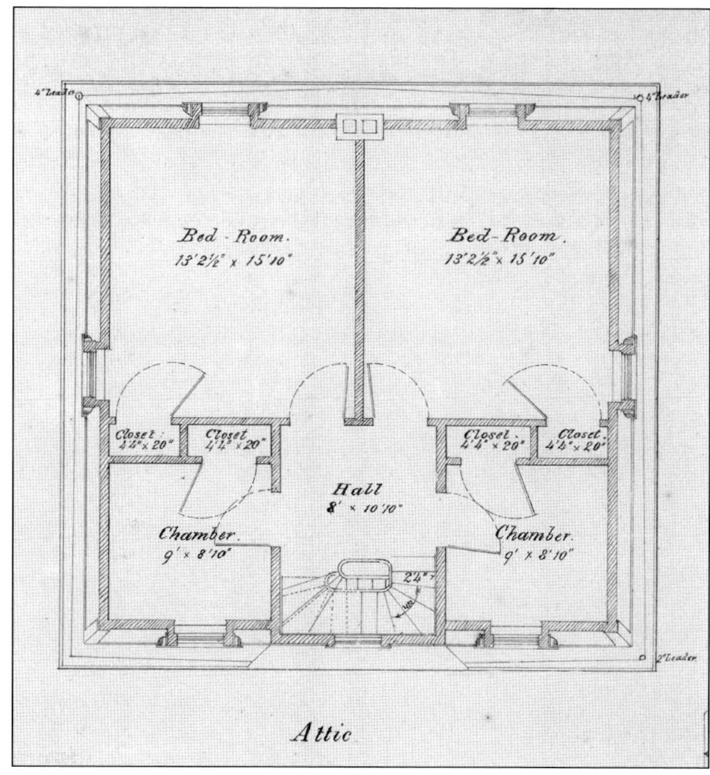

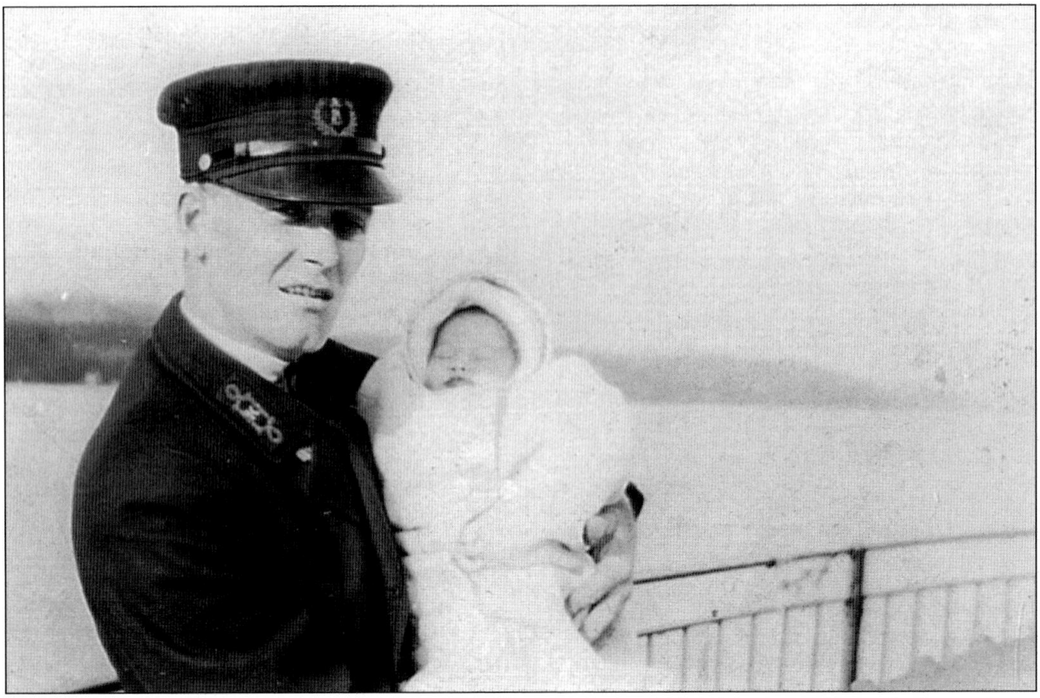

Keeper Andrew McClintock; his wife, Rebecca; and their daughter Doris lived at the lighthouse from 1922 to 1933. Here, Andrew holds a two-week-old Doris, called "Dorie," in his arms at the lighthouse with the Hudson River in the background. (EML.)

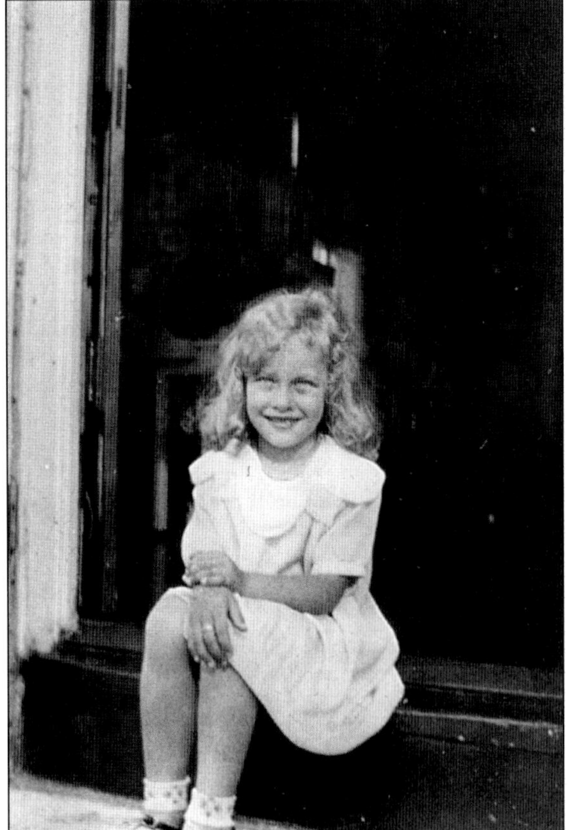

Dorie was always very well dressed as Rebecca was a talented seamstress and milliner. The family had made friends throughout the Mid-Hudson Valley, including at some of the great estates. Although she only lived at the lighthouse until age six, Dorie had very vivid memories of life on the water. (EML.)

Here, the Esopus Meadows Lighthouse is seen in winter sometime before 1933. Note the fog bell installed in the second-story window and the metal ladder bypassing the stone steps on the foundation. In 1933, Emanuel and Sylvia Weber became keepers and were succeeded in 1936 by Manuel and Elsie (Hilden) Resendes. (EML.)

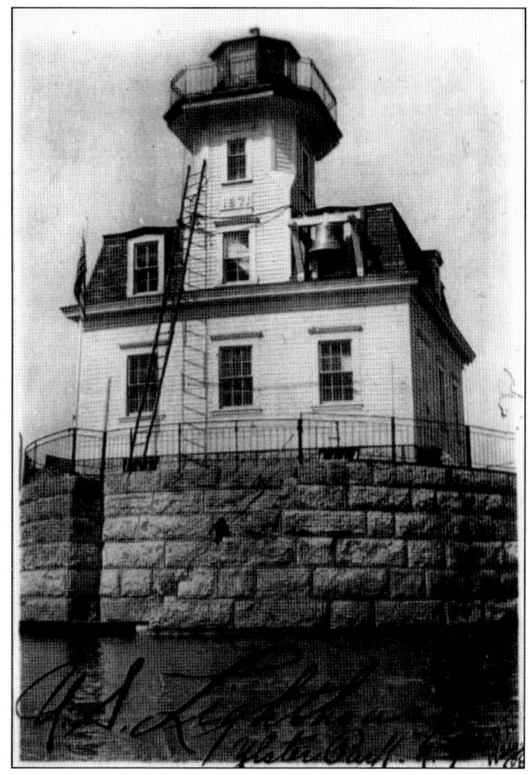

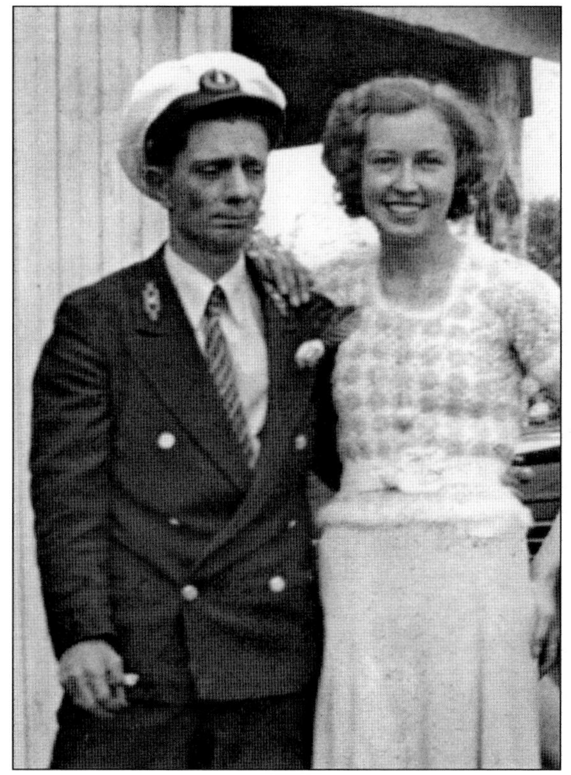

In the 1930s, a small enclave of Portuguese immigrants lived on the bluffs overlooking the Meadows. Elsie, who went by "Ellie," lived there with her family. The family felt sorry for the lonely lightkeeper and so when Ellie was just 18 years old, she found herself in an arranged marriage with Manuel "Manny" Resendes, aged 35. However, Manny seemed to prefer life on shore, especially horse racing, to the lighthouse and often left Ellie to manage lightkeeping alone, sometimes for weeks on end. (EML.)

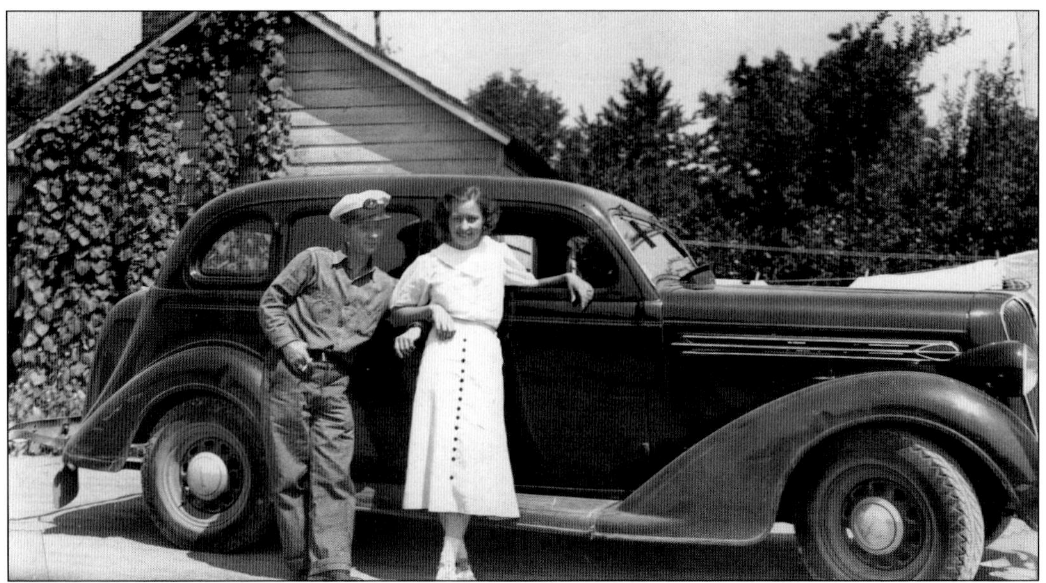

Manny eventually disappeared altogether, and in 1944, Ellie moved back on shore to a house on the hill overlooking the lighthouse. She was never able to claim his pension and lived in relative obscurity and poverty until her death. The Coast Guard had taken over in 1939. Two temporary keepers, John Olsen and John Bretz, both served in 1944. (EML.)

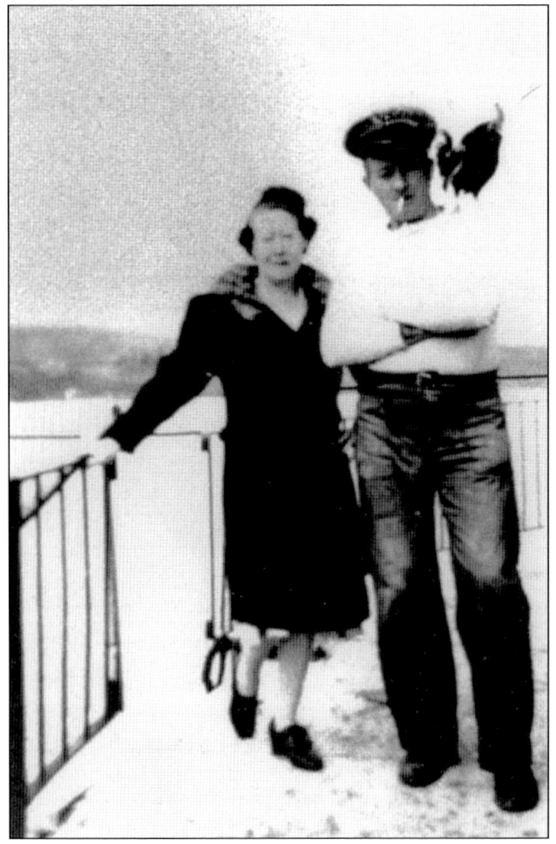

Keeper John J. Kerr served from 1944 to 1959 as the last civilian keeper of the Esopus Meadows light and indeed any light on the Hudson River north of the Tappan Zee. He was known for his love of animals (note the pet chicken on his shoulder). In 1949, a visiting seal spent several days off of the lighthouse, conducting a "flirtation" with Kerr's dog by barking at each other, much to his consternation. (EML.)

Kerr was succeeded by a series of Coast Guardsmen on one- to three-year rotation until 1965, when the light was automated and decommissioned. Here, the Coast Guard boat *Firebush* passes the lighthouse. Note that the fog bell has been removed from the upper window. (EML.)

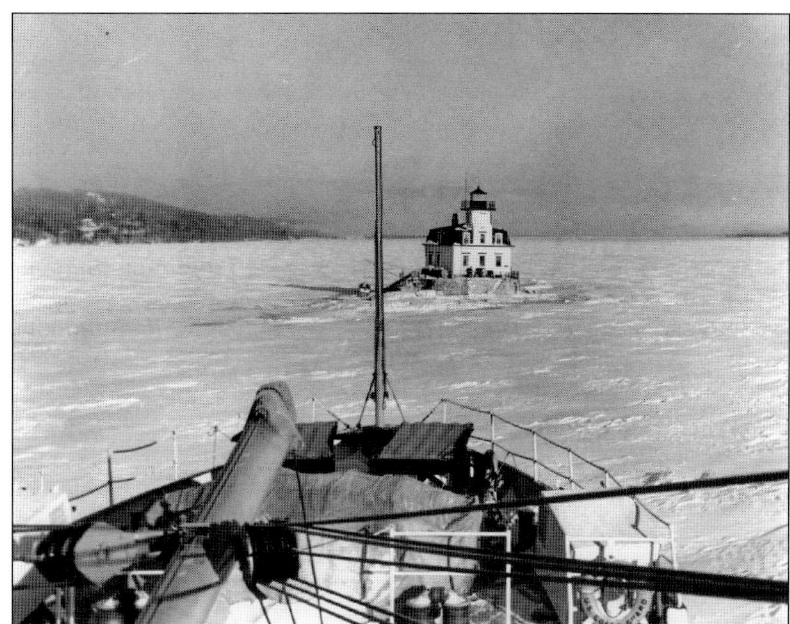

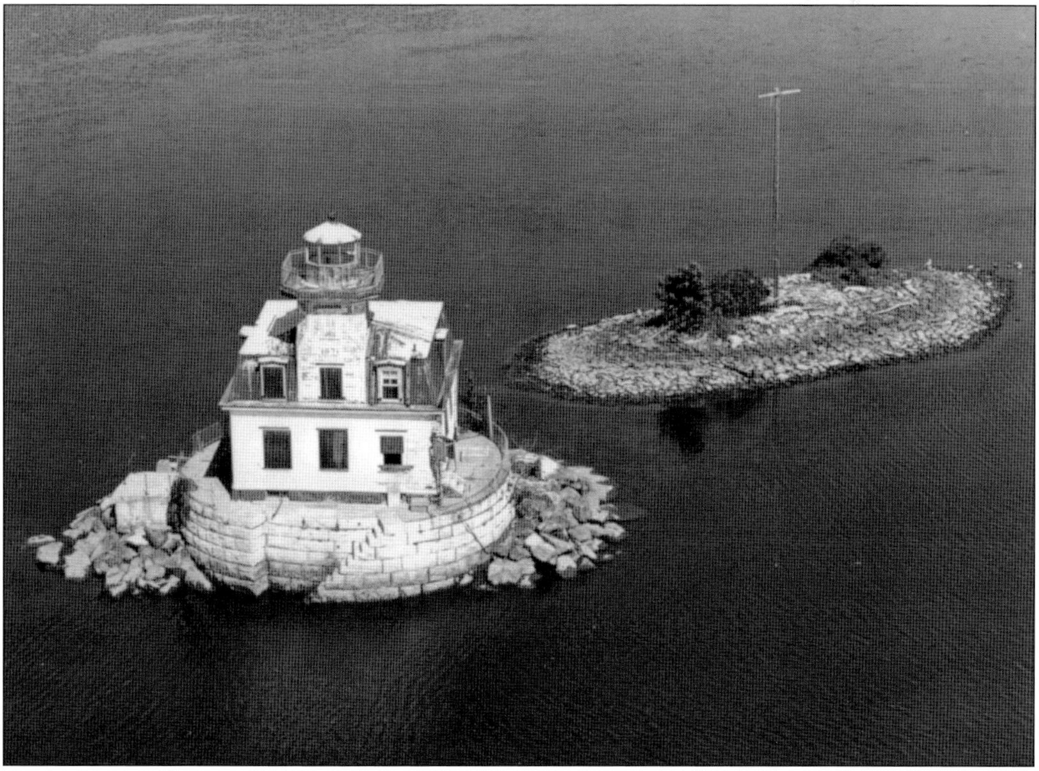

In 1965, the lighthouse itself was abandoned in favor of an automated light stationed on a pole outside the building. Here, the lighthouse is shown shortly after the Coast Guard abandoned the structure; the automated light can be seen on the front right corner of the building. Note the boarded-up windows, one of which had already been broken by the time this photograph was taken. (HRMM.)

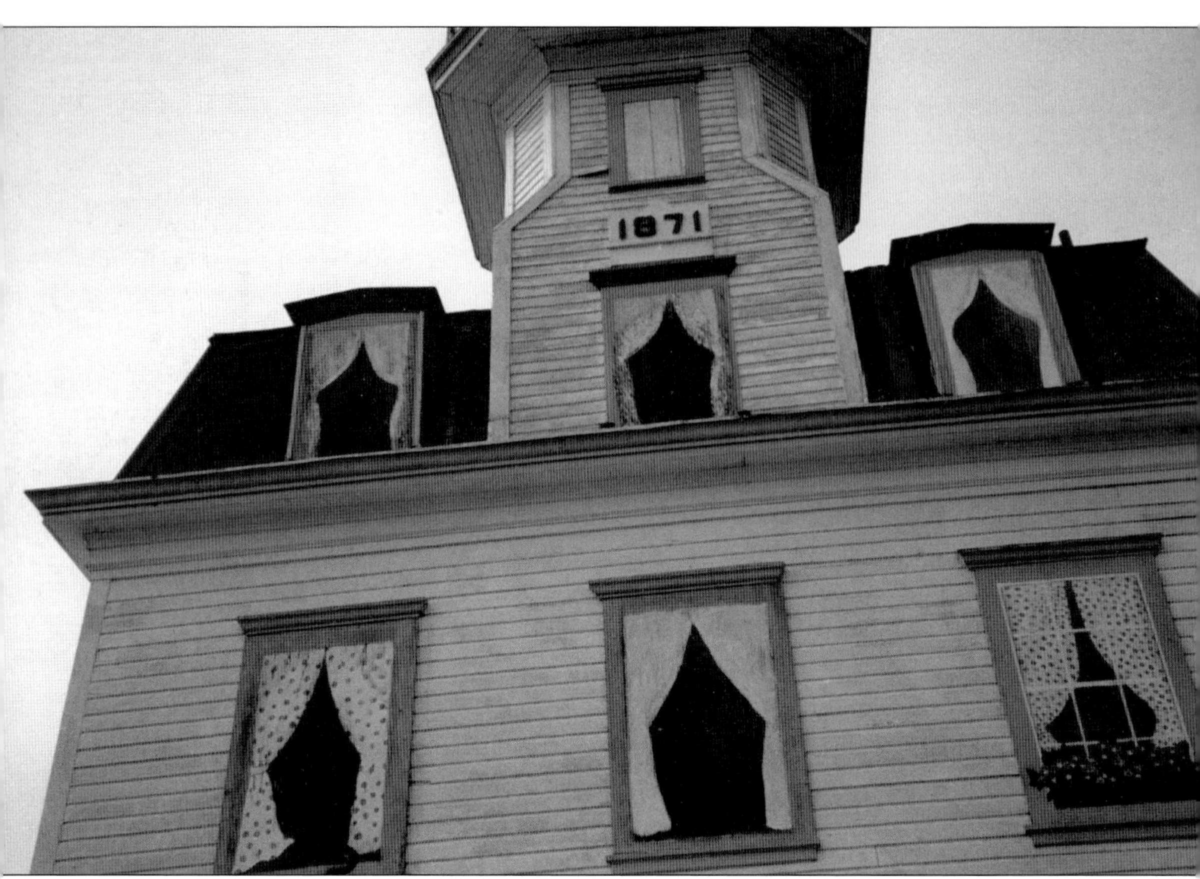

As the abandoned structure grew more and more deteriorated, a group of concerned citizens banded together to attempt to save the light. These groups, including volunteers from the Hudson River Maritime Museum and Hudson River Sloop *Clearwater*, started the work to save her and repaired her terne (a tin-lead alloy) plate roof to prevent further damage to the interior, put a coat of paint on her exterior, and installed trompe l'oeil painted window boards to replace broken windows. These preliminary efforts helped improve her image on the Hudson and started to pave the way for more extensive restoration down the road. (EML.)

Five

Rondout Creek

Rondout Creek is unique among most tributaries of the Hudson River in that it is navigable for a considerable distance inland. When Dutch colonists first came to the valley, the settlement that would become known as Kingston was one of the three major settlements in New Netherland. With the Rondout Creek a natural, deepwater port well-protected from the winds and waves of the mighty Hudson, it became an important industrial port in the 19th century with the opening of the Delaware & Hudson Canal in 1828. The D&H Canal, which terminated at Rondout, brought massive amounts of coal from eastern Pennsylvania to be shipped throughout the northeast. Bluestone, bricks, Rosendale cement, natural ice, and agricultural products were also shipped out of the port of Rondout in enormous quantities. It was this increase in shipping that led to the construction of the first Rondout lighthouse in 1837.

Rondout is one of the few ports on the Hudson to have had three separate lighthouse structures over the years and the only one to have them in three separate locations. The exact location of the original 1837 lighthouse, made of wood, is unknown, but was likely near the center of the harbor entrance. The 1867 lighthouse was built on the south side of the mouth of Rondout Creek, off of the village of Sleightsburgh (now Port Ewen). The 1915 lighthouse was constructed on Army Corps of Engineers jetties on the north side of the creek starting in 1913 and remains in use today.

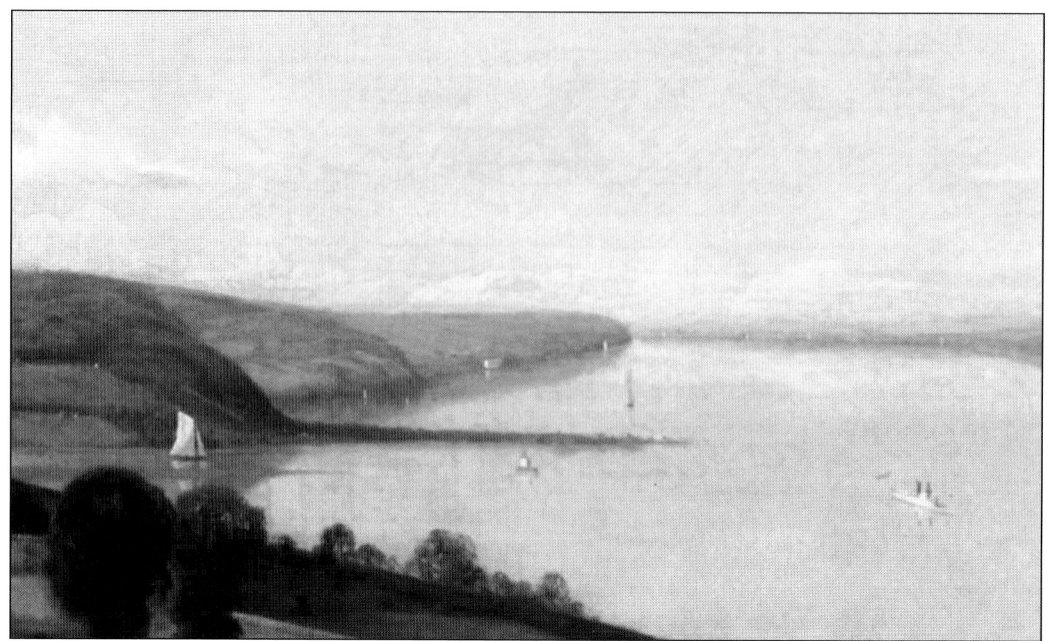

This Hudson River School painting of the entrance to Rondout Creek, by Jervis McEntee, contains the earliest known image of the first Rondout Lighthouse, completed in 1838. Although the lighthouse structure was completed by December 1837, a small scandal erupted as the man contracted by the government to furnish lamps and oil cans had failed to do so by July 1838, despite the fact that lighthouse keeper James McCausland had begun service in March. The lighthouse was finally lit by the end of the year. (Richard Sharp.)

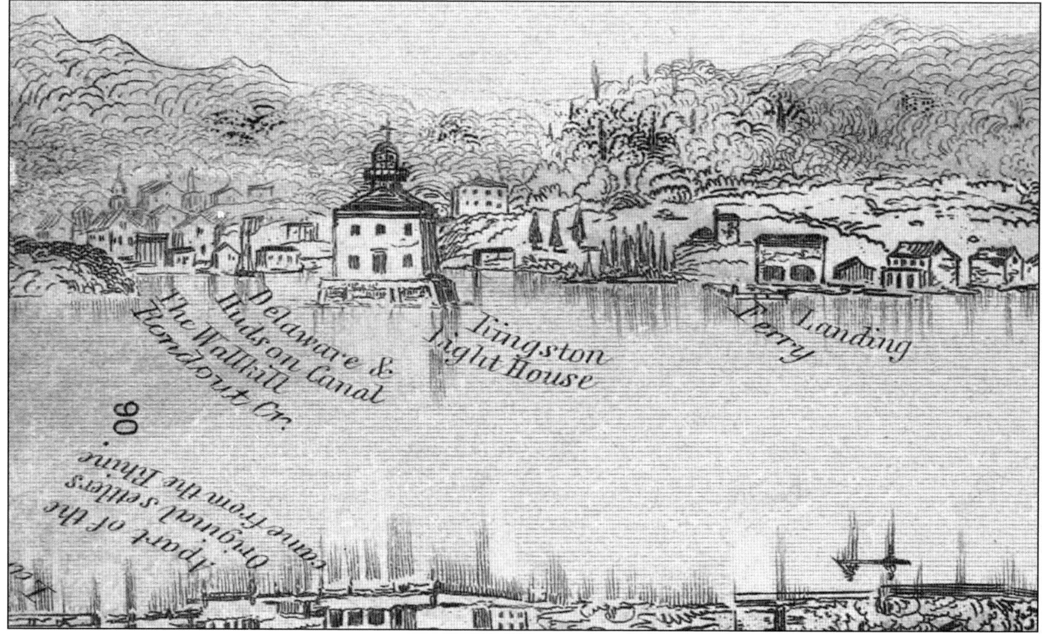

Taken from the 1847 Wallace & Croomes *Panorama*, this is the second-known image of the early wooden Rondout Lighthouse. Note the lighthouse's location in the center of the Creek. (ARC.)

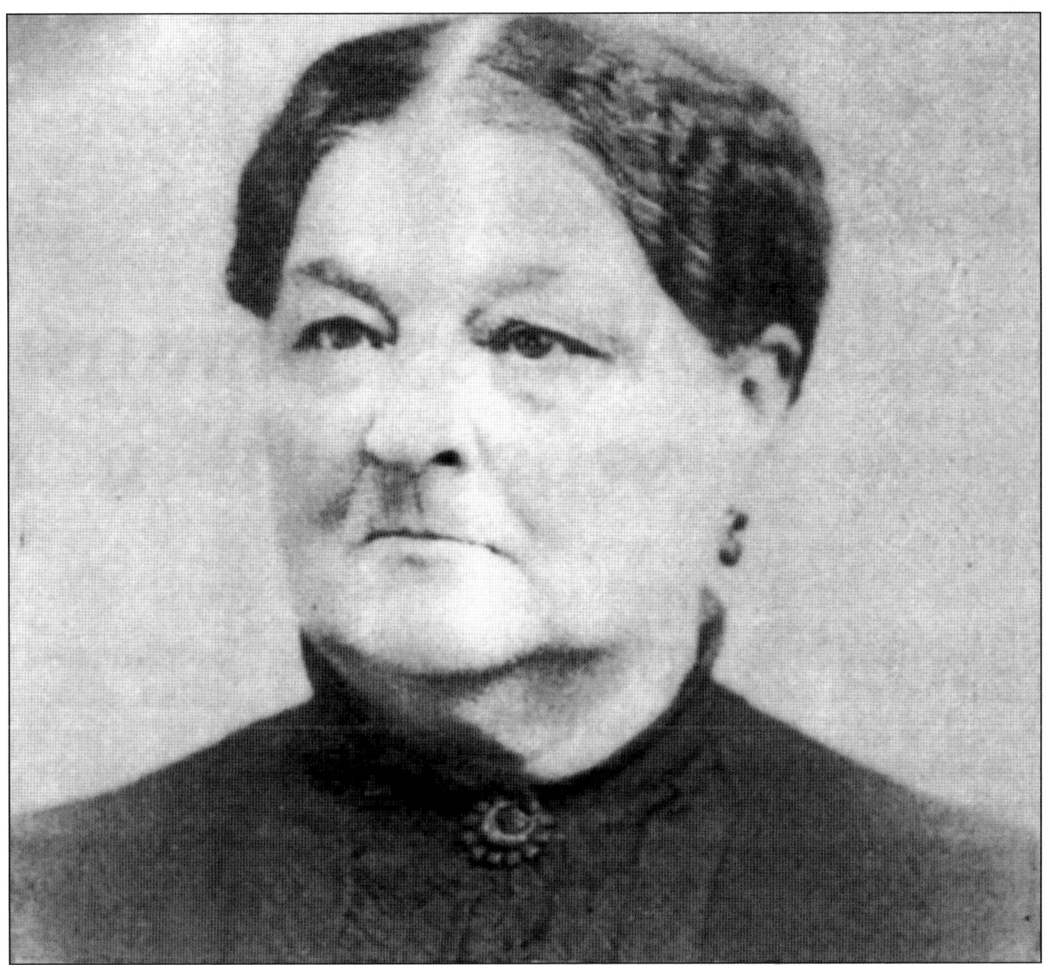

Although there were several single male lighthouse keepers at Rondout in the early years, George Murdock was the first family keeper. He was appointed in 1856 by Pres. Franklin Pierce after serving as a prison guard at Sing Sing Prison. He and his wife, Catherine (pictured), and their children George Jr. and Emma moved into the first wooden lighthouse. Catherine was pregnant at the time. On May 27, 1857, George went ashore for groceries and was never seen alive again. His body was found floating in the creek the next day and the cause of death ruled "accidental drowning while intoxicated." Left a widow with three young children, Catherine Murdock took her newborn son James (who had been born in the lighthouse) down to the US Lighthouse Board in Washington, DC, to petition in person to be made keeper, bringing letters of recommendation from family and friends in nearby Port Ewen. She argued that baby James could have no better training to become a lighthouse keeper himself than to be raised in a lighthouse. The board apparently agreed, and she was appointed keeper at the end of the year. (HRMM.)

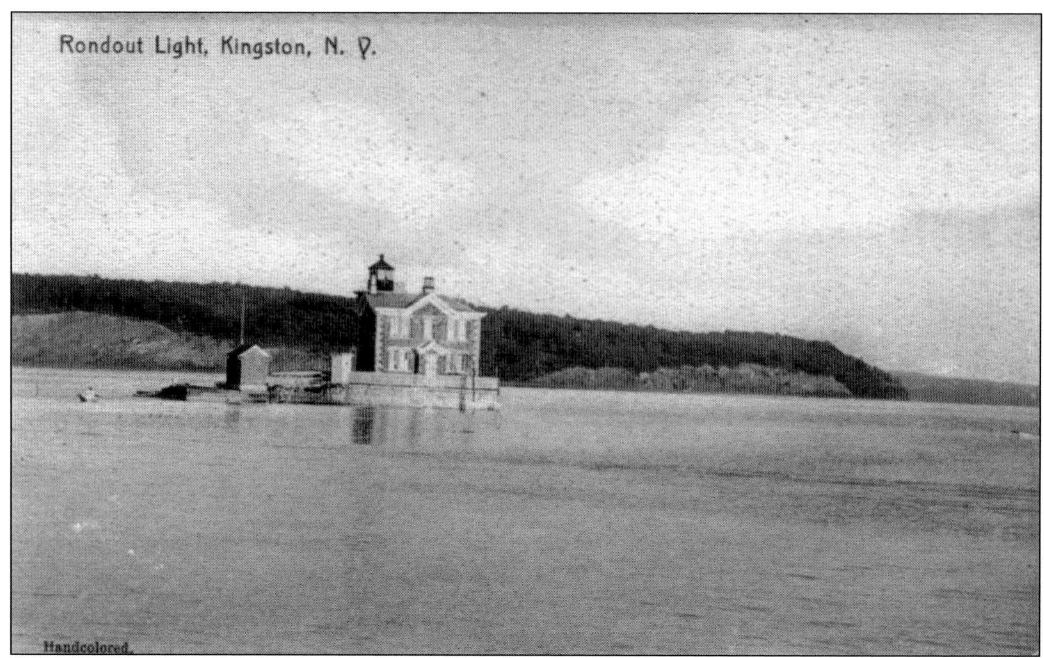

Catherine later married Jeremiah Perkins, who worked on steamboats; they had a son named William Perkins. Sadly, in 1865, Jeremiah died from a fall from a ladder while coming up out of the hull of a barge. Catherine was widowed again, and the wooden lighthouse in the middle of the creek was not faring so well either. In 1867, construction began on a new, sturdier lighthouse made of bluestone, seen here. (HRMM.)

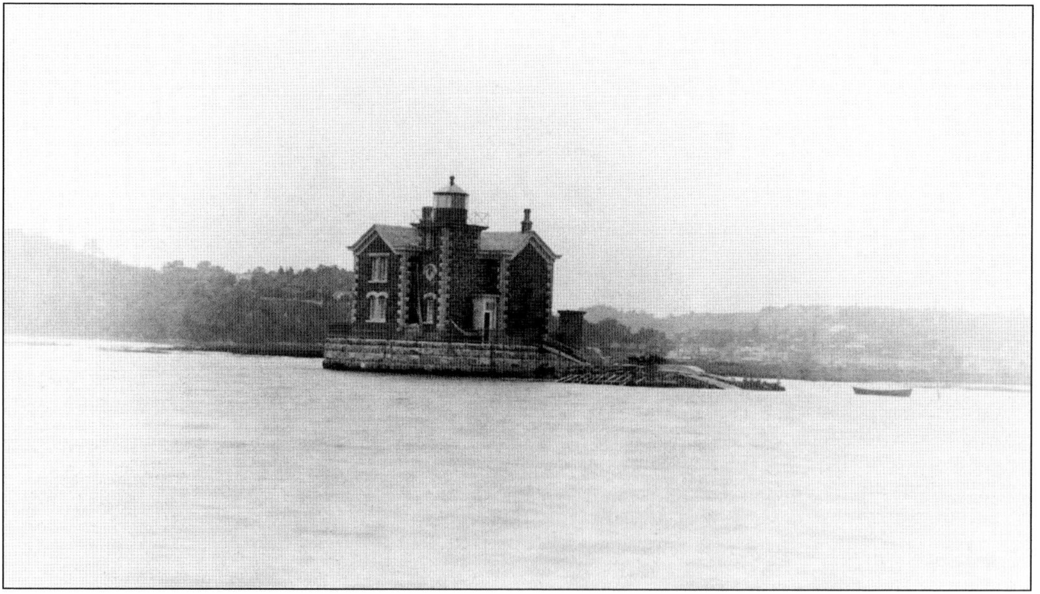

Situated just to the south of the entrance to the creek, off of the village of Sleightsburgh, the new lighthouse sat on an enormous round stone pier, to better withstand heavy ice floes in winter and spring flooding. Here, the unusual design of the lighthouse can be seen, with the light tower in the center and the two-story house wrapped around it. The wooden outhouse is at right, along with a boat ramp. A hammock is strung near the back door. (HRMM.)

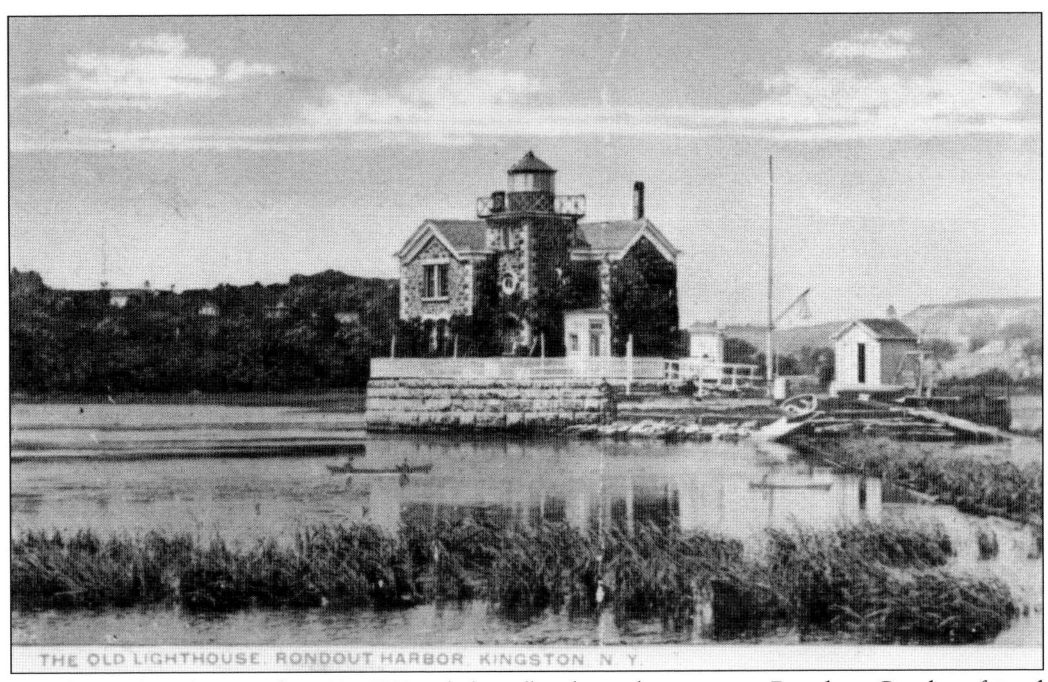

On the night of December 19, 1878, while a flood was brewing on Rondout Creek, a friend urged Catherine to come ashore. She replied, "I will never desert my post of duty. I am a woman, I know, but if the Lighthouse goes down tonight, I go with it." Catherine and the lighthouse survived the flood, but dozens of buildings along Rondout Creek were destroyed, and vessels struck loose from their moorings. The section of breakwater jetty pictured here was completed in 1877. (HRMM.)

This view of the lighthouse from Port Ewen bay looking northeast shows how Catherine Murdock and her family went ashore—the curved metal poles to the left are davits, which were used to raise and lower the lighthouse tender. Just to the left of the davits is a large stone staircase set into the foundation. An American flag flies near the back door. (Cordts Family Collection, HRMM.)

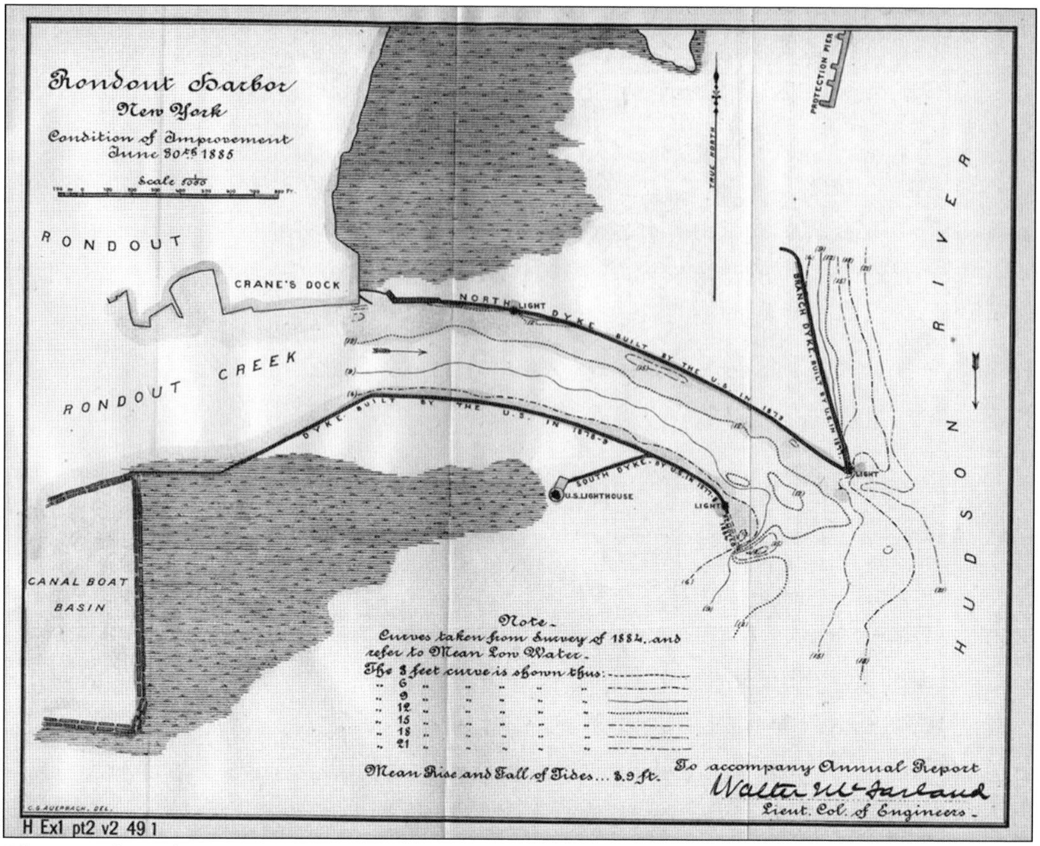

Rondout Harbor
New York
Condition of Improvement
June 30th 1885

RONDOUT
CRANE'S DOCK
RONDOUT CREEK
CANAL BOAT BASIN
U.S. LIGHTHOUSE
PROTECTION PIER
TRUE NORTH
HUDSON RIVER

Note.
Curves taken from Survey of 1884, and refer to Mean Low Water.

Mean Rise and Fall of Tides... 3.9 ft.

To accompany Annual Report
Walter McFarland
Lieut. Col. of Engineers.

H Ex1 pt2 v2 49 1

This map from the Army Corps of Engineers shows improvements made to the mouth of Rondout Creek. The dikes are dated, with the first completed in 1877–1878 from the lighthouse curving out into the river. The others were completed in 1878 and 1879. With the creation of these new dikes came the installation of red stake lights to warn mariners of the modifications to the entrance to Rondout Creek. (HRMM.)

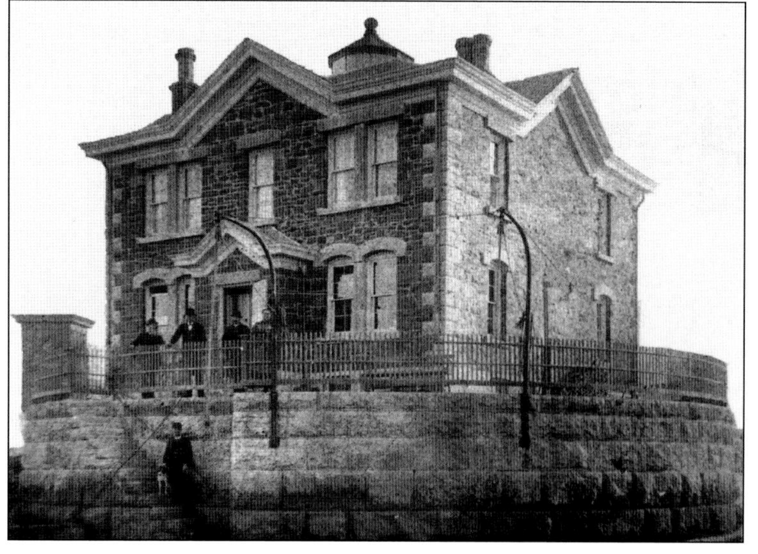

Although the faces of the people pictured here are slightly blurred, the woman to the far right is almost certainly Catherine Murdock herself, and the man in what appears to be a US Lighthouse Service uniform with the dog on the stairs is likely her son James Murdock, who became assistant keeper in 1880 after the completion of the breakwater jetty. (G.M. Mastropaolo.)

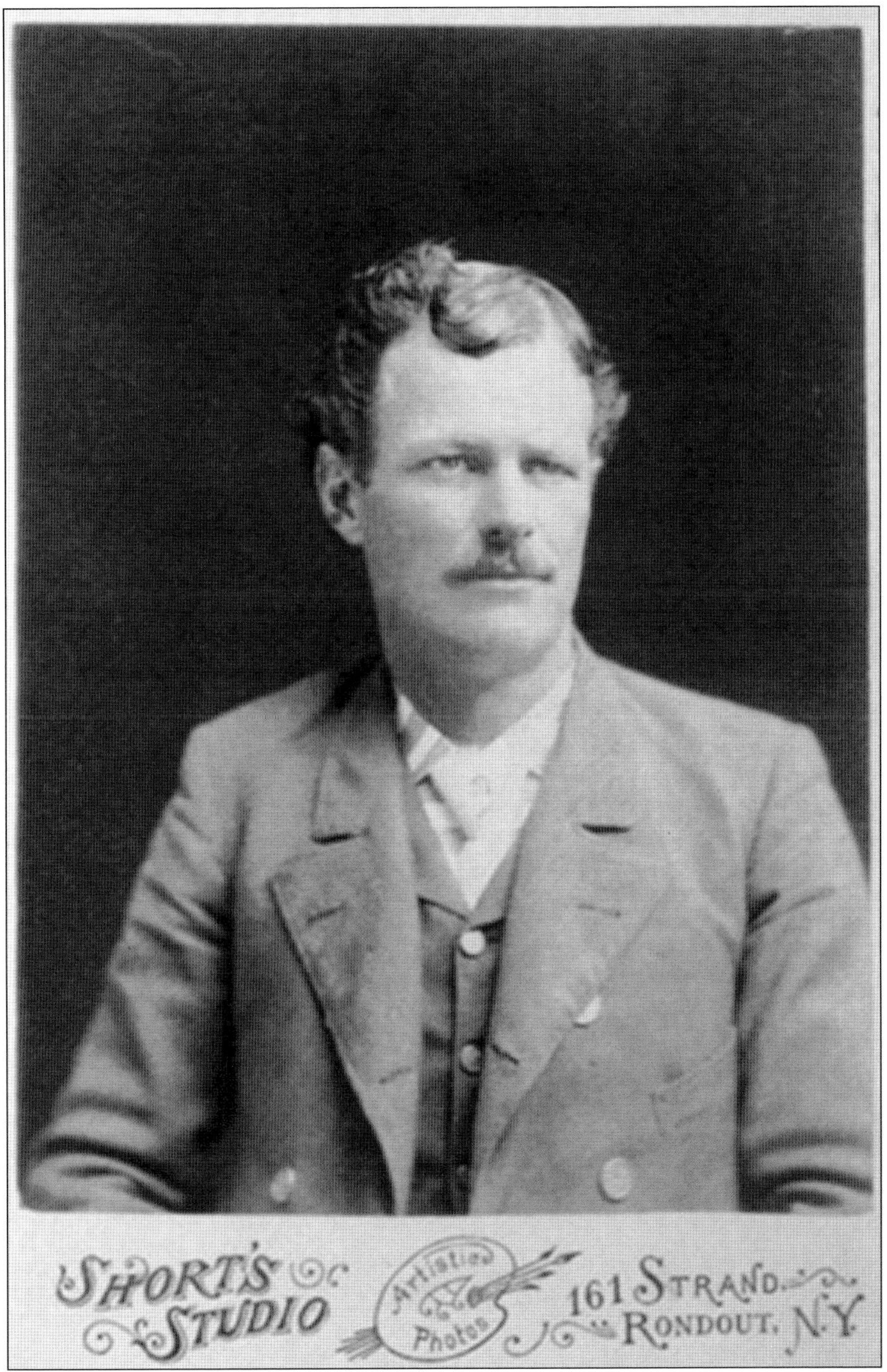

James Murdock became assistant keeper in 1880 and was charged with maintaining the stake lights along the newly installed dikes at the entrance of Rondout Creek. He likely also assisted his mother with her own lightkeeper duties. In 1907, after 50 years of service, Catherine retired and moved ashore to Ponckhockie. James became the full-time lighthouse keeper and remained in the lighthouse with his wife and children. Catherine died in 1909 at the age of 81. (G.M. Mastropaolo.)

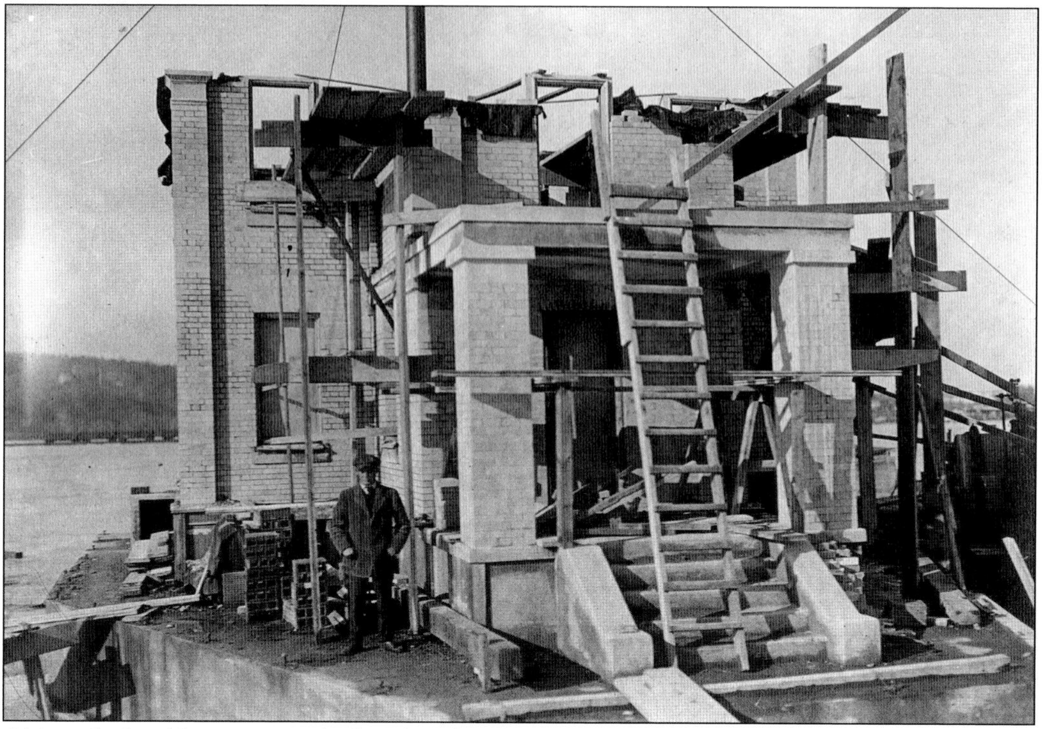

Although the dikes were marked with red stake lights, many mariners were unhappy with the arrangement and complained that the lighthouse was now too far back to be of any use. They petitioned New York congressman George Fairchild, who introduced a bill in 1910 to build a new lighthouse for Kingston. The bill passed and construction began in 1913 on a new lighthouse to be located at the very tip of the north dike, well out into the Hudson River. By early 1915, the enormous steel and cement pilings had been completed, and work on the yellow-brick lighthouse was underway. (Both, NARA.)

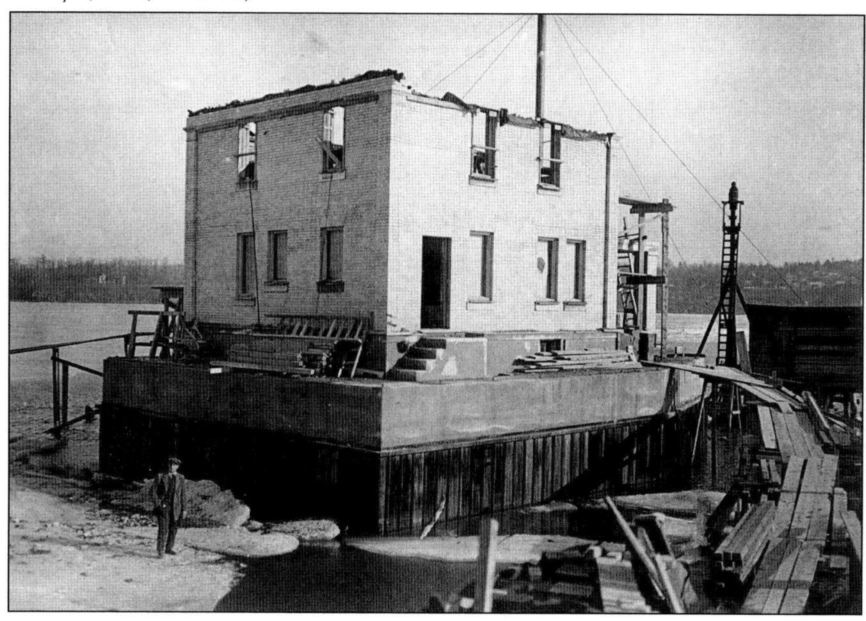

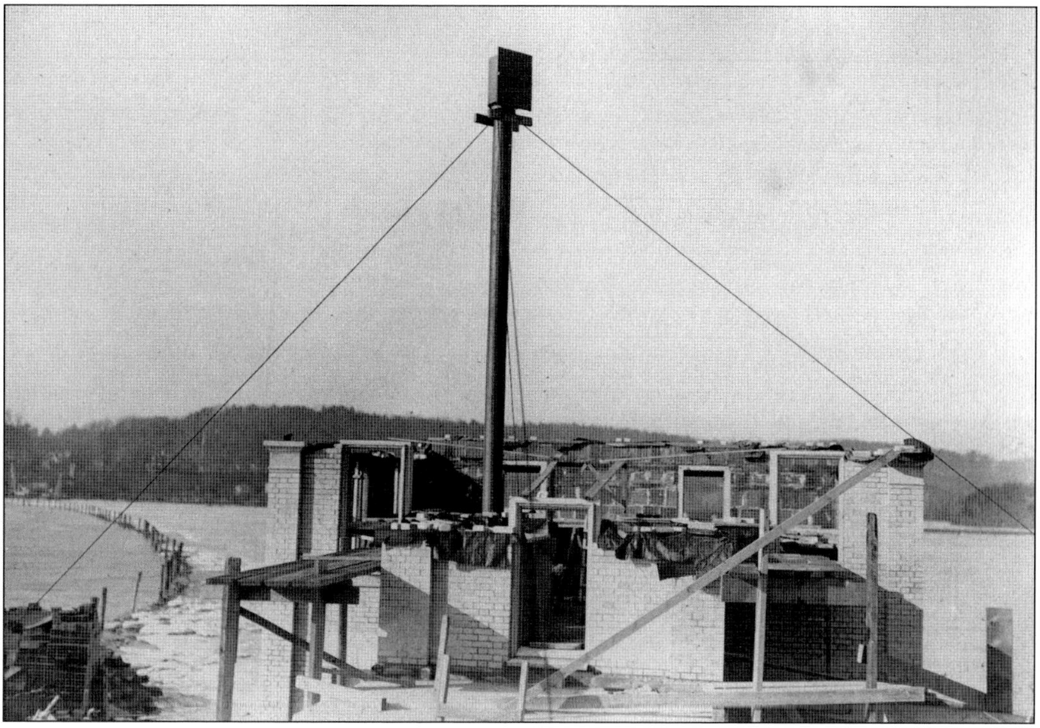

Working through the winter months of 1914 and 1915 was not easy, but progress was slowly made. Here, the weight well for the lantern turning mechanism is being installed in advance of the tower construction. (NARA.)

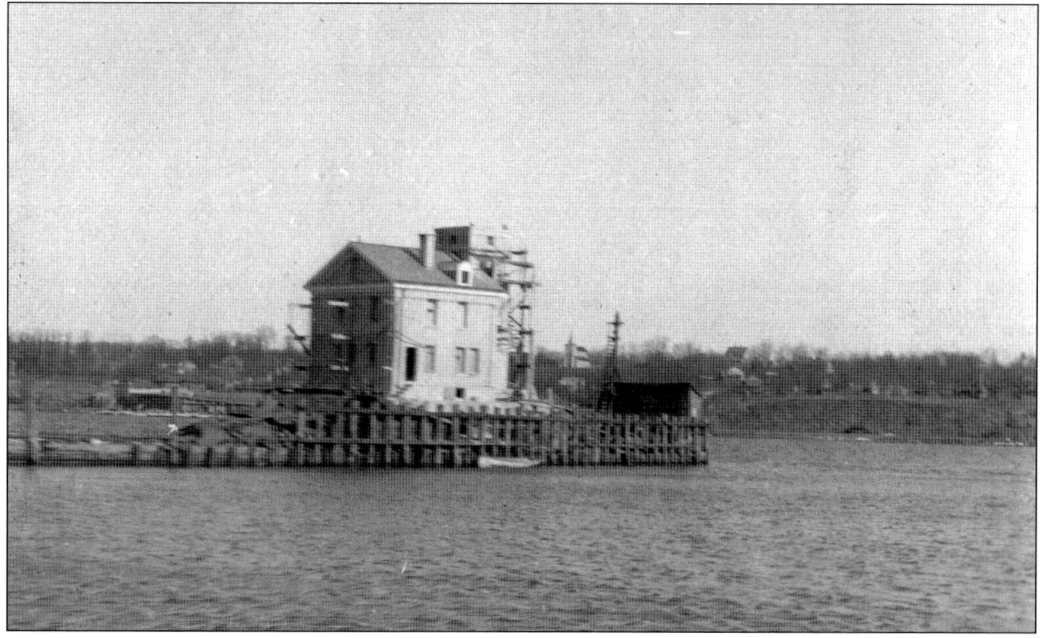

Here, the lighthouse nears completion in early 1915. The wooden shack at right might be crew housing. Note the tall wooden pilings designed to help keep stone riprap in and ice away from the steel and cement foundation. (NARA.)

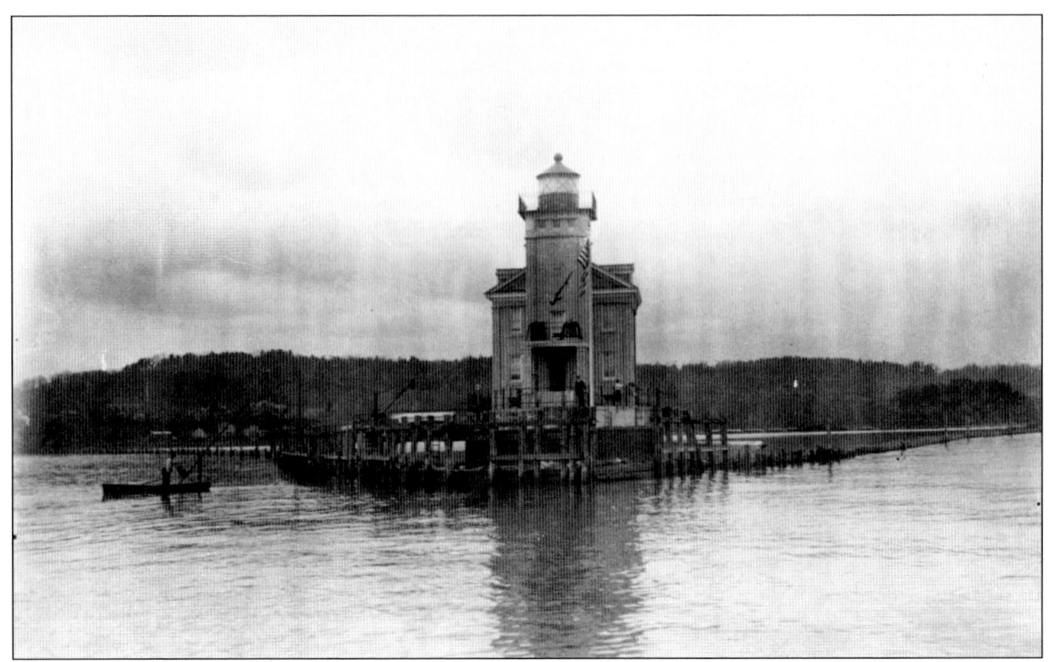

The lighthouse was completed by summer 1915, and in August, the light was lit. In this photograph, taken in April 1916, James Murdock and his wife, Emma, stand on the foundation of the lighthouse looking south. James retired in 1922 at the age of 65 after 42 years (and a lifetime) of service. His retirement marked the end of the Murdock dynasty, where one family had kept the lights burning for 66 years in all three of the Rondout Lighthouses. (NARA.)

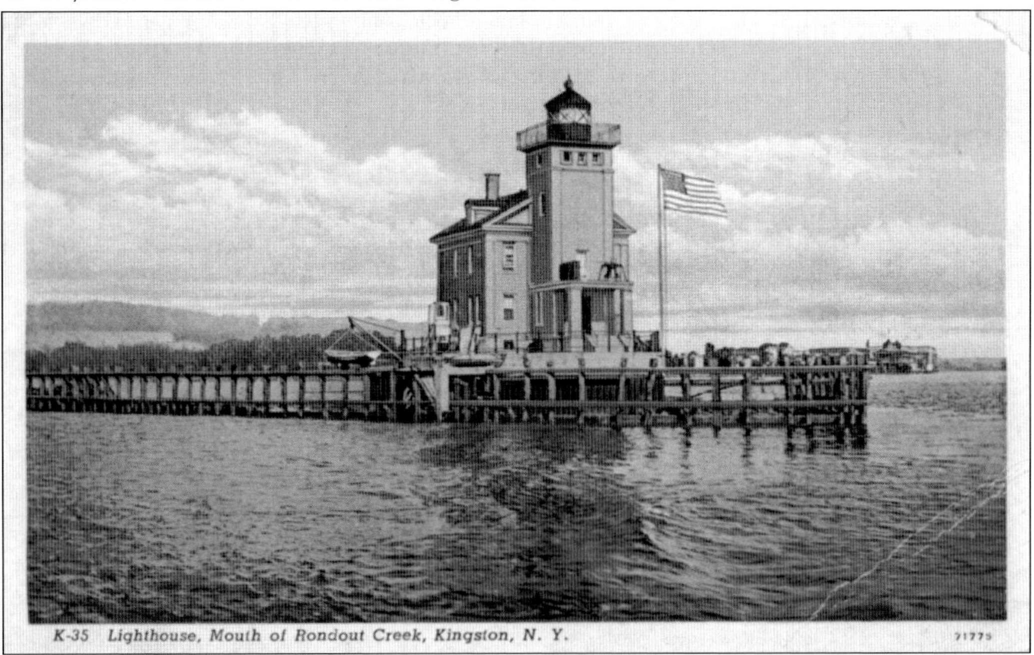

After James Murdock's retirement in 1922, several single men became lighthouse keepers, but no one stayed for long. In this detailed postcard, note the high wooden pilings, the lighthouse tender suspended by davits, and the fog bell on the roof of the front portico. (HRMM.)

In 1938, keeper Robert Howard moved in with his wife, Mathilda (right), and their two children, Lila (the elder, below left) and Esther (the younger, below right). Robert had served at other lighthouses before. (Both, HRMM.)

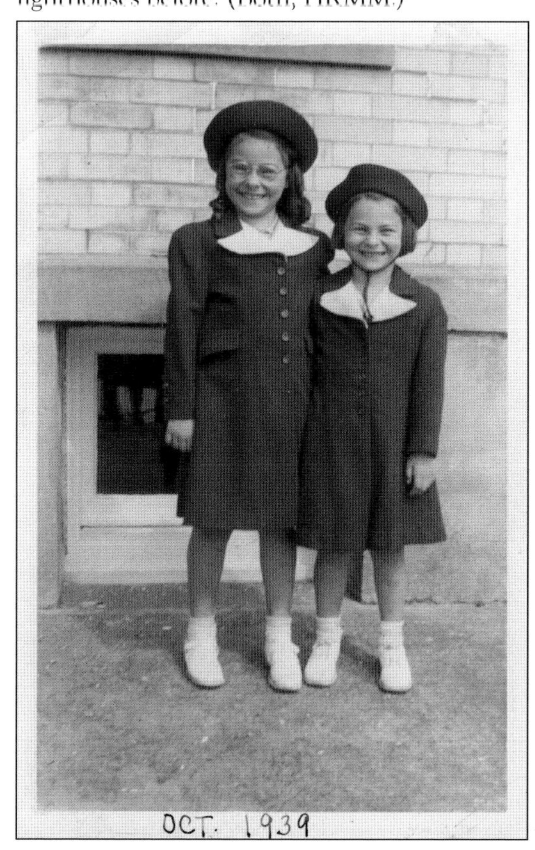

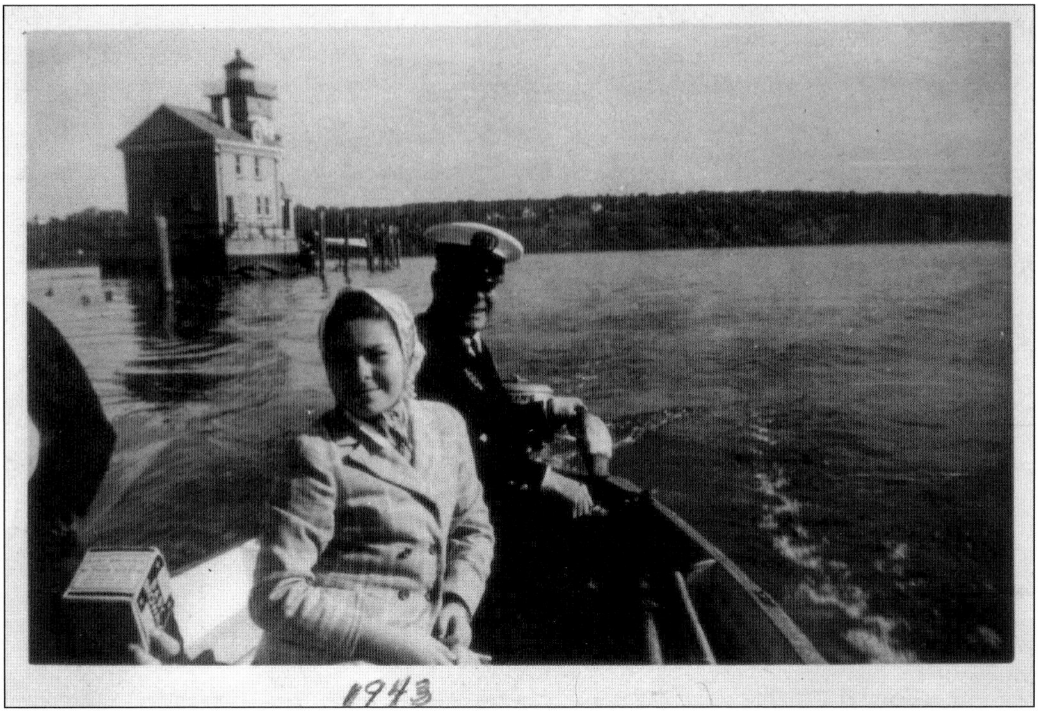

The Howard family spent several years at the lighthouse, with Robert taking Lila and Esther to shore for school during the warmer months in the lighthouse tender. In winter, they walked across the frozen shallow flats behind the north dikes. (HRMM.)

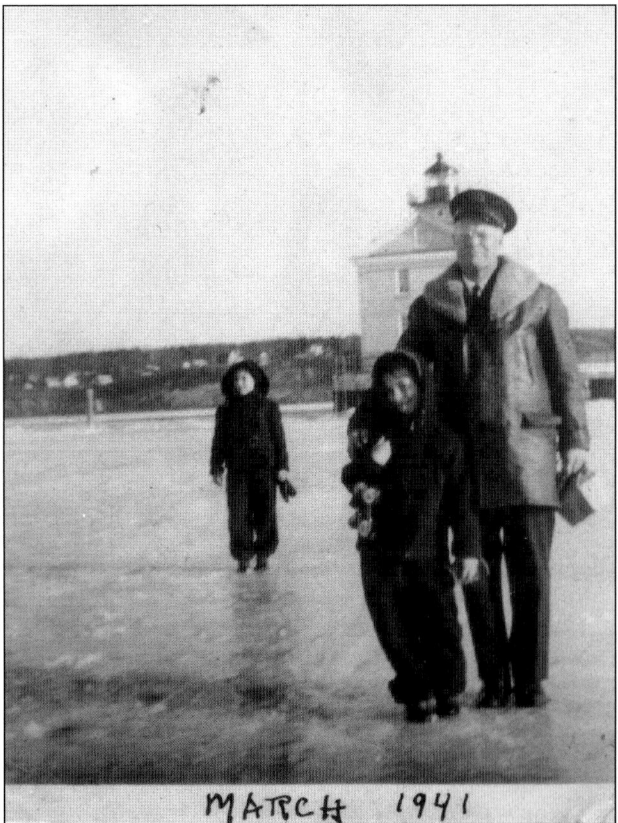

When walking to school one day, Esther fell through the ice and was rescued by Lila. They made their way back to the lighthouse to get warm and dry, and then their mother sent them back out again to go to school. (HRMM.)

Always in his US Lighthouse Service uniform, Robert Howard is pictured here with Mathilda and the girls, posing on the upturned hull of a rowboat. The family stayed at the Rondout Lighthouse until Robert's accident in December 1945. (HRMM.)

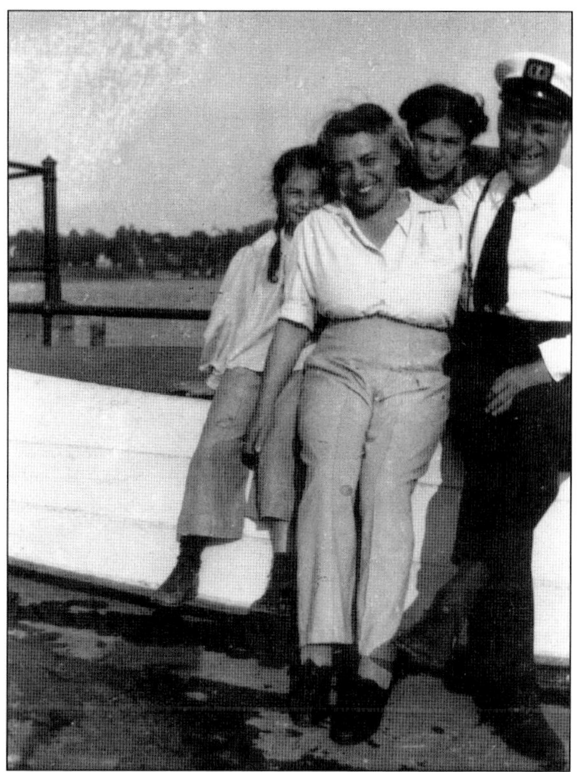

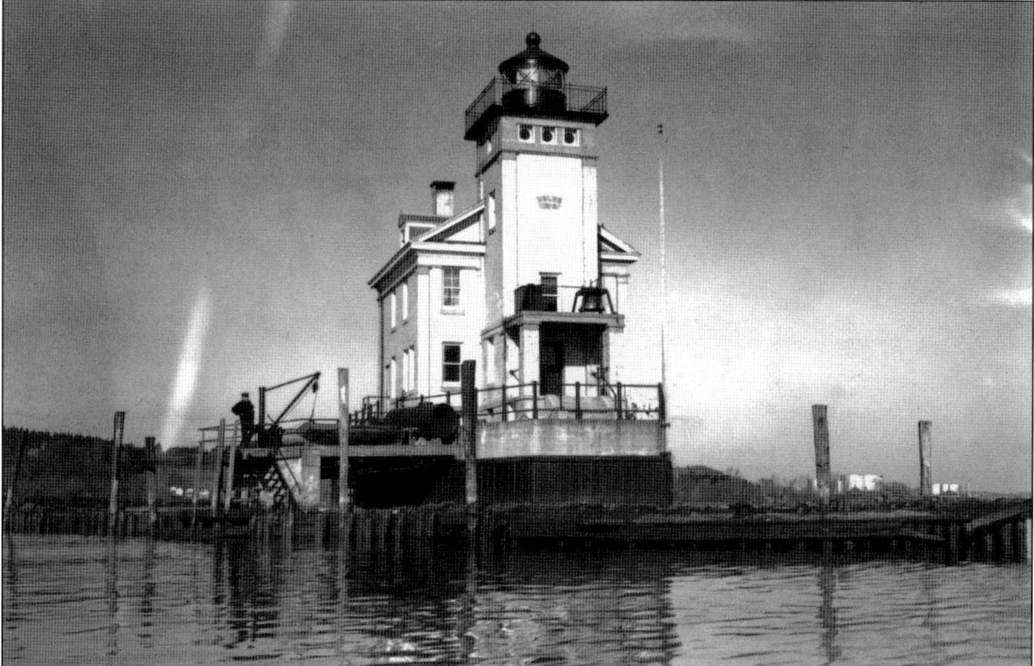

Robert Howard, pictured here on the deck at far left, had been assisting with the rescue of a boat stranded in the ice when he slipped and fell and hit his head. He had a stroke and later died in the hospital. He was the last civilian lighthouse keeper in the Rondout Lighthouse. (HRMM.)

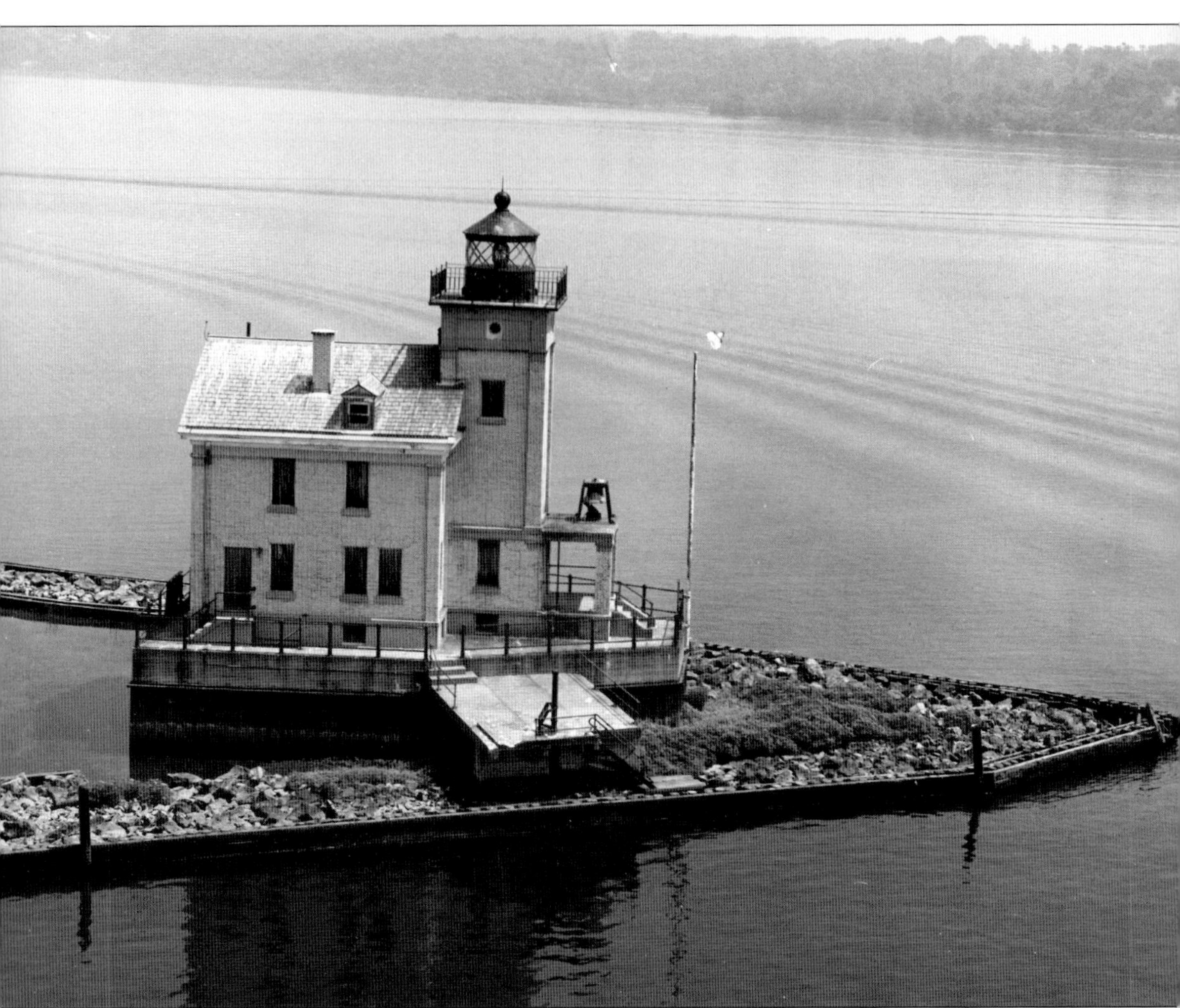

Following the end of World War II, the Coast Guard, which had absorbed the US Lighthouse Service in 1939, began replacing civilian keepers with enlisted men. The Rondout Lighthouse had electricity installed in 1948 and was fully automated in 1954. Upon automation, the lighthouse was cleared and boarded up, as seen in this photograph. In the 1980s, the Hudson River Maritime Museum got permission from the Coast Guard to access the building for tours and has been running public tours ever since. Although the light is now solar-powered LED, Rondout remains a functioning lighthouse. (HRMM.)

Six

SAUGERTIES

North of Rondout Creek, the channel narrows, beset by shoals and other obstacles to navigation. Over 80 percent of the 19th-century lights on the river were located within the 50-mile stretch from Rondout to Troy. Today, two-thirds of the numbered buoys and channel markers on the tidal Hudson are located along these upper reaches. Among them, the Saugerties Lighthouse marks a submerged hazard—the Saugerties flats, which extend a half mile into the river from the west bank and constrict the channel for some distance. It also marks a destination—the entrance to the mouth of Esopus Creek and Saugerties Harbor. Like many other Hudson River lighthouses originally built in the 1830s, the Saugerties Lighthouse had several incarnations. The light was first equipped with five whale oil lamps and reflectors. After a catastrophic fire in 1848, the apparatus was replaced with four secondhand lamps. In 1854, the station's light was upgraded with a sixth-order Fresnel lens, which was transferred to the new tower in 1869. In the 20th century, a Coast Guard light attendant station was established at Turkey Point, approximately halfway between Rondout and Saugerties, to service buoys and other aids to navigation. The Saugerties Lighthouse remains in operation today.

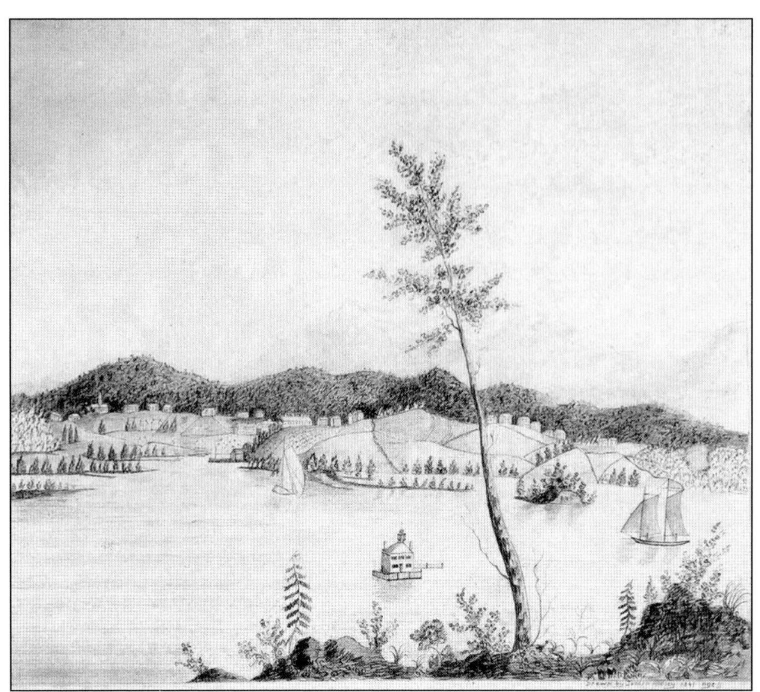

The first Saugerties Lighthouse was built in 1835 to mark the Saugerties tidal flats and entrance to Esopus Creek. Drawn at age 11 by Joseph Hidley, who later grew to be a prominent folk artist and landscape painter, this 1841 drawing is one of the few depictions of the original lighthouse. A two-story dwelling with a "birdcage" lantern centered atop a hipped roof, the lighthouse stood 37 feet tall on a pier of wooden cribbing with stone fill. (SLC.)

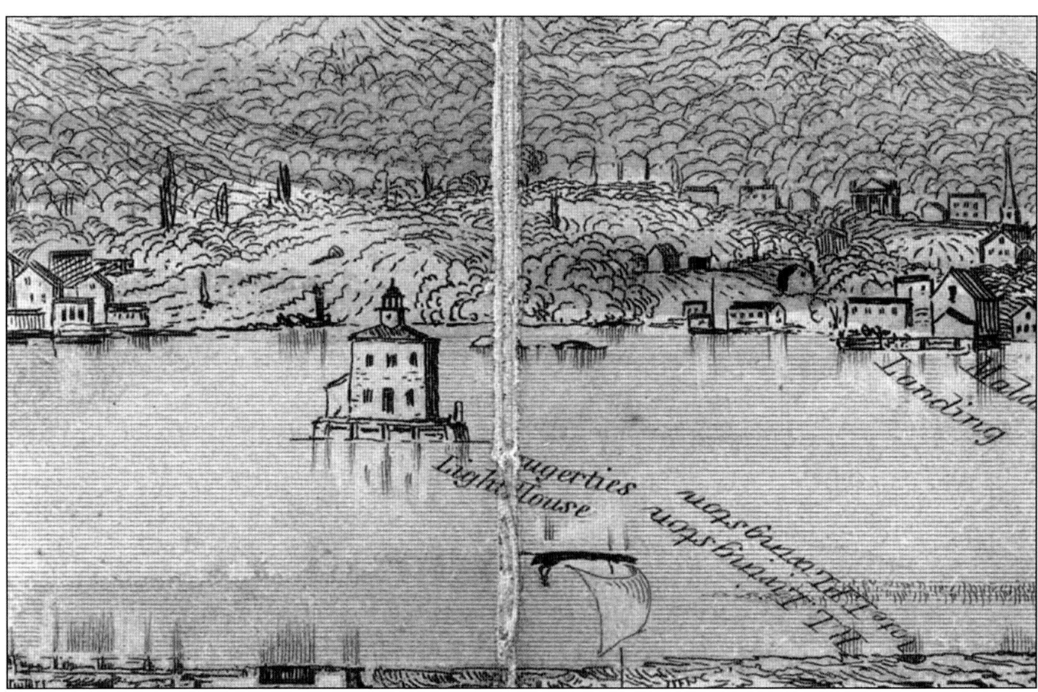

Abraham Persons was the first keeper in 1835 but was soon dismissed from office for hiring out the lighthouse and residing elsewhere. He was replaced by George Keys in 1838. In 1842, Joseph H. Burhans was appointed keeper by Pres. John Tyler, but when Tyler lost reelection to James Polk, Burhans was replaced by Abram Schoonmaker in 1845. This image is from the 1847 *Panorama*. (ARC.)

Abram Schoonmaker died in 1846 at age 49. During his ailing final year, his wife, Dorcas, performed the keeper's duties "with such marked regularity and attention as to receive the universal commendation of the boatmen on the river," as reported in the Saugerties *Daily Telegraph* on July 21, 1849. She was made an official keeper and served until 1849, when Pres. Zachary Taylor reappointed James Burhans in her stead. Her family gravestone is pictured here. (SLC.)

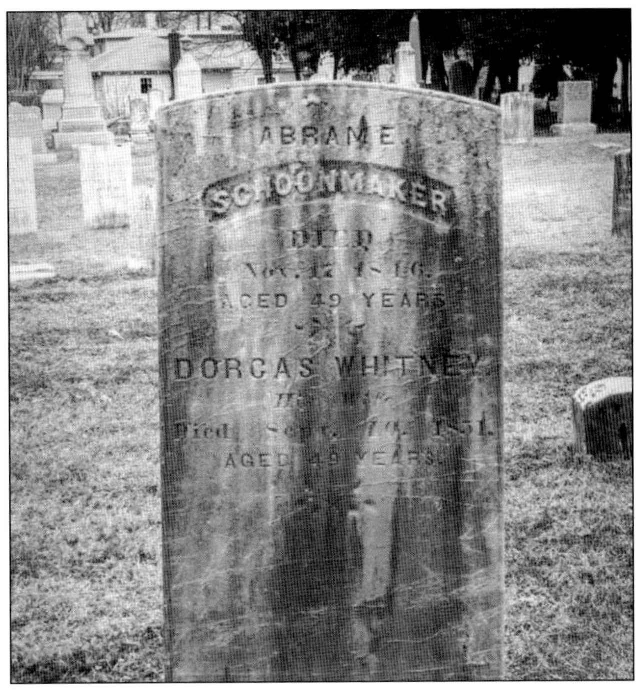

HUDSON RIVER HEROINES.

The Ida Lewis and Grace Darling of Saugerties—The Maidens of the Lighthouse

A writer in the *Jersey City Churchman*, under the signature of "A. N. Z.," relates these facts:

It was a bright, starlight night, and the writer sat in the pilot house talking to the steersman, who guided the steamer through the shadows of the frowning peaks of the Highlands and answered questions or voluntary infomation between rotations of the wheel. As we turned a bend in the river a light which looked like a star of the first magnitude, twinkled and shone upon us far away in the distance. "That's fifteen miles away," said the man at the wheel. "That's Saugerties light. We'll lose it again a dozen times in the turns of the river. Do I know who keeps it?" Well, no; not to speak to 'em, but I know it's two gals as has got grit enough, for I've seen 'em on the river many a time by day-light pulling away a great heavy row boat that no two river men would care to handle, in one of those gales that comes sweepin' down through the mountains like great flues in a big chimney. It ain't like a tumultuous sea, hey? Well, that jist shows how little you know about these North river storms. Why, when we get some of these hurricane blasts, that sweep down through these gaps from the north, and another current comes up from the south, then Heaven help the vessel that gets caught in the mælstrom when they meet. Well, it was one of those occasions. I was comin' up the river on the old Columbus after she'd got off carryin' passengers and took to the towin' business. Let me see—that was about five years ago. We'd got a little north of Rondout, and I was all alone at the wheel; I heerd a tumblin' behind me, and I looked around, and when I saw a great big cloud with thunder heads rushin' up from the south, I knew we were going to catch a ripper. This was nothing, however, to the heavy clouds that came sweeping down from the north, in an opposite direction; and then I saw that the two storms would meet. I hollered down the trumpet to the engineer to slower the engine, and made up my mind to keep headway and stay in the river, as it would be unsafe to try and make a landing or get fastened to a dock. In a few minutes the two storms struck us. The boat cavorted like a frisky horse, and in the foaming water plunged and reared, and shook in every timber as if it had the agur. We were then pretty near abreast of Tivoli, and Saugerties lighthouse was only about two miles ahead. A sloop loaded with blue stone, which had just emerged from the mouth of Esopus creek, and was standing down the river, went over when the squall struck her as suddenly as if a great machine under the water had upset her; and soon I saw two men struggling in the water. Hardly a minute elapsed before two female forms were fluttering around the small boat by the lighthouse.—In another minute it was launched, and it bobbed up and down in the seething, foaming waters.

The two gals, bareheaded, with a pair of oars apiece, began pulling toward the men in the water. The waves ran so high, the gale blew so madly, the thunder roared so incessantly and the lightning flashed in such blinding sheets, that it seemed impossible for the women to ever reach the men, to get headway or to keep from being swamped. But they never missed the opportunity of a rising billow to give them leverage, and they managed, by steady pulling to get ahead until they reached the men in the water. The great danger was that the tossing boat would strike the sailors, and end their career, but one of the gals leaned forward over the bow of the boat, braced her feet beneath the seat on which she had been sitting, stiffened herself out for a great effort, and, as her sister kept the bow of the boat crosswise to the waves, caught one of the men beneath the arms as he struck out on top of a billow, lifted and threw him, by main force, into the middle of the boat, and then prepared for the other man.

He had got hold of the sloop's rudder, which had got unshipped and was floating on the water. He let go and swam towards the row boat, and was hauled in also by the woman and his half-drowned comrade. I tell you," said the pilot, "those gals are bricks, and no mistake. You couldn't have got any river boatman to do what they did."

It was just 4 o'clock in the morning when the steamboat landed at the little insular dock which is called Saugerties. The light from the light house, however, full a mile away, shone down upon it like the eye of a great ogre, illuminating the surrounding country.

Dennis Crowley became keeper in 1862, but due to cataracts, he was soon replaced by first his son Daniel, and later daughter Kate Crowley. The story pictured here, featuring Kate and her sister Ellen executing a daring rescue during a storm, was published throughout the country. Kate served until 1885, when James Crowley took over. (SLC.)

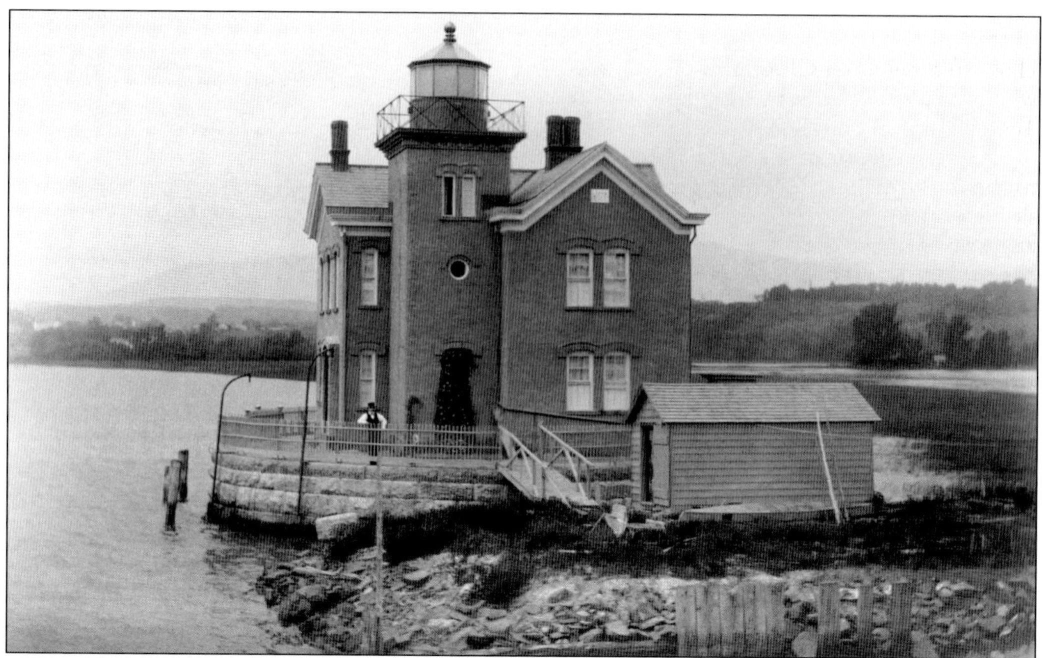

This c. 1886 image is the oldest known photograph of the 1869 Saugerties Lighthouse with keeper James Crowley. James was the fourth member of the Crowley family to serve in succession at the lighthouse. After the original lighthouse was damaged by ice floes, this one replaced it with a massive stone platform to protect from the river ice. Note the footbridge connecting the new lighthouse to the piled stone foundation of the old. (NARA.)

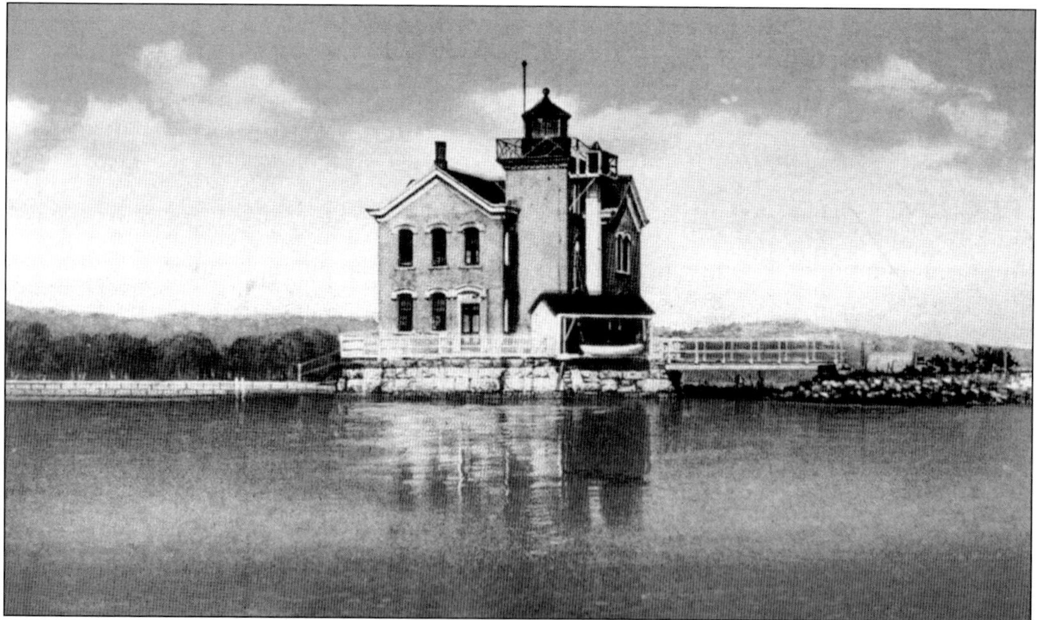

This c. 1912 image was featured on a postcard produced by the Kingston Souvenir Company. The iconic cantilevered boat shed, relocated from the outer island in 1899, can be seen in front of the light tower. Also in view is the bulkhead built as part the Saugerties Harbor channelization project on Esopus Creek from 1888 to 1892. (SLC.)

In this image from May 14, 1939, keeper Conrad Hawk and neighbor Chester B. Glunt, who was in charge of the light attendant station at Turkey Point in Saugerties, sit in the boathouse overlooking the keeper's Lighthouse Service rowboat. Provisions were hauled by rowboat or sledded across the ice. To supplement his modest keeper wages, Hawk took odd jobs, like ice harvesting. To fill out their rations, the family tended a garden and fished. (Patrick Kaufmann.)

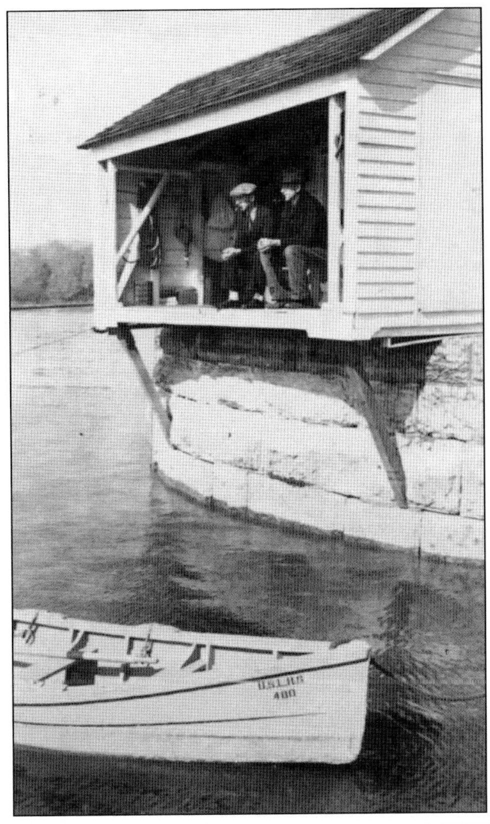

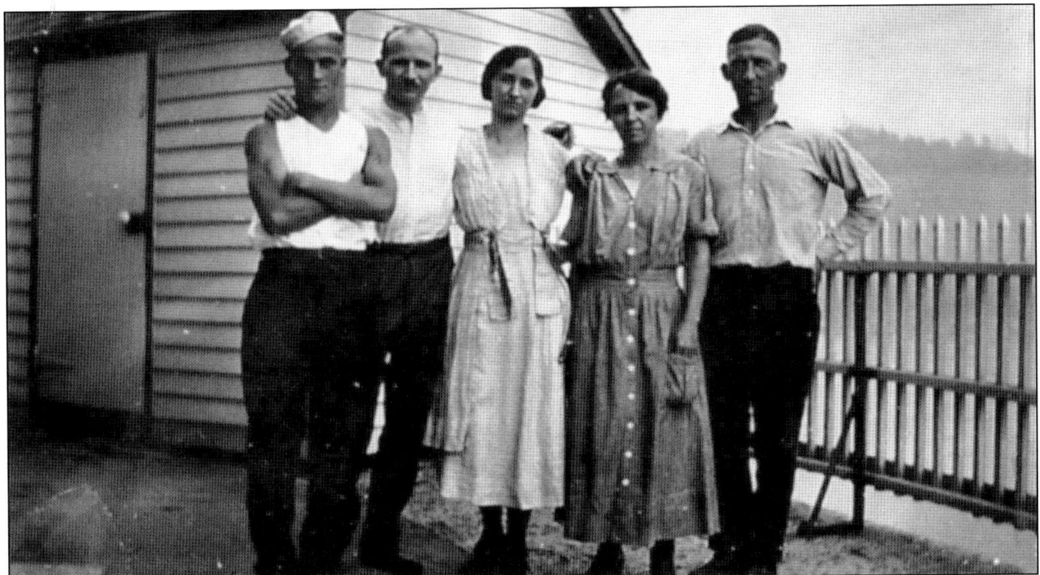

Keeper Conrad Hawk and his wife, Thyra (shown at right in this image from 1921), were the longest-serving keepers at Saugerties, keeping the light from 1914 to 1940. They often enjoyed having company at the Saugerties Lighthouse, which was less isolated than Conrad's previous offshore keeper assignments at Peck's Ledge, Stratford Shoals, and Falkner's Island in Long Island Sound. (Patrick Kaufmann.)

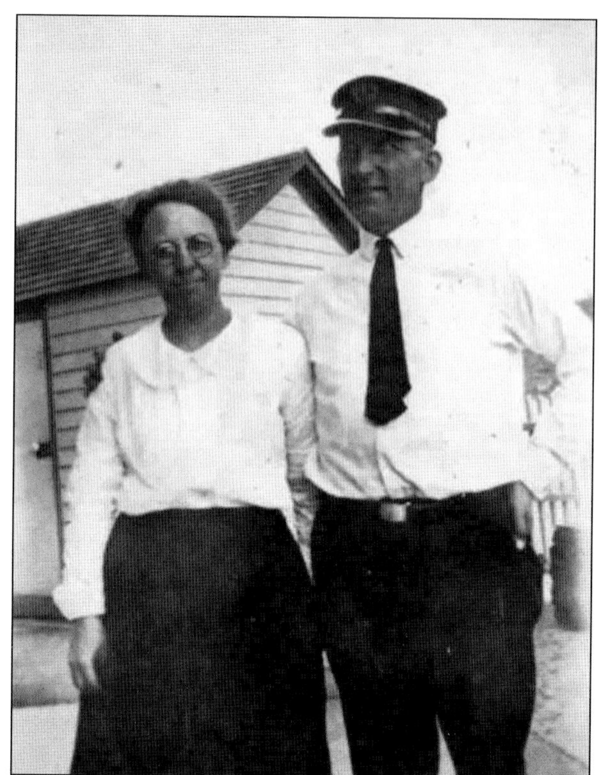

Keeper Conrad Hawk, seen here, was born in Oslo, Norway, March 20, 1877, and emigrated to America at age 16 on the sailing vessel *Bianca*, a trip of 51 days at that time. Later, he joined the US Navy, serving on the battleship *Indiana* in the Spanish-American War. He married Thyra Burnmark (pictured here) in Brooklyn in 1904. She was also born in Olso. (Patrick Kaufmann.)

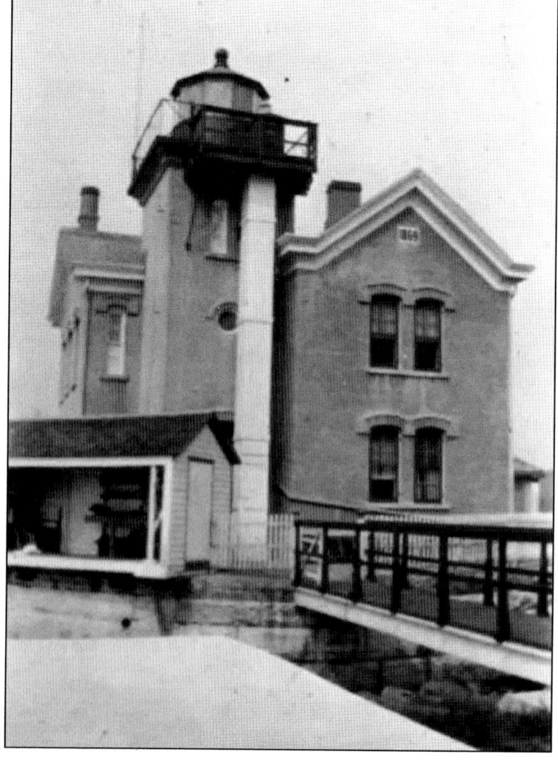

Before the installation of an automated fog bell in 1909, the keeper (including Kate Crowley) manually sounded a fog horn. In this view of the east face of the lighthouse, the white fog bell weight box running the length of the tower can be seen. The fog bell was struck by clockwork machinery; heavy weights suspended below the clockwork mechanism were enclosed in the weight box to prevent them from swinging in the wind. (SLC.)

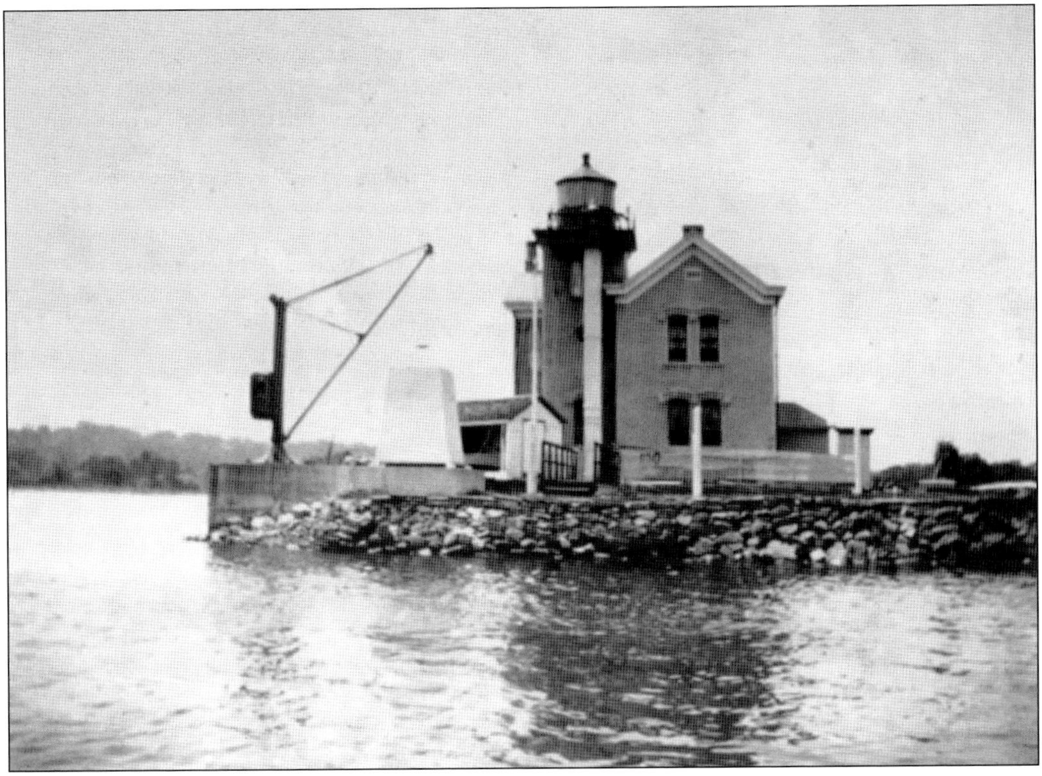

In the 1940s, the Coast Guard modernized the lighthouse and added several improvements, including an electrically actuated fog bell, seen enclosed in the white wooden pyramid structure, and a davit crane with winch for hoisting the keeper's boat out of the water. (SLC.)

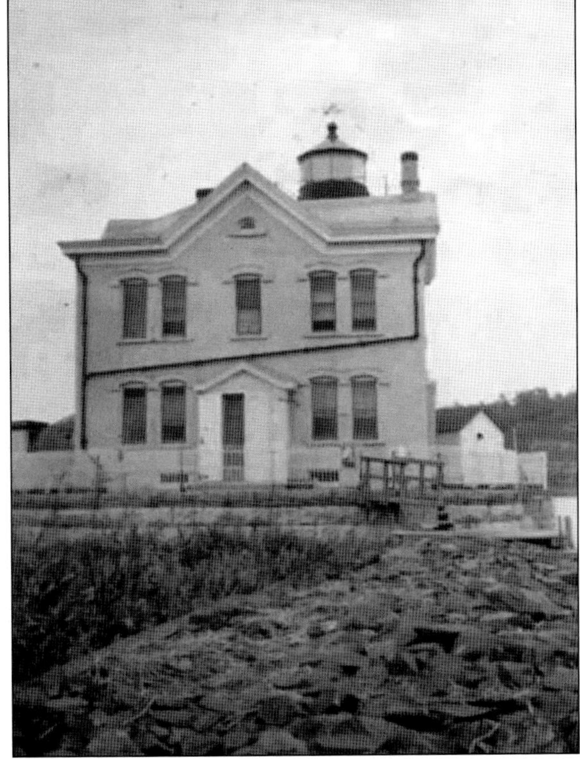

This 1939 view of the west face of the lighthouse illustrates the use of downspouts that collected rainwater from the roof and channeled it into the cistern. The original downspouts were replaced with cast-iron. Once the building was vacated, the cast-iron rusted, leaking water against the brick walls and hastening the deterioration of the lighthouse. The lateral pipe running across the western wall was especially troublesome. (Patrick Kaufmann.)

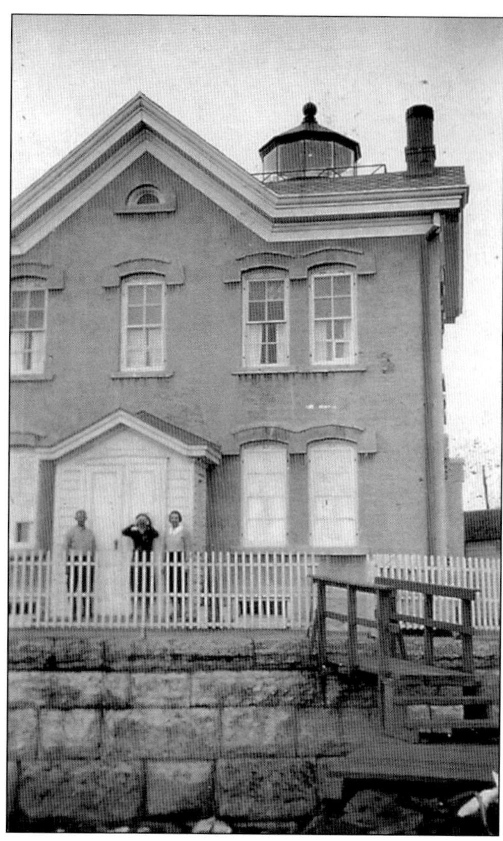

Since the dwelling was not modernized until after Conrad Hawk's tenure, daily life at the lighthouse remained unchanged from the 19th century with no plumbing, electricity, or telephone. The family still relied on oil lamps and used an outhouse perched over the water. In the evenings, they read books, played cards or board games, or listened to the phonograph. (Patrick Kaufmann.)

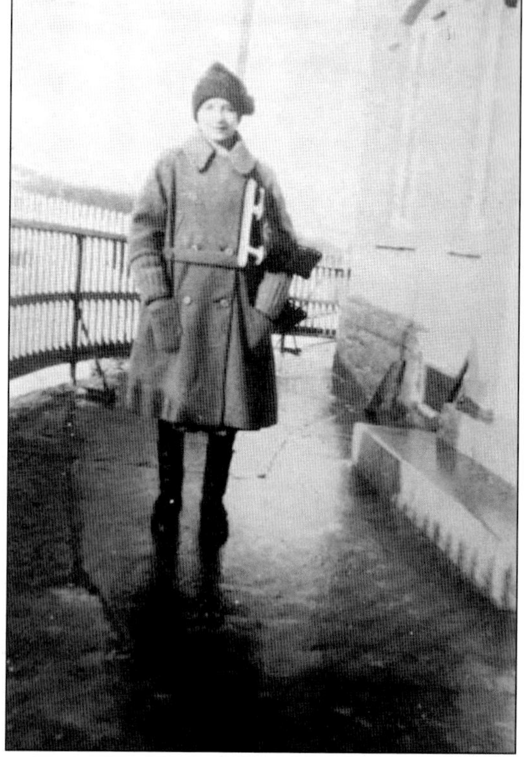

Ilah Hawk, daughter of Conrad and Thyra Hawk, is seen here with ice skates in 1923. For residents of the lighthouse, ice-skating was not just a pastime. To attend school in the village, Ilah and her brother Earle made the trip on their ice skates in winter. Both were excellent skaters like their father, winning competitions on the frozen Hudson River. (Patrick Kaufmann.)

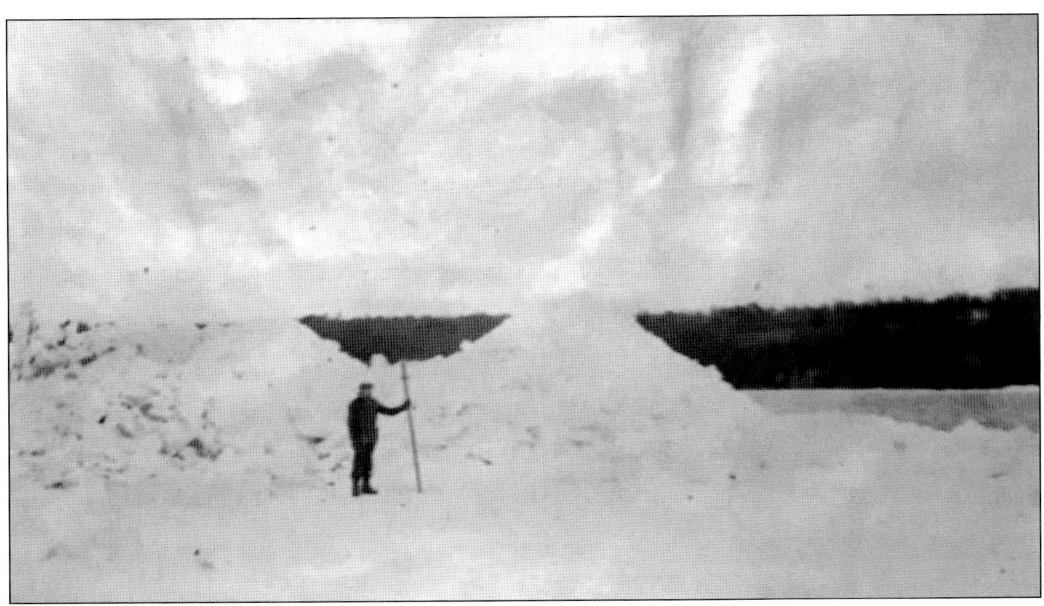

The ice floes seen in these photographs taken by the Hawk family in the spring of 1939 illustrate the necessity for solid foundations to protect the lighthouse. Above, a man illustrates the height of the piled ice. Below, the force of the ice pushing against the shore of the old foundation destabilizes the outbuilding, which has been propped up with boards. (Both, Patrick Kaufmann.)

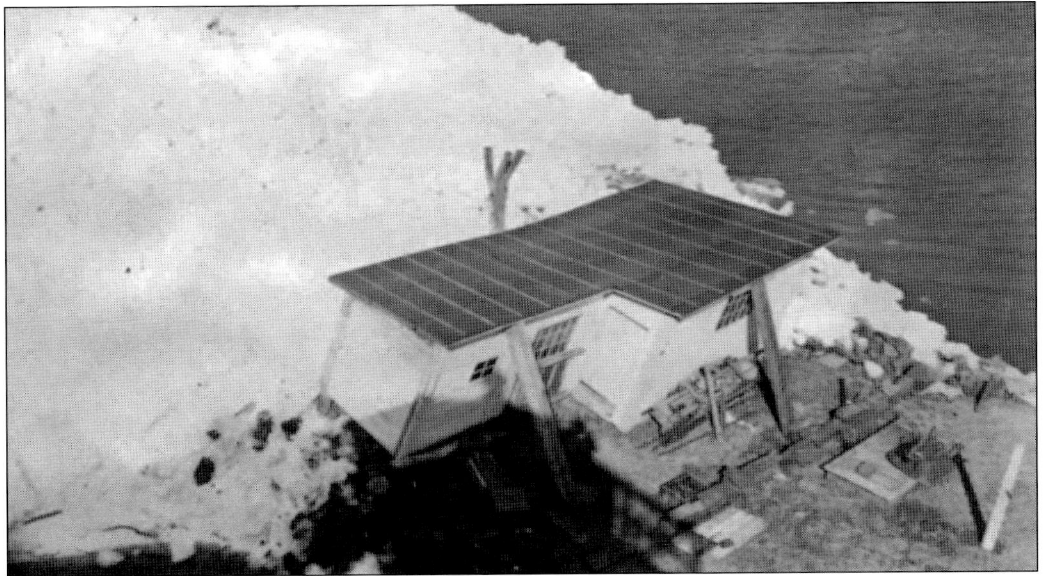

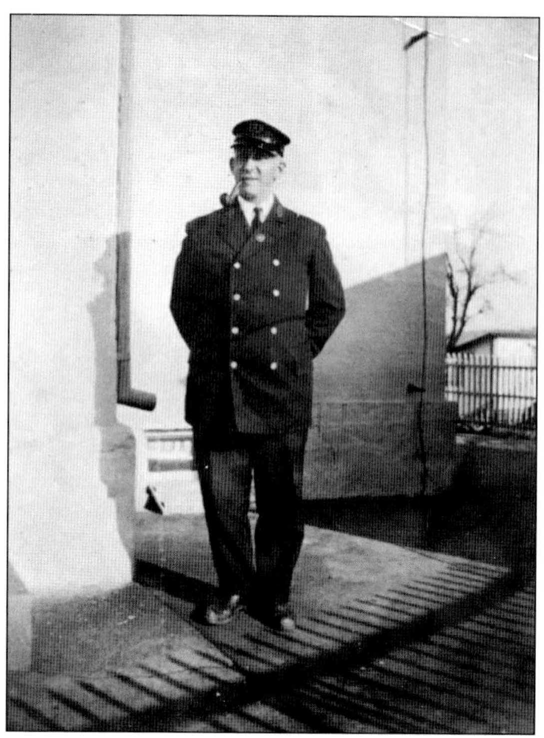

Conrad Hawk served as lighthouse keeper at Saugerties until his death in January 1940. He had been ill for several months with stomach ulcers and while at the US Marine Hospital in Stapleton, Staten Island, passed away suddenly, to the shock of many. He had kept the Saugerties Lighthouse for nearly 26 years. (Patrick Kaufmann.)

Chester Glunt, seen here, supervised the Coast Guard's Turkey Point Light Attendant Station. He and his wife, Ruth, were neighbors and close friends of the Hawk family. Turkey Point, located on a small outcropping halfway between Rondout and Saugerties, was opened in 1938 as a supply warehouse for the Coast Guard. Chester and his wife, Ruth, were instrumental in saving the Saugerties Lighthouse from demolition and getting the building listed in the National Register of Historic Places. (HRMM.)

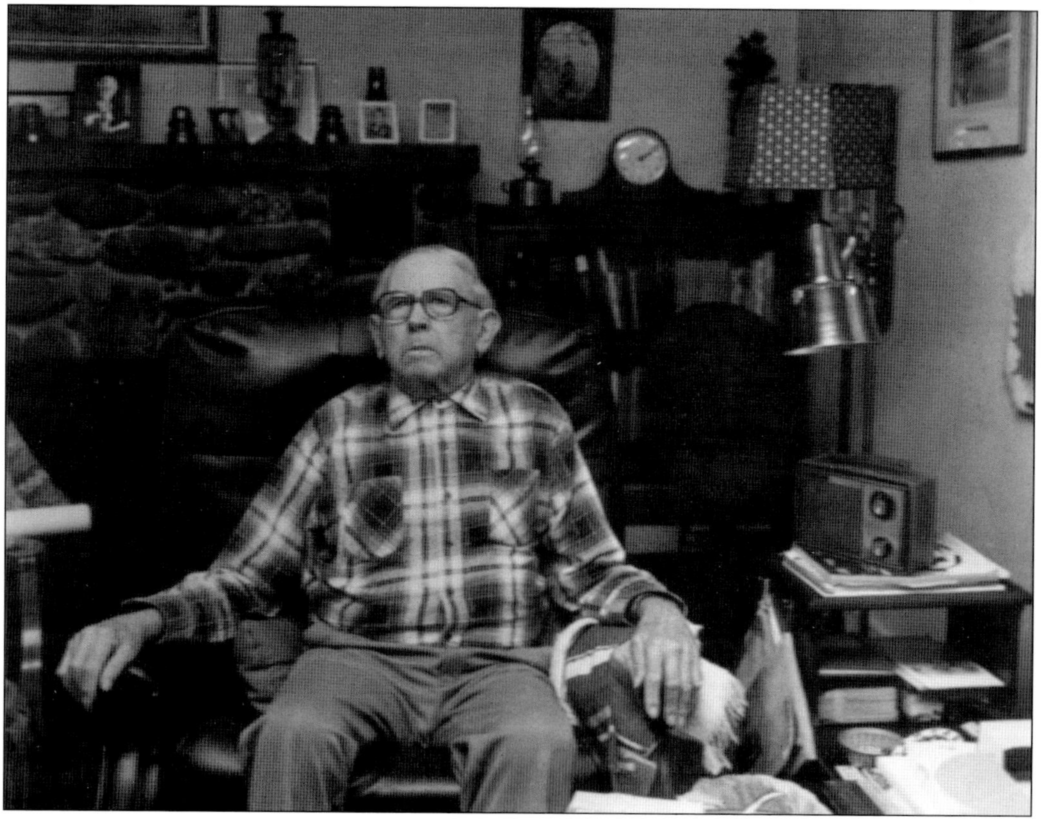

Seven

Catskills

The stretch of river from Saugerties north to Hudson had a few more natural obstacles to avoid, with hooks, islands, and mud flats. This section of the river really marks the beginning of the Upper Hudson, which is beset with all sorts of navigational obstructions, but also destinations. A stake light marked the entrance to Livingston Creek, and both Catskill and the city of Hudson were important destinations throughout the 19th century—Catskill for its famous mountain houses, and Hudson as an industrial port. Enormous ice houses also dotted the shoreline and a constant stream of cargo boats carrying ice south to New York City and elsewhere ran throughout the summer months.

Some obstructions include Rogers Island near Catskill, numerous shallow flats and bays, a mid-river shoal one-half mile above Germantown marked by a stake light called Upper Coal Beds, and flats along the western shore south of Athens marked with the West Flats stake light. Of particular danger were the Middle Ground Flats, a long string of narrow islands and mud flats that bisected the river from the twin towns of Hudson and Athens north for four miles. Historically a low sandbar visible only at low tide, in the late 19th and 20th centuries it became a convenient dumping ground for dredging operations by the Army Corps of Engineers, expanding it to its more substantial island-like form today. Located at the southern end of the Middle Ground Flats, the Hudson-Athens Lighthouse continues to warn mariners away from the obstruction and marks the split in the river.

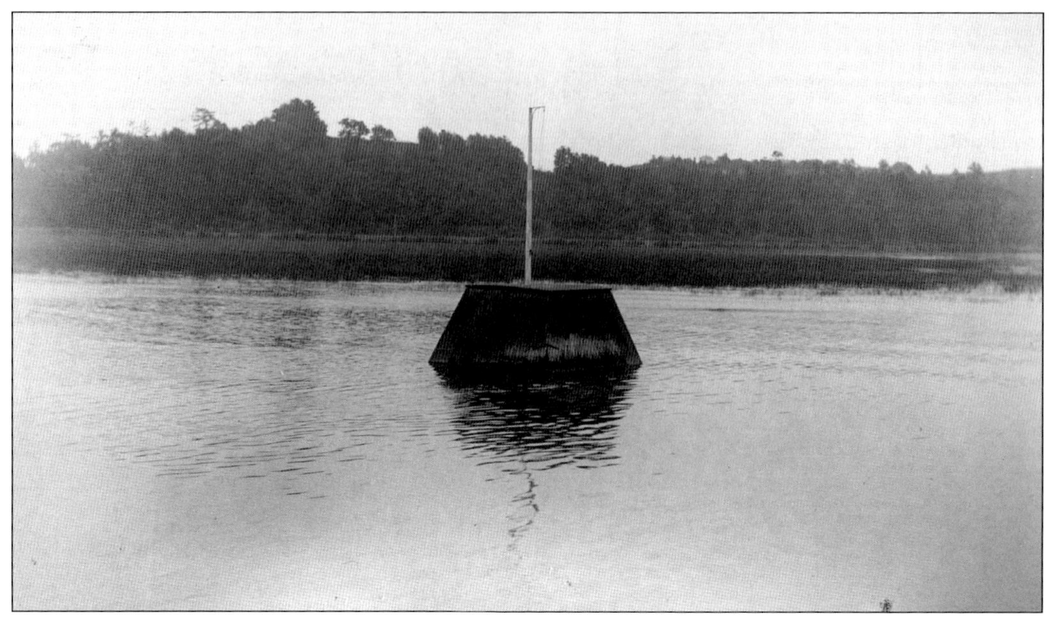

Livingston Creek (known today as Roeliff Jansen Kill) is a tributary of the Hudson that terminates at Linlithgo in the town of Livingston. At one point, a light was installed to mark the entrance to the creek. In 1885, it was listed as a stake light with a wooden foundation. In this undated image, the foundation appears to have been upgraded to concrete. (NARA.)

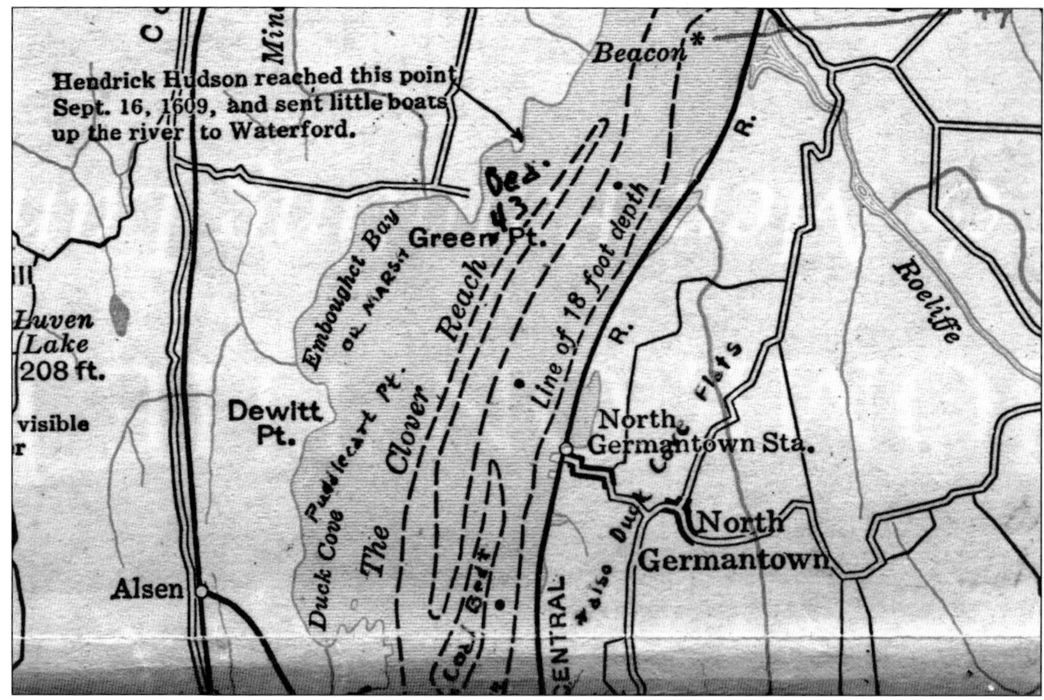

In this 1924 map, "Coal Beds" was hand-written on the shoals near the bottom opposite North Germantown. A beacon, Livingston Creek Light, is marked near Linlithgo. A beacon is also marked near Catskill—known at the time as the Catskill Lighthouse, although it was, in fact, a stake light. (HRMM.)

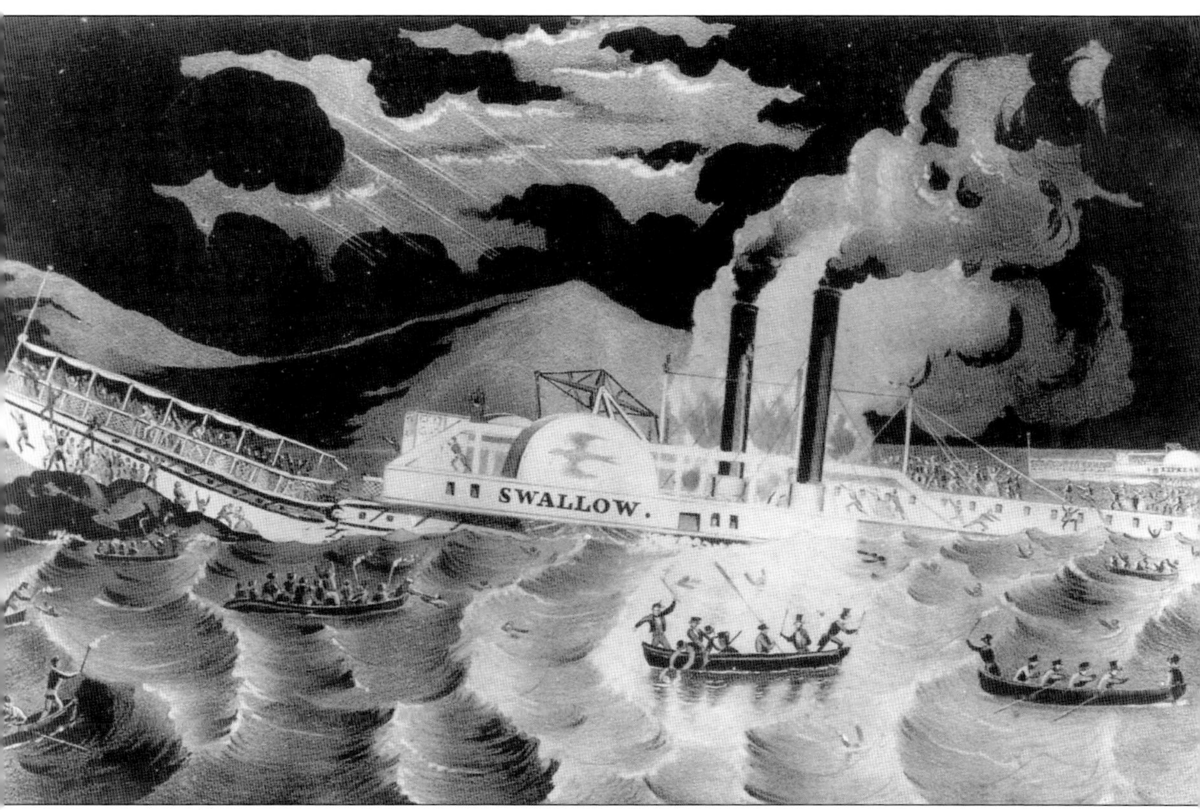

On the night of April 7, 1845, the steamboat *Swallow* was running at night, carrying over 250 passengers to Albany. Approaching the village of Athens in a frigid wintry storm, the *Swallow* ran aground on a small island, breaking her hull with a crack heard on shore. She soon caught fire. Berths below decks quickly filled with icy water, endangering those who had turned in for the night. Church bells rang in nearby Hudson, calling local residents to assist in the evacuation of the wrecked vessel in the freezing weather, and bonfires were built on shore to help make passengers in the water more visible. In total, between 15 and 25 people died (the number is unclear in part because the company kept poor passenger records), and the wreck was later blamed on the captain, who was said to be operating at full speed despite the inclement weather. The wreck of the *Swallow* became famous and helped spur calls for a lighthouse to be installed between Hudson and Athens. (HRMM.)

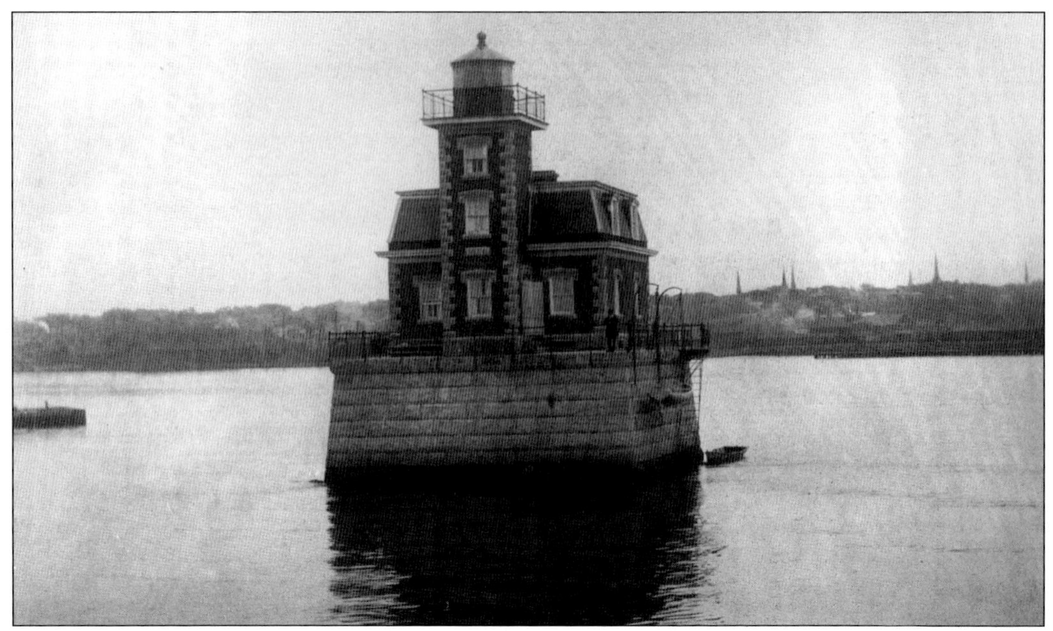

Completed in 1874, the Hudson-Athens Lighthouse (also known as Hudson Light and Hudson City Light) was built to the south of the Middle Ground Flats to warn mariners of the divided river. Built of brick on a high stone foundation (seen here at low tide), the architecture is reminiscent of Esopus Meadows. (HRMM.)

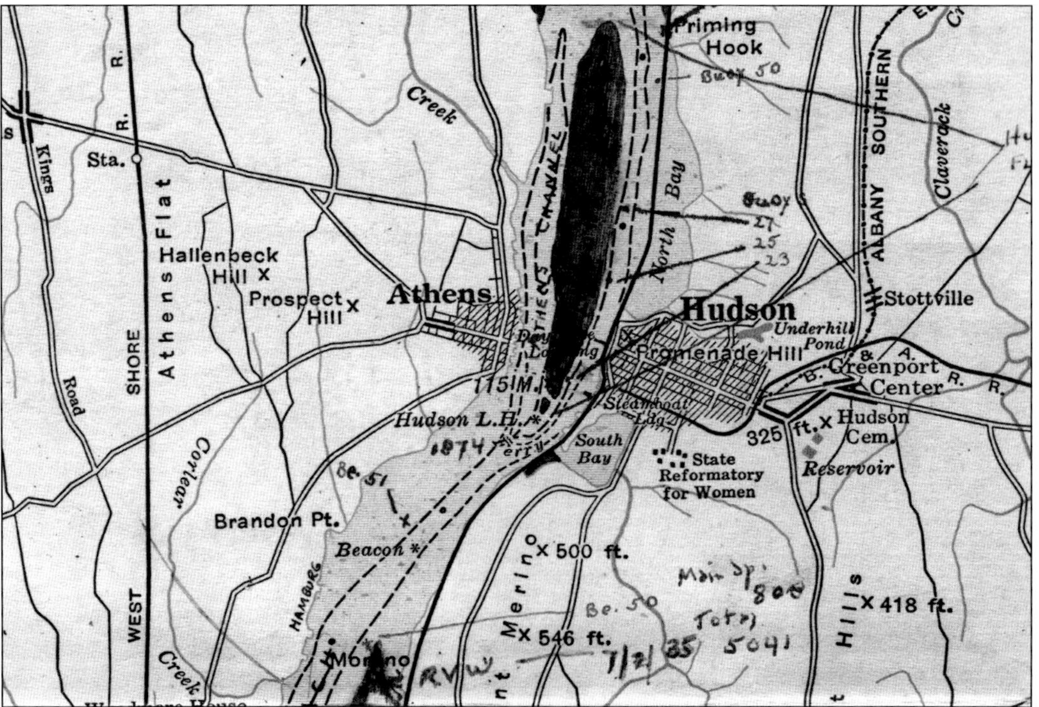

The Middle Ground Flats were hand-colored by the owner of this map. The flats bisect the river and offer a navigational obstacle between the cities of Hudson and Athens. Note the Hudson Lighthouse marked just south of the tip of the flats. (HRMM.)

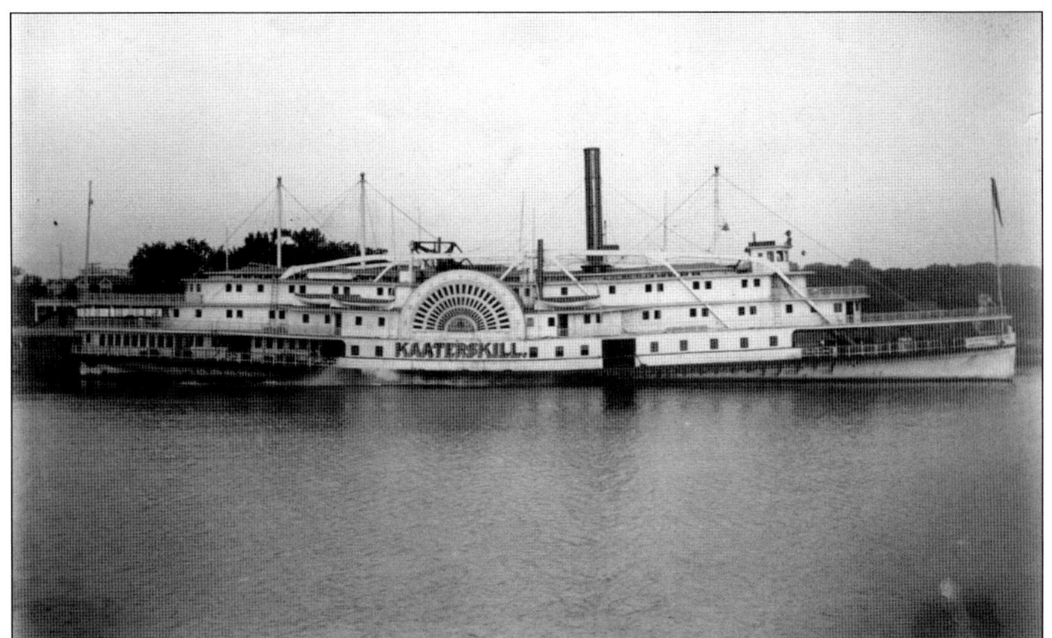

In September 1892, the steamer *Kaaterskill* collided with the Hudson-Athens Lighthouse, damaging the lighthouse platform, stairs, and "some twenty feet of iron railing," according to the Saugerties *Weekly Post*. The *Kaaterskill* was only slightly damaged and was able to make her way to the wharf at Hudson. (HRMM.)

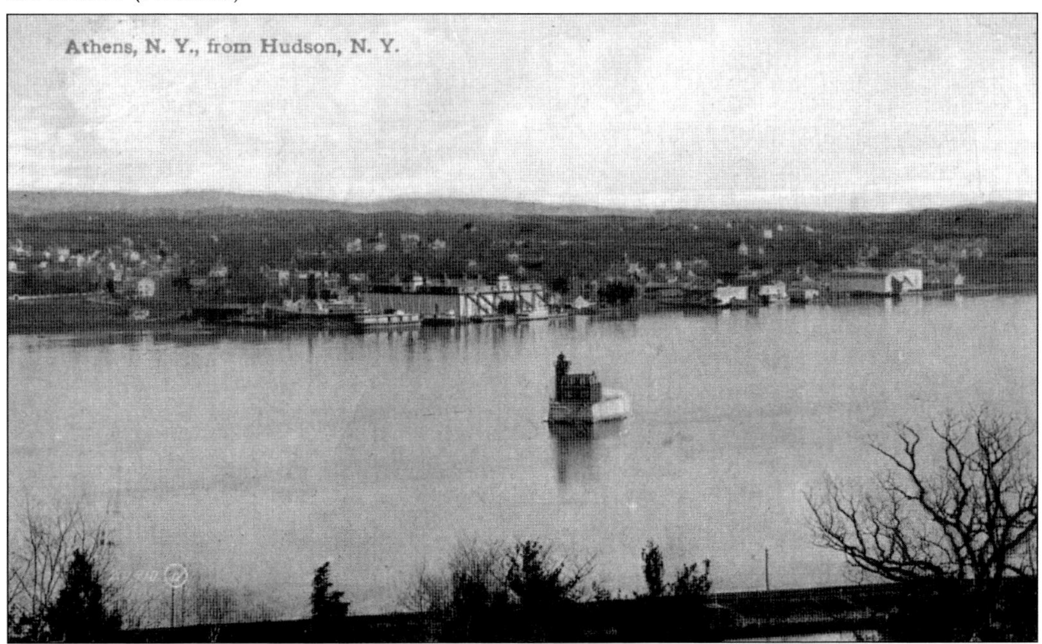

In December 1892, Henry D. Best, who had been keeper since the lighthouse opened in 1874, passed away at the age of 69. His son Frank took over in 1893 and continued until 1918, when he was killed after a fall from an electric power line tower he was helping construct. Frank's widow Nellie kept the light for the remainder of 1918 and although she was offered the position, gave it up to move ashore. (HRMM.)

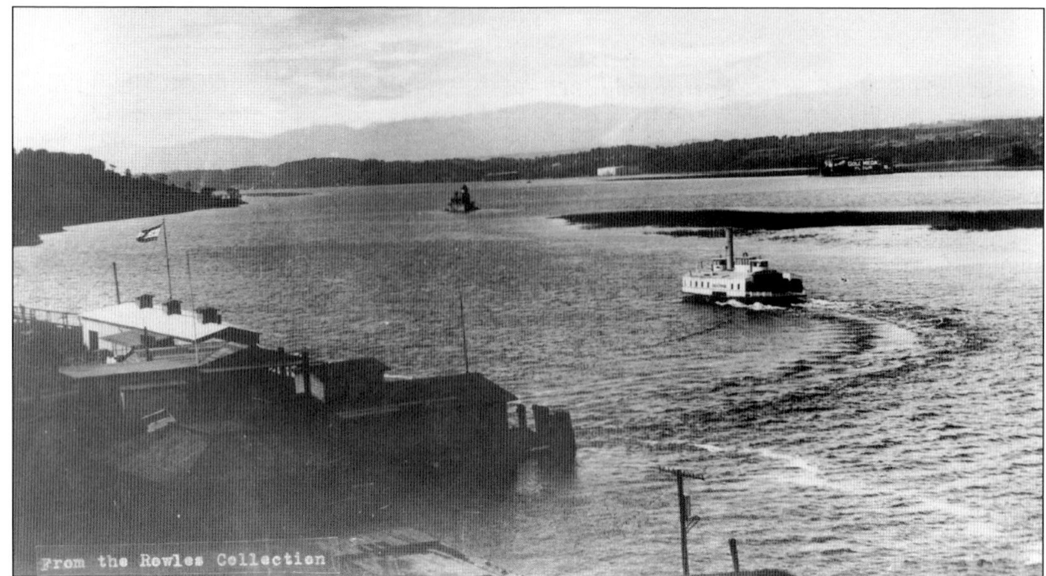

This image clearly illustrates the division in the river produced by the flats. The boat in the foreground is the Hudson-Athens ferry the *George H. Power*, which had to wind its way around both the flats and lighthouse to get from one shore to the other. (HRMM.)

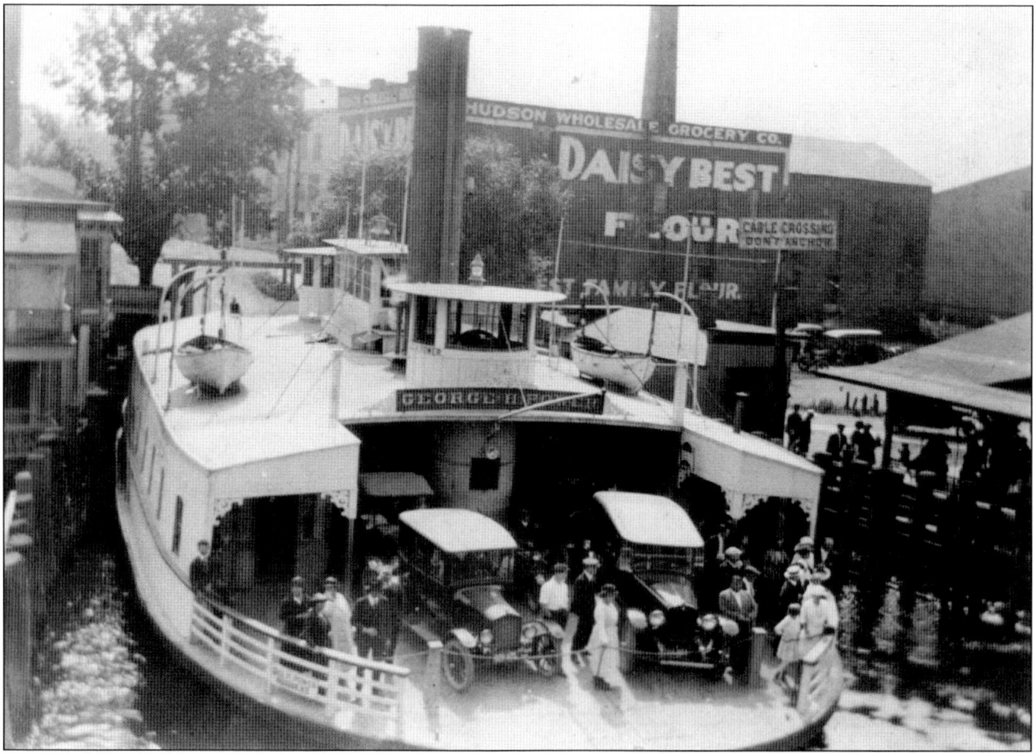

The flats could be treacherous even to experienced boatmen. In November 1906, the ferry *George H. Power* ran aground on the flats. The ferry had already made one trip across the river without mishap, but on the return trip, a fog "settled upon the river unexpectedly" so thick that even the lighthouse could not be seen, according to the Kingston *Daily Freeman*. (HRMM.)

The ice floes on the upper Hudson were severe enough that the north side of the pier was shaped like the bow of a boat to help cut through ice buildup from spring freshets. By 1912, the Best family moved ashore during the winter, although Frank continued to maintain the light. He complained in 1913 that he got no winter vacation because the night boats kept running to Troy. (HRMM.)

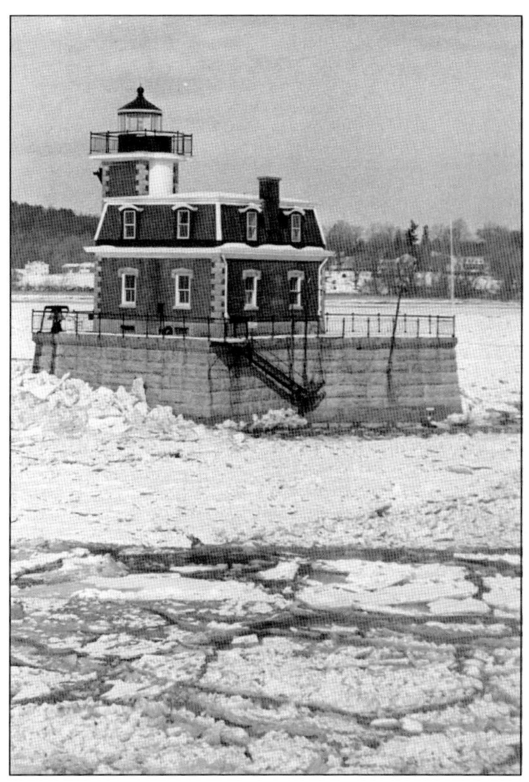

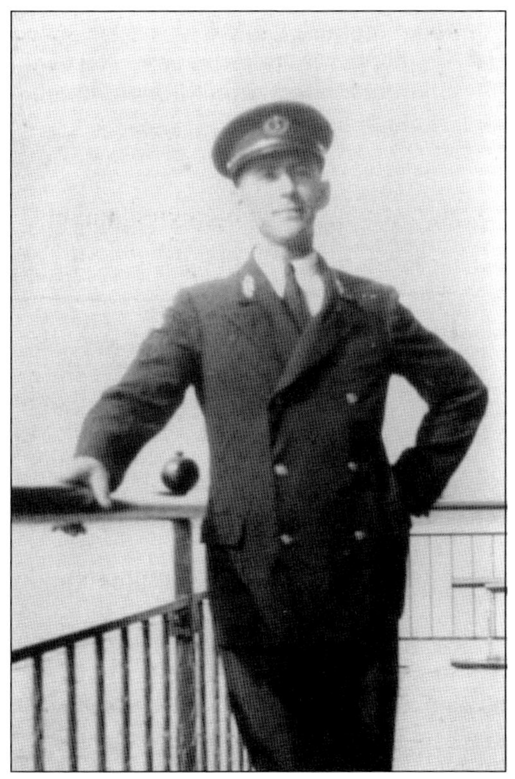

Nellie Best was succeeded at Athens by William Murray (1918–1920) and August Kjelbert (1921–1930). In 1930, Emil J. Brunner (pictured) took over as keeper. (Lynn Brunner.)

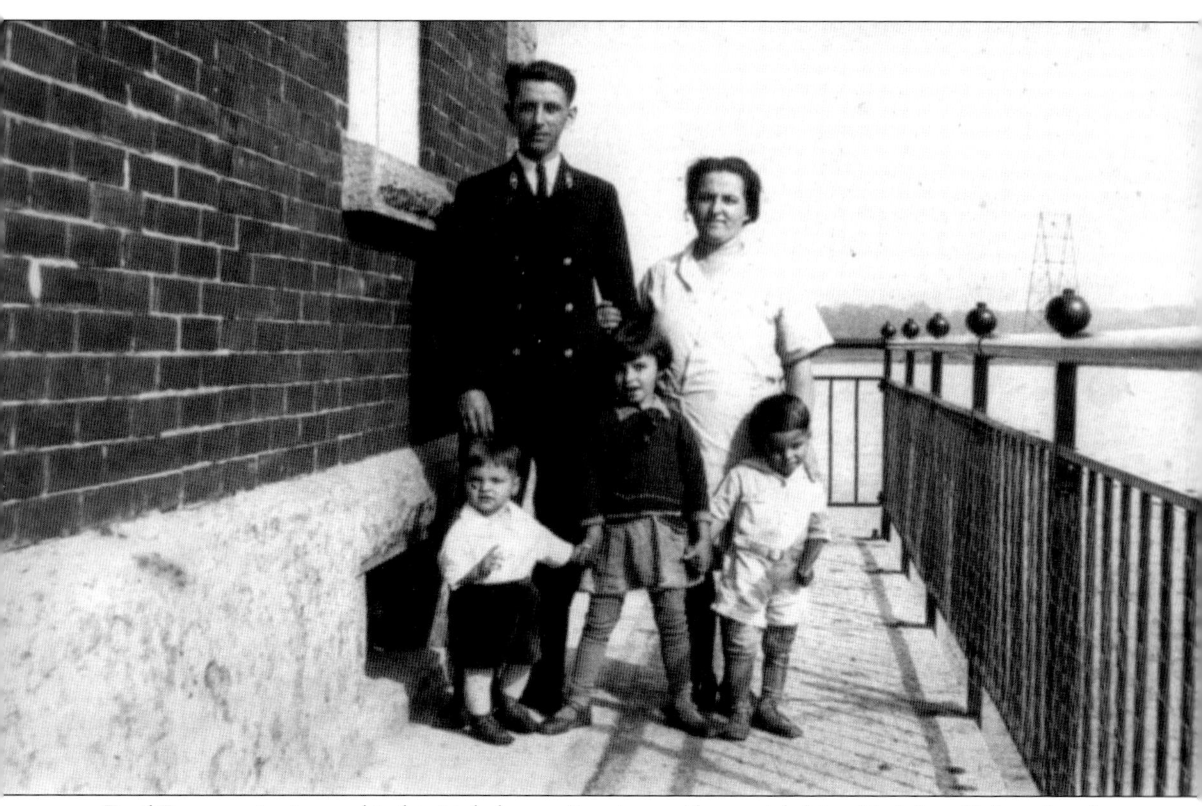

Emil Brunner is pictured in his Lighthouse Service uniform with his wife, Mary Helen, daughter Emily (center), and sons John (left) and Richard. All three children were age five or younger. Emil was a Coast Guard employee and had formerly served as keeper of lighthouses in Huntington on Long Island Sound and Perth Amboy, New Jersey. (Lynn Brunner.)

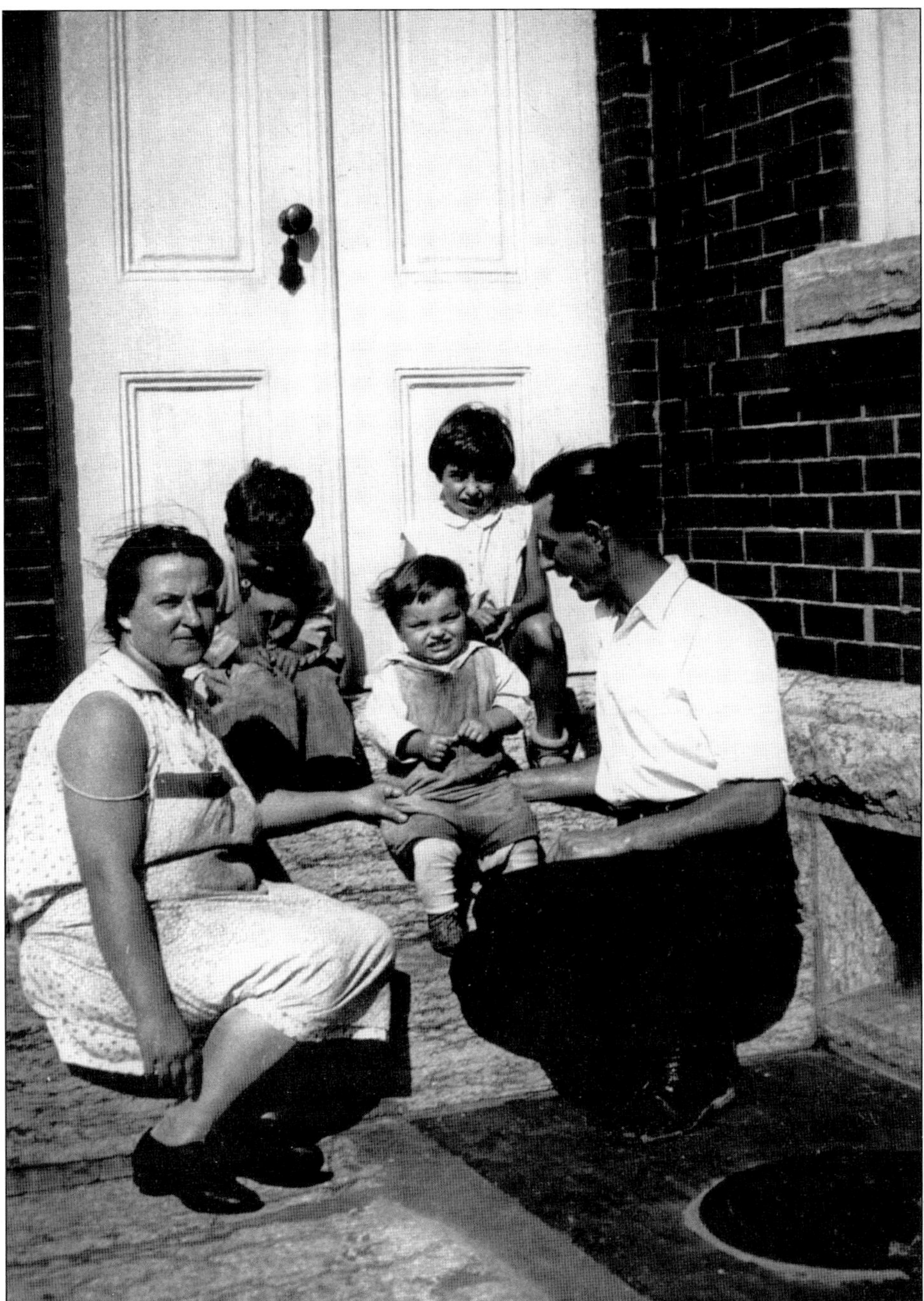

As an adult, Emily Brunner recalled the many games they played and the mischief they got into. On one occasion, young John fell asleep beneath an overturned boat, and his father thought he had fallen into the water. Emil went ashore to Hudson to gather a search party, which combed the river banks until John awoke and "popped from his hiding place." Other games included "Telephone," which involved climbing the marble quoins to the roof and yelling messages down the cistern drain spout, and "In and Out," which involved dangling over the outside of the foundation's fence rail and moving hand-over-hand. Luckily, the children escaped any real harm or serious accidents, even when walking across the winter ice to school. (Lynn Brunner.)

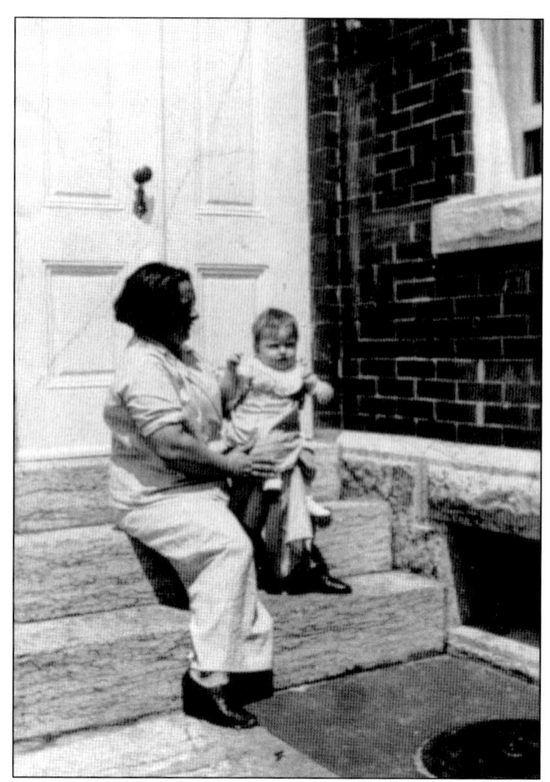

In September 1933, little Robert Brunner, seen at left and below, was born at the lighthouse. Emil rowed ashore to get Dr. Norman Cooper to attend the birth. Robert was followed by brother Norman, who was born in Catskill, a few years later. The family lived at the lighthouse until 1936, when they moved ashore to Athens at the behest of the school district, because the Brunner children were missing too much school due to winter weather and ice floes. Emil continued to man the lighthouse alone, sometimes stranded on the water for days with only his Coast Guard radio to keep him company. (Both, Lynn Brunner.)

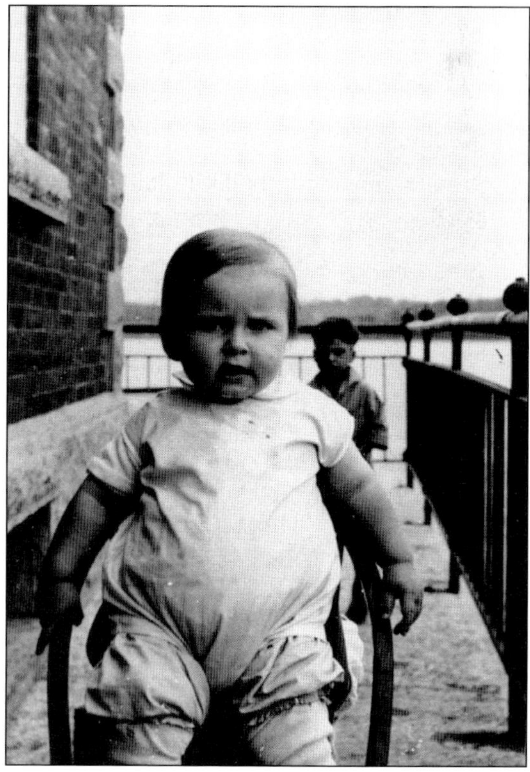

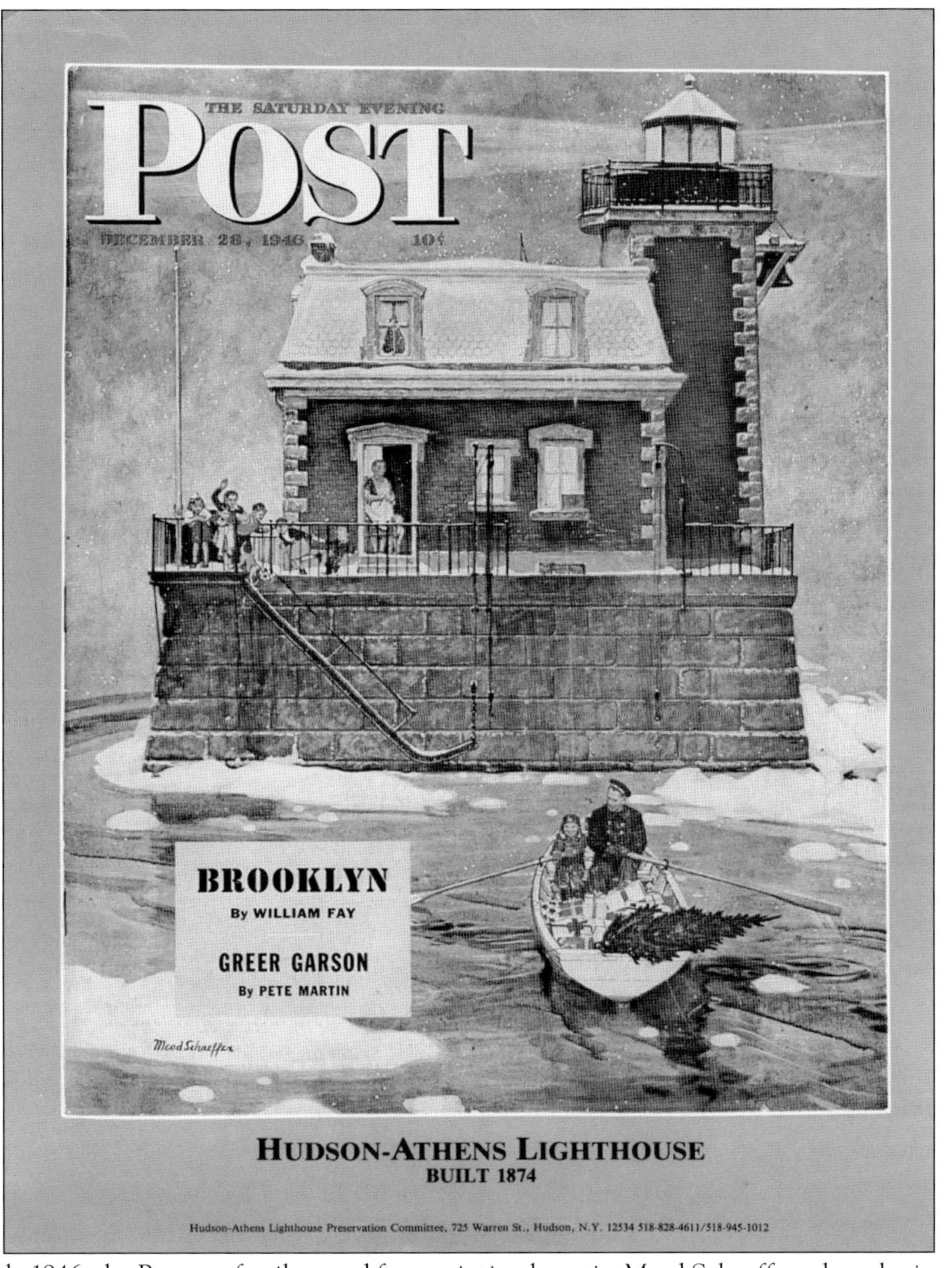

In July 1946, the Brunner family posed for a painting by artist Mead Schaeffer, who submitted it to a contest sponsored by the *Saturday Evening Post*. Schaeffer, of Vermont, had spotted the red and white lighthouse from a train and thought the picturesque lighthouse "should be under a Christmas tree." He hurriedly gathered the family and some props and posed Emil and Norman in a boat rowing toward the light, with Mary Helen Brunner, Emily, and the boys at the light. At the time, Norman asked why they had to wear winter clothes in the summer. With the artistic addition of three extra children and a dog, Schaeffer's painting won the contest and was featured on the cover of the December 26, 1946, issue of the *Post*, making the Hudson-Athens Lighthouse and the Brunner family famous. The cover was featured in several local newspapers and was recalled in many articles thereafter. (HRMM.)

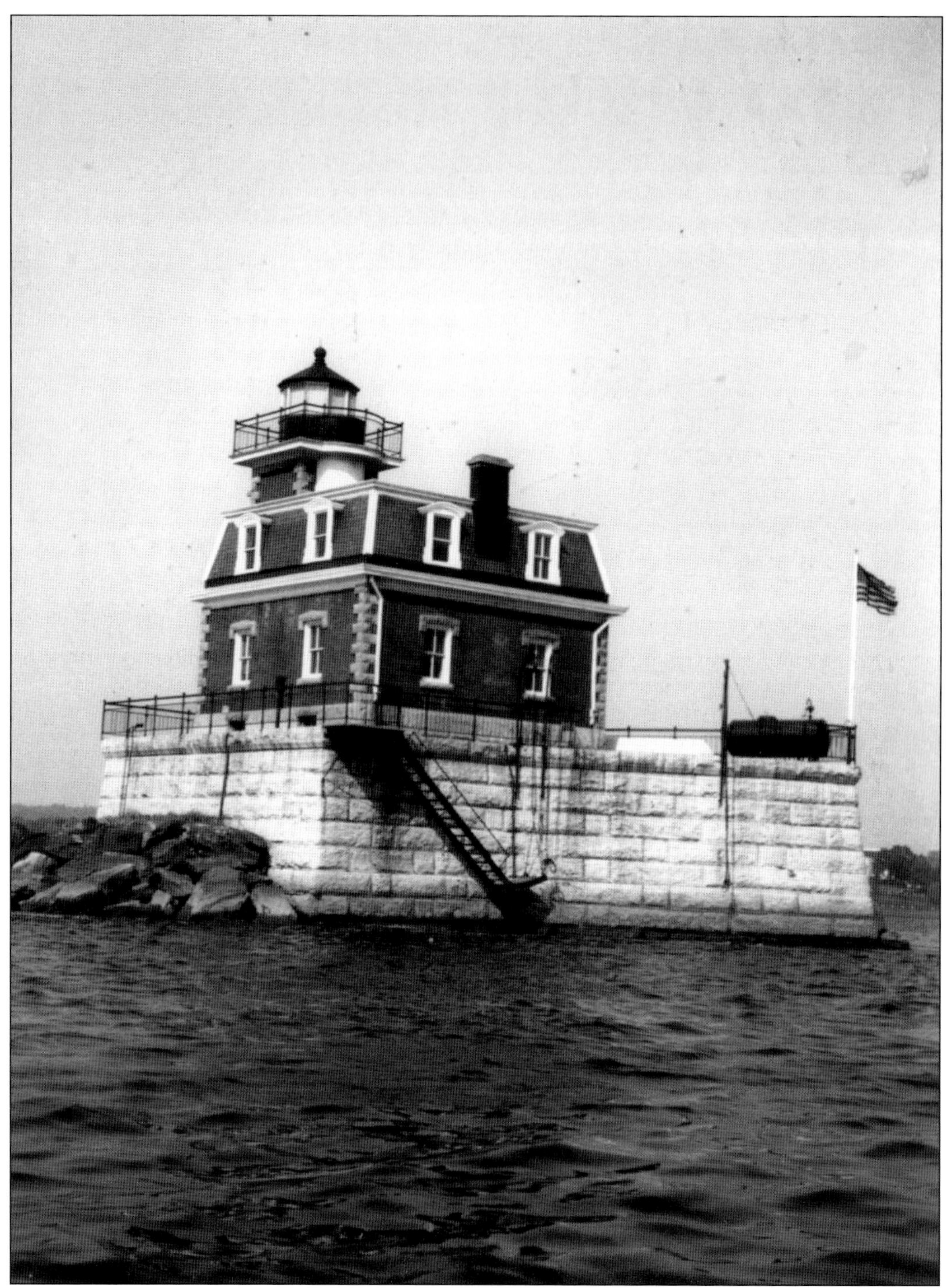

Emil Brunner left the service in 1949 and was replaced by G.E. Speaks (1949–1957), Perry Peloubet (1957–1966), and William Nestlen (1966-1986). The lighthouse was automated in 1949, relieving the later keepers from such onerous duties as before. (HRMM.)

Eight

Lost Lighthouses North to Albany

Today, the Hudson River shipping channel can accommodate large freighters as far north as Albany, but this was not always the case. Laden with sediment from the upper reaches of the watershed, the Hudson River between Albany and Hudson-Athens was broad, shallow, and filled with islands and sandbars that shifted frequently through the course of spring freshets and storms. Many of these problems were concentrated in the area between New Baltimore and Glenmont referred to as the "Overslaugh." Until the 19th century and the advent of greater traffic, pilots were often content to wait for high tide, or if necessary, discharge passengers and freight south of Albany for travel by road. Accounts of this period describe periodic groundings, with travelers taking the delays in stride.

Sporadic and limited efforts were made to clear obstructions in the river in the late 18th and early 19th centuries, but major public commitments did not begin until 1828 when New York State developed a plan to dredge a uniform 10-foot channel through the Overslaugh. The project filled 1,100 scows with sediment. The 10-foot deep channel, when achieved, was adequate in facilitating regional freight and passenger traffic, but as oceangoing ships grew in size, Albany became inaccessible to most. By 1868, the US Army Corps of Engineers had assumed responsibility for maintaining the channel. The corps initiated a series of dredging, blasting, and dike building projects that continues today. Throughout these alterations to the navigation channel near Albany, a series of lighthouses and beacons were installed marking the dikes and islands. As the channel changed, so too did the lights, and none of the original lighthouse structures nor their sibling beacon and stake lights survive.

H. D. Best, keeper.

13. West Flats, stake light, white; Charles Lee, keeper.

14. Four Mile Point, stone building, iron tower detached; keeper, Moses Waters, resides in building.

15. Narrow channel or Lamphear's dock, wood beacon; keeper, George Houghtaling.

16. Coxsackie, brick building, stone foundation; Frank Hoos, keeper; resides in building.

17. Stuyvesant, brick building, stone foundation, Ed. M. Allister, keeper

18. Sands Spit, stake light; George Woodbeck, keeper.

19. New Baltimore Island, wood foundation, stake light; De Witt Bailey, keeper.

20. New Baltimore dyke, wood foundation, portable beacon; De Witt Bailey, keeper.

21. Vive Hook, wood foundation, portable beacon; De Witt Bailey, keeper.

22. Coeymans bar, wood foundation, portable beacon; De Witt Bailey, keeper.

23. Rohn Hook, wood foundation, stake light; De Witt Bailey, keeper.

24. Schodack channel, wood foundation, stake light; Geo. Schaeffer, keeper.

25. Mull's west dyke, lower end.

26. Mull's west dyke, upper end, stake lights; Geo. Schaeffer, keeper.

27. Nine Mile Tree, wood foundation, portable beacon; George Schaeffer, keeper.

28. Cow Island, wood foundation, stake light; Jas. Jenkins, keeper.

29. Baeren Island, or Parda Hook, stake light; Jas. Jenkins, keeper.

30. Van Wie's Point, stone beacon; W. Welsh, keeper.

31. Crossover, wood foundation, portable beacon; Peter Gans, keeper.

32. Cuyler's dyke, wood foundation, portable beacon; Peter Gans, keeper.

33. Bath dyke, stake light; Mason, keeper.

From the above it will be readily seen

The upper Hudson River between Hudson and Troy, New York, were full of navigational beacons. This newspaper article from 1885 lists nearly all of these lights, some of which have no recorded history other than on maps or in references in newspapers. (HRMM.)

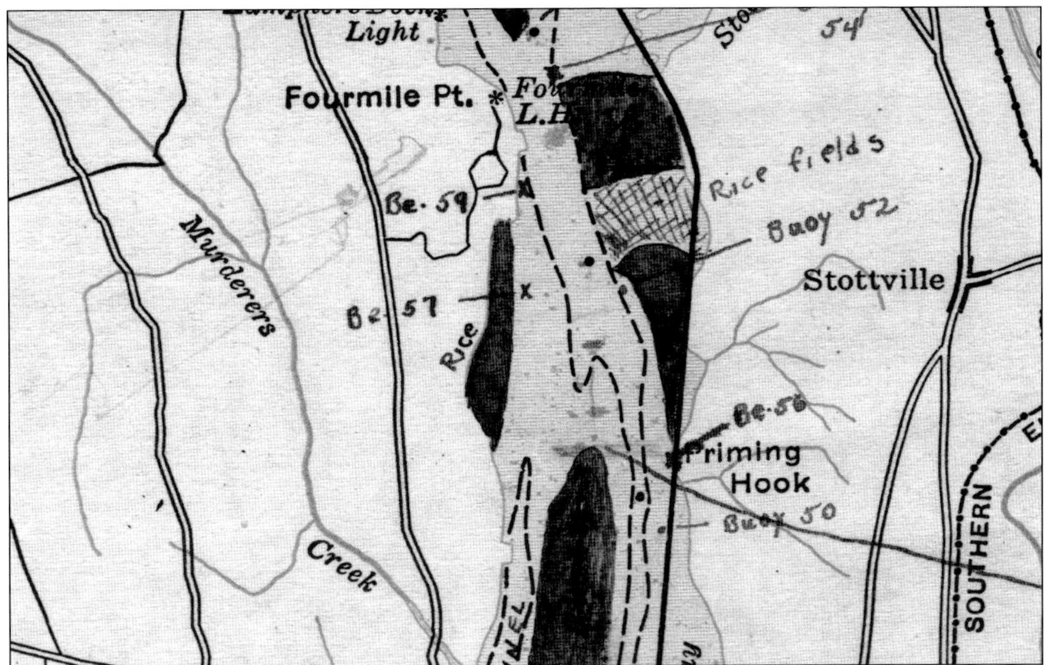

Four Mile Point, so called because it is four miles north of Hudson, is a steep cliff overlooking the west side of the Hudson River. North of the treacherous Middle Ground Flats, a lighthouse was installed at Four Mile Point in 1831 because the navigation channel skirted the cliff edge. A stone tower similar in design to Stony Point, this lighthouse had a separate keeper's residence built of the same stone. The original stone tower was demolished in 1880 and replaced with an iron sparkplug-style lighthouse. In 1928, the light on the cliff was decommissioned, although a skeleton light was installed at river level near the same location. The iron tower was torn down between 1928 and 1939. The original stone keeper's house still exists as a private residence. (Above, HRMM; below, ARC.)

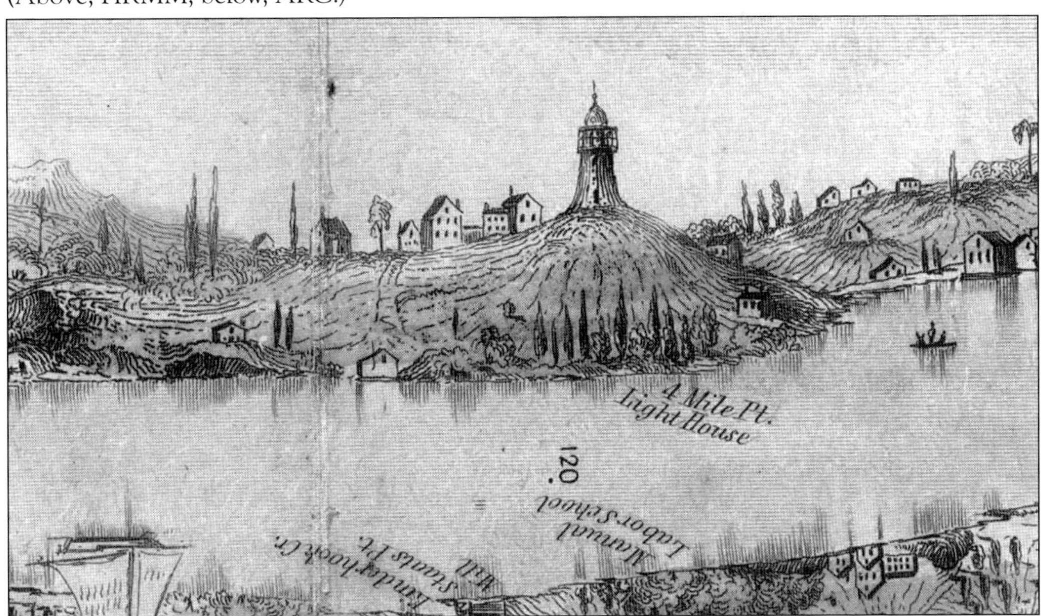

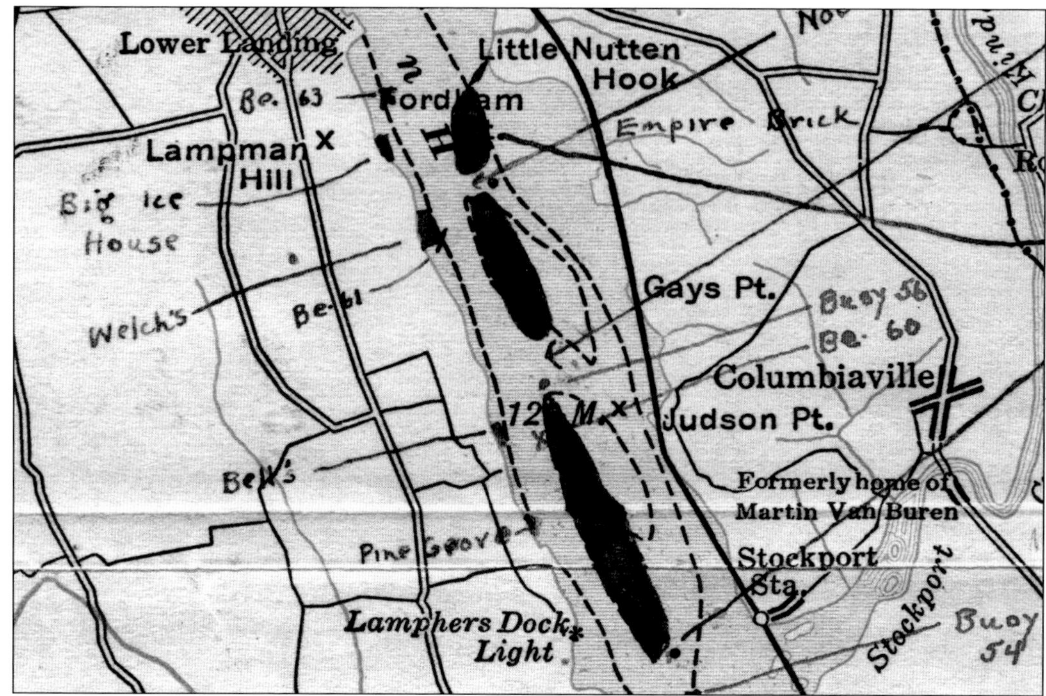

Installed in 1884, Lamphere's (or Lamphear's) Dock light was a hexagonal frame portable beacon tower placed on a brick foundation located on land three miles south of the Coxsackie Steamboat Landing. Measuring just 12 feet high in total, this comparatively small beacon helped mark the channel. In 1885, the keeper was George Houghtaling. (HRMM.)

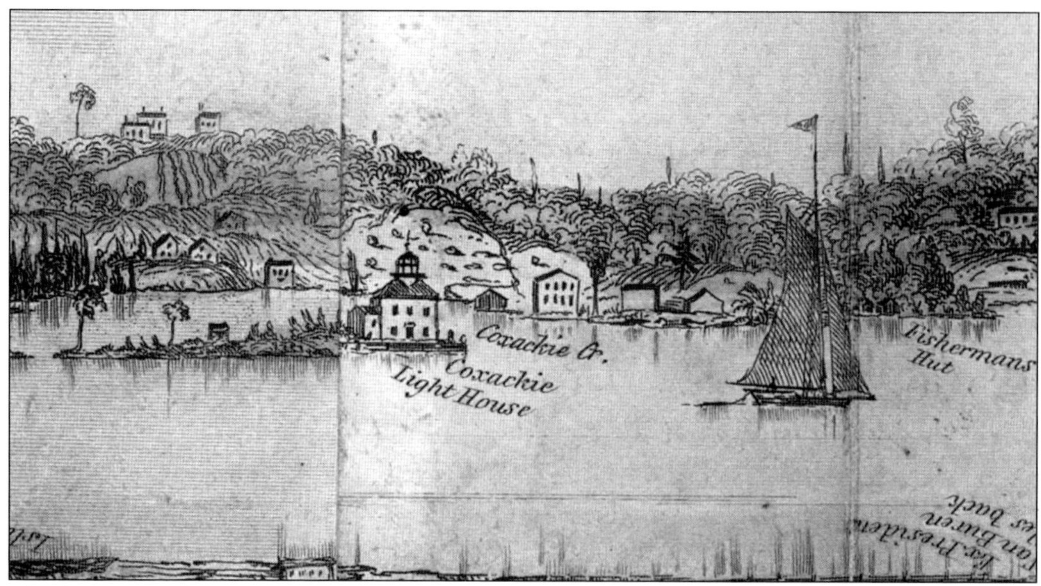

The first Coxsackie Lighthouse was built in 1828 on a small river island called Rattlesnake Island, which led to the auxiliary name of "Rattlesnake Island Lighthouse." Little is known about its keepers, although William Craig kept the light from 1842 to 1845. This is the only known image of this first Coxsackie lighthouse. (ARC.)

In 1868, the original lighthouse at Coxsackie was replaced by an Italian villa–style house designed in an L shape wrapped around a central tower. The stone foundation was also rebuilt out of enormous stone blocks. In this undated photograph, the faint outlines of the keeper's family sitting in front of the house, along with the outhouse at center left and an elaborate birdhouse on a white pole at left, can be seen. The stone riprap and solid stone foundation are clearly visible. (NARA.)

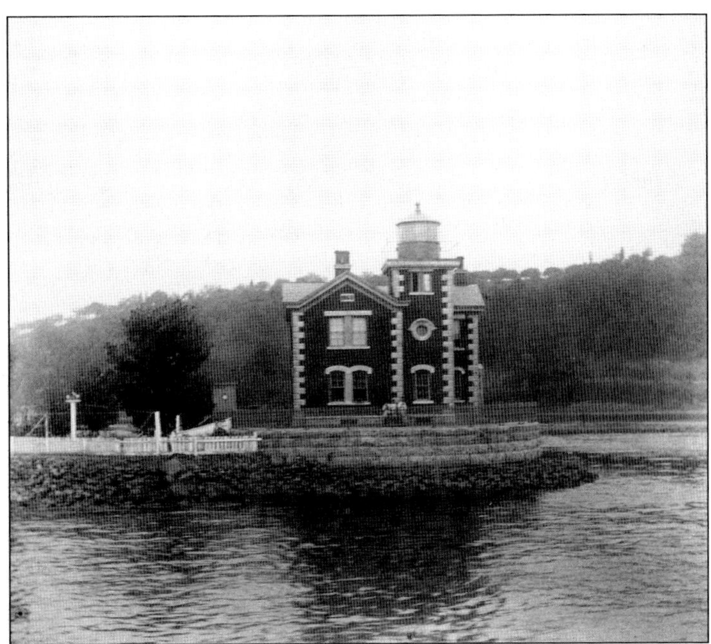

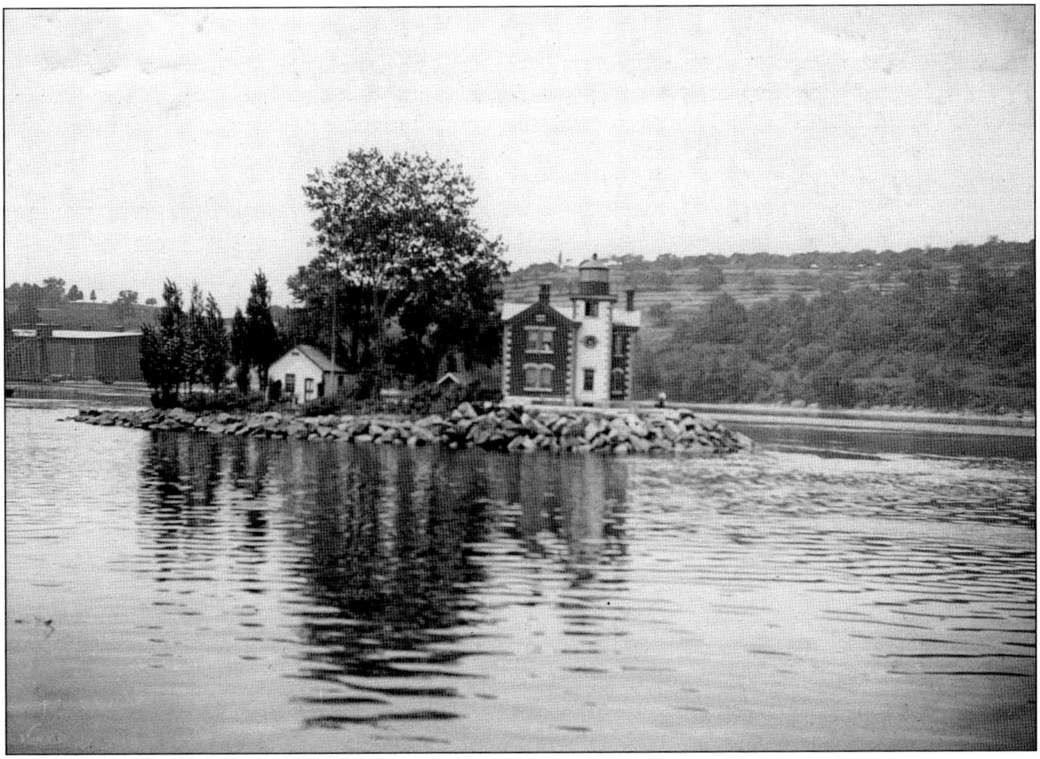

In 1902, an ice dam formed and broke, sending huge blocks of ice slamming into the lighthouse, damaging the structure, destroying the outbuildings, and flooding the first floor. The buildings were later replaced, and the tower was painted white. In this image, the additional stone riprap piled around the edge of the island to protect from ice can be seen. At left are the rebuilt outhouse and coal storage shed. (HRMM.)

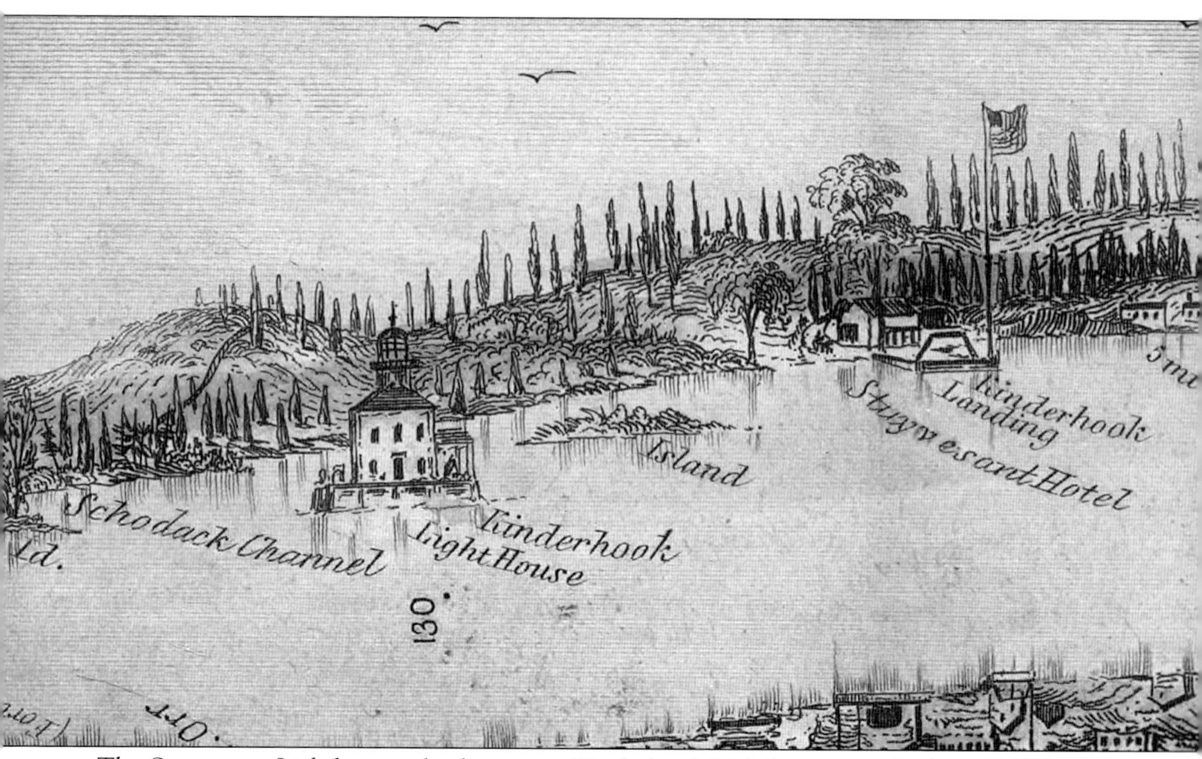

The Stuyvesant Lighthouse, also known as Kinderhook Lighthouse, was built in 1829. Volkert Witbeck was the first keeper in 1830, but he and his family suffered terrible loss during the breaking of an ice dam on the Hudson in 1832. He and nine other family members were inside the house during an attempted evacuation when the dam broke, and the rush of ice collapsed the stone structure. Two young daughters and two grandsons were swept away and killed. Kinderhook native Pres. Martin Van Buren, at the behest of locals, allowed the Witbecks to stay on the payroll until a new lighthouse was built in 1835. Volkert was succeeded as keeper by his wife, Christina (1841–1853), and later daughter Ann Whitbeck (1853–1866). (ARC.)

By the 1860s, the original Stuyvesant Lighthouse had destabilized enough that a new foundation and lighthouse were built in 1869, in the same Italian villa style as Rondout, Saugerties, and Coxsackie. Henry McAllister was the first keeper in the new lighthouse, succeeded in 1884 by his son Edwin. (NARA.)

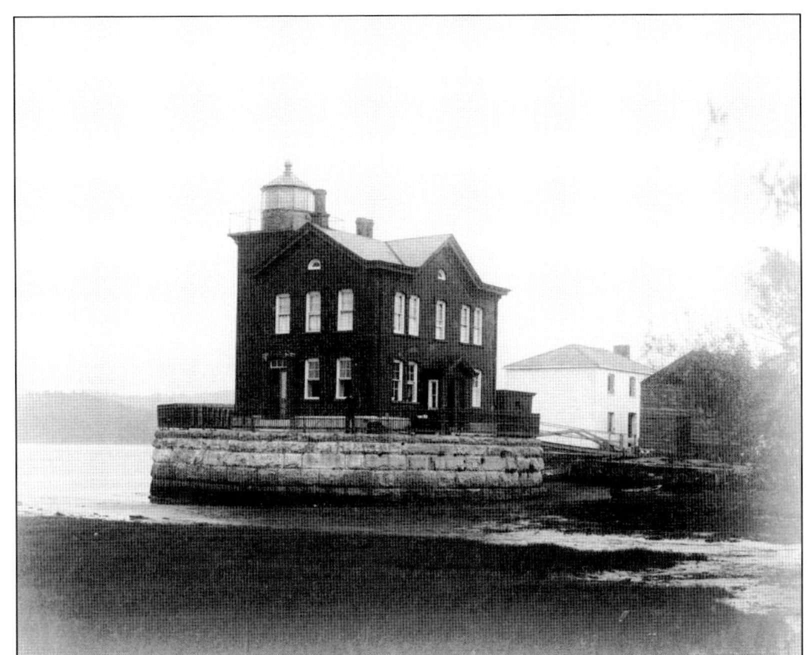

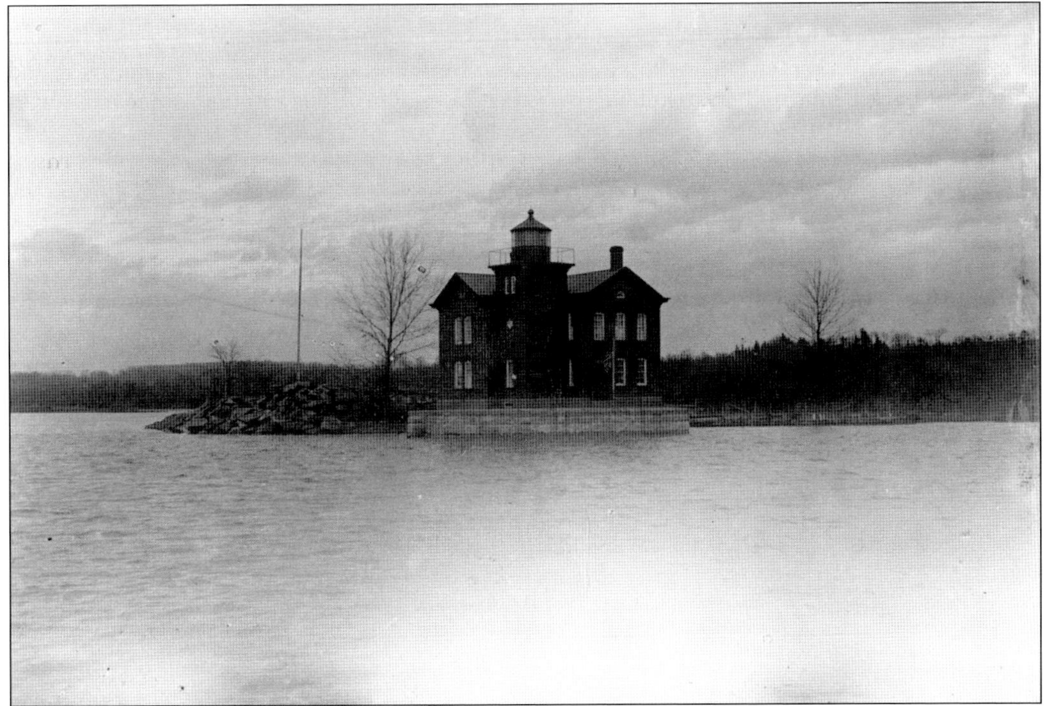

Edwin and Josephine McAllister were present during the March 1902 freshet that sent ice blocks hurtling down the flooded Hudson and severely damaged the lighthouse and destroyed outbuildings. Repairs were completed by November 1902 with stone riprap added to protect the base from future ice floes. In this photograph, taken November 20, 1915, the riprap can clearly be seen at left, and the former outbuildings are no longer present. An automated skeleton light was added in 1933, and the building was demolished in 1936. (NARA.)

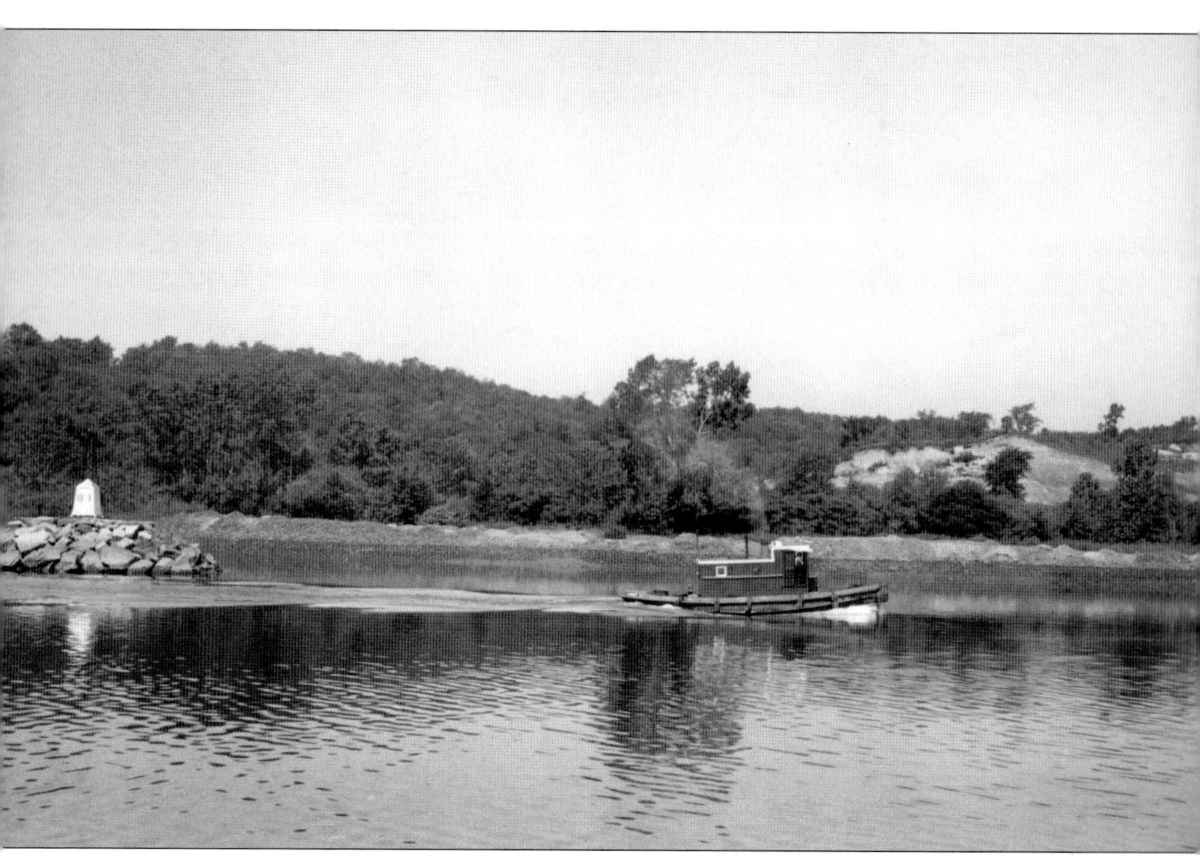

Just north of Stuyvesant, Bronck Island was marked by a small temporary beacon shown here. Sometime in the mid-20th century, Bronck Island was filled in on the back side, uniting it with the west shore. It is still labeled Bronck Island on maps today and boasts a Scenic Hudson Unique Area, but the little beacon is no more. (HRMM.)

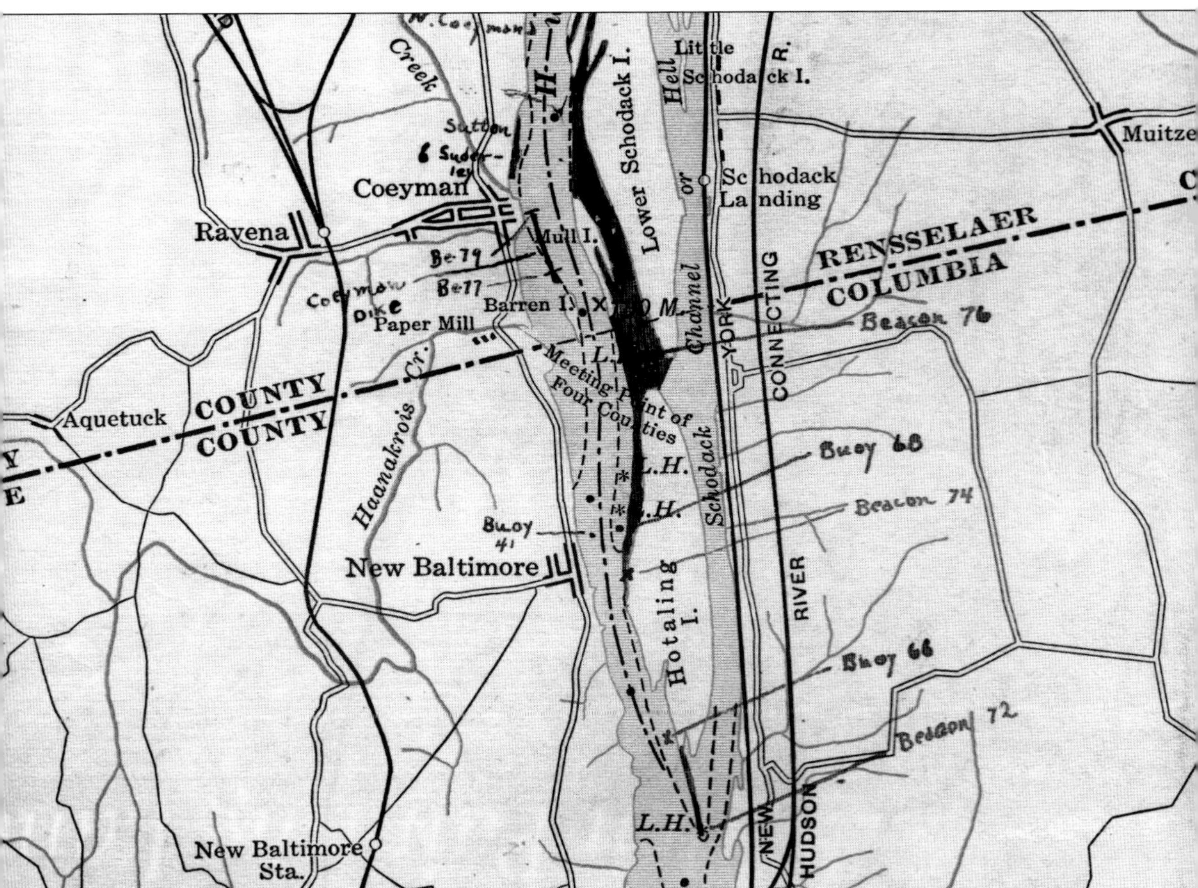

This map is one of the few remaining clues to the origins of the lights between Stuyvesant and Albany. Although not named on this map, Sands Spit (1884), New Baltimore Island, New Baltimore Dike, Five Hook, Coeymans Bar, Roha Hook, Schodack Channel, and Mull's Island (1884) Lights were present along this stretch of river. All were either portable beacons or stake lights. Schodack Channel had a female keeper, Joanna Lawton (1860–1873). New Baltimore also had a female keeper, Eliza Smith (1864–1870). In 1885, De Witt Bailey kept both New Baltimore lights, as well as Five Hook, Coeymans Bar, and Roha Hook. As can be seen on the map, the large islands in the center of the river made for treacherous navigation. Exact installation dates for most of these lights is unclear, but all are mentioned in an 1893 report. In 1916, Nine Mile Tree, Roha Hook, Five Hook, and New Baltimore were rebuilt. (HRMM.)

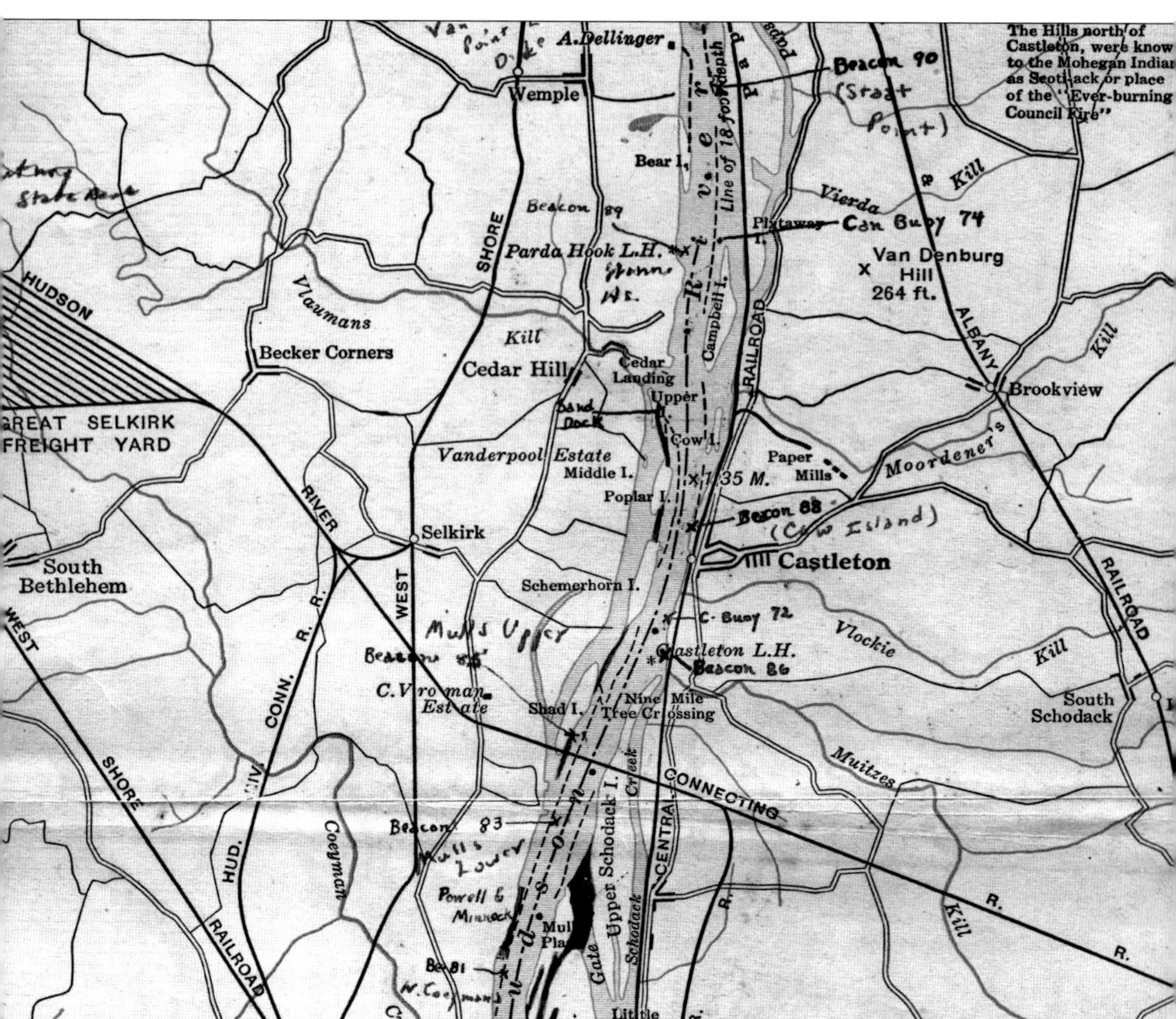

In this section of the same map, the Mull Island, Nine Mile Tree/Castleton, Cow Island/Campbell Island, Parda Hook (also known as Baeren Island), and Staats Point Lights are listed. Like their southern neighbors, all were portable beacons or stake lights. In 1885, George Schaeffer kept Schodack Channel, both Mull Island, and Nine Mile Tree lights. That same year, James Jenkins kept Cow Island and Parda Hook. In 1893, Mull, Nine Mile Tree, Cow Island, Bear Island, and Staats Point Lights were updated, and in 1916, Bear Island and Cow Island were rebuilt. In 1933, the widening of the navigation channel meant that several hooks including Parda Hook were shaved off. Many of these islands and shoals were removed or consolidated during the Army Corps of Engineers' effort to widen the river for ocean shipping between the 1930s and 1960s. (HRMM.)

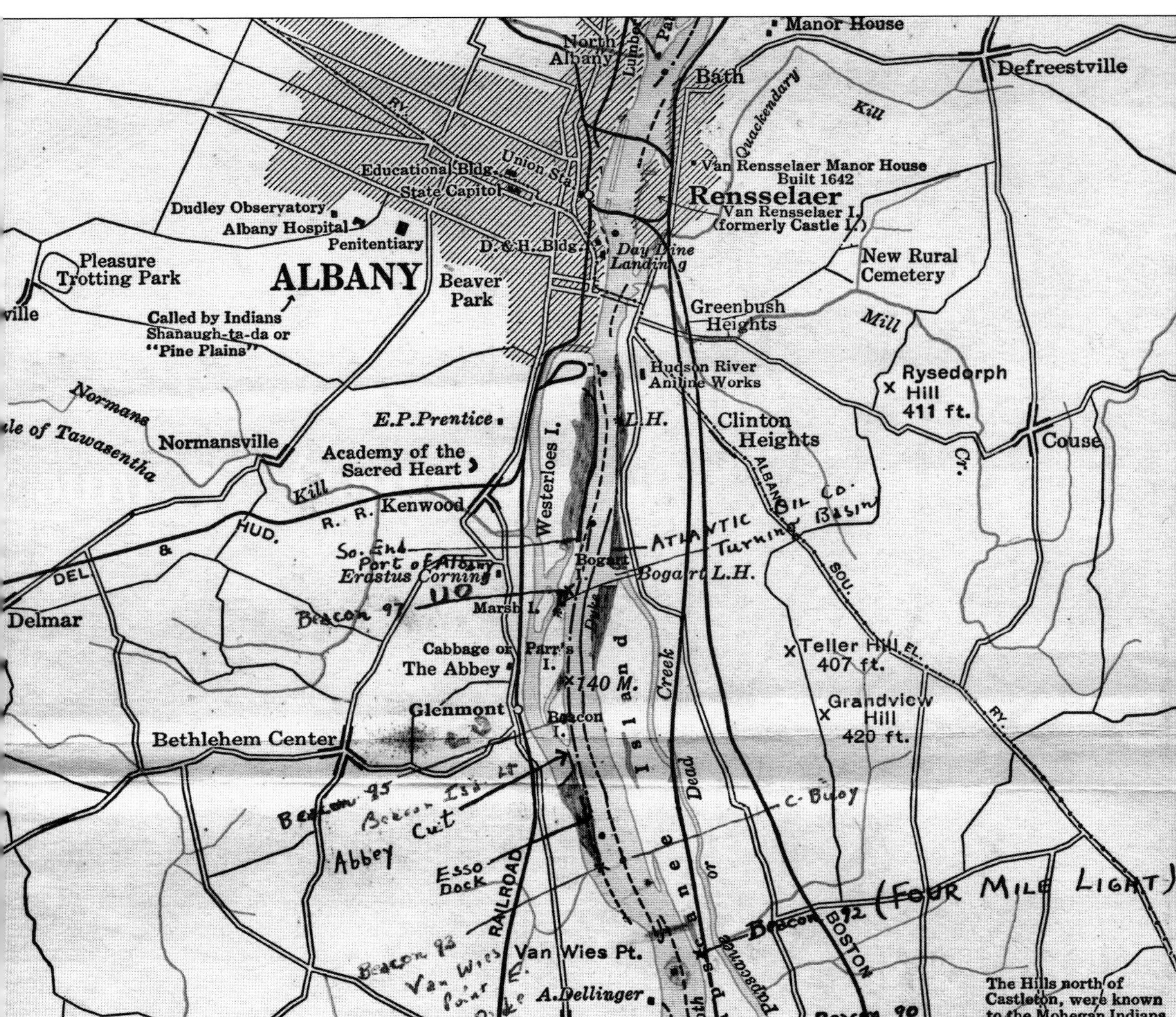

In this section of the map, evidence of Van Wies (sometimes spelled Wie's) Point Lighthouse, Bogart Lighthouse, and Beacon Island and Bath Dike lights can be seen. Bath Dike, in particular, was in a tough spot and was frequently destroyed by freshets and ice floes, including in 1885 and again in 1886. Van Wie's Point Lighthouse was a stone tower standing 21 feet tall on the south end of a stone dike off the point, built in 1854. William Welch was keeper at Van Wie's Point Lighthouse from 1858 until his death at age 93 in 1910. At the time, he was the oldest keeper in the country and served for 52 years. His son Franklin was appointed keeper in his place and served until the 1930s. Van Wie's Point and Bath Dike were updated in 1893, and Van Wie's Point was updated again in 1916. In 1885, a man named Mason kept the Bath Dike stake light. Almost no record of Bogart Island Lighthouse and Beacon Island Light exist; starting in the 1920s, they were merged with Cabbage, Marsh, and Westerlo Islands to become a single island. (HRMM.)

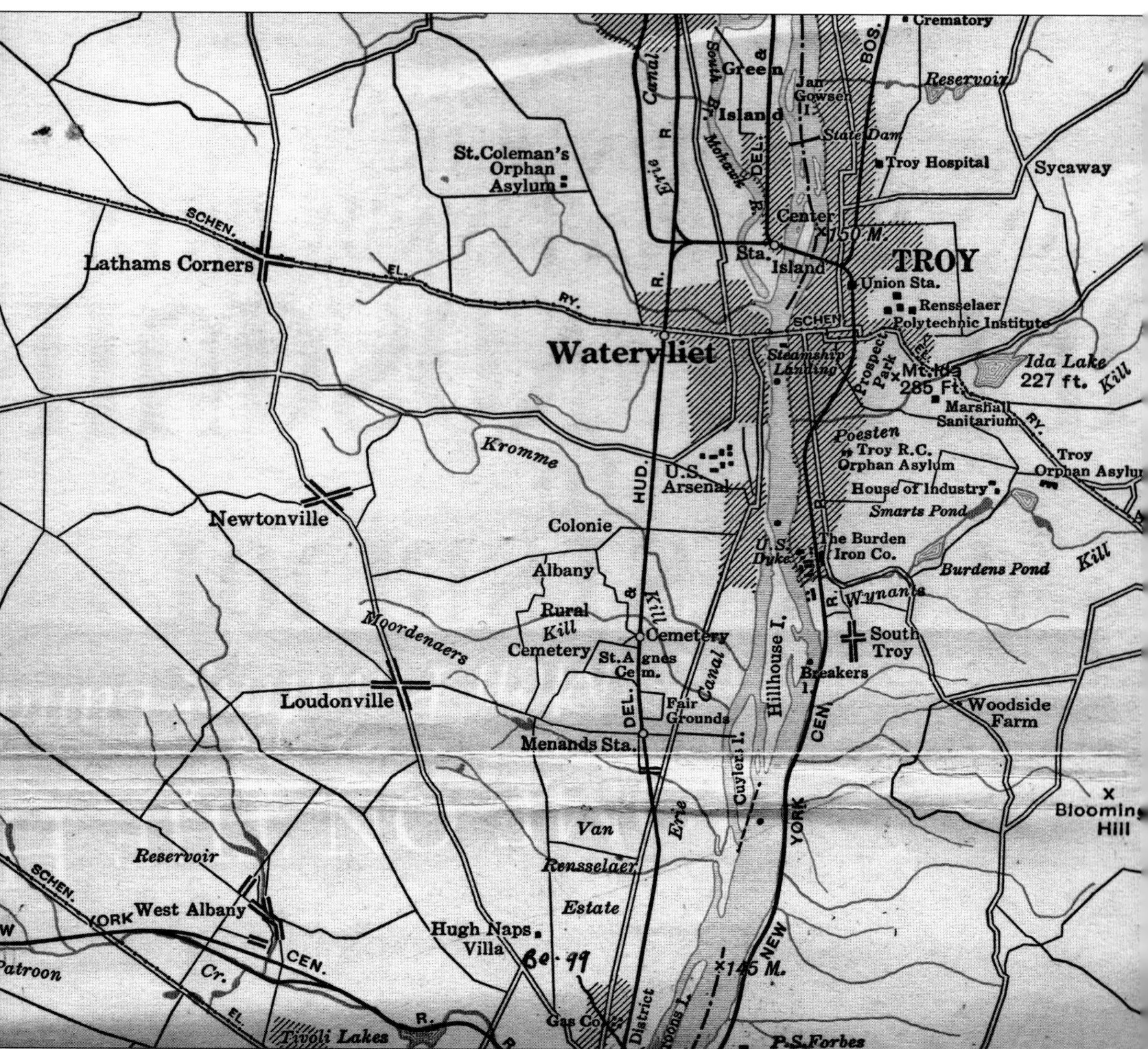

North of Bath, Patroon Lower Island and Cuyler's Island (also known as Cuyler's Dike) Lights were also located on this section of the river. Cross-Over Light, on the north end of Westerlo Island just south of Albany, and Cuyler's Dike were often manned by the same person. From 1869 to 1872, Cyrenius C. Craig was the "lampist" for both Cuyler's and Cross-Over Lights. By 1885, Peter Gans was keeper of both beacons. (HRMM.)

Nine

PRESERVATION

Hudson River lighthouses were, for the most part, products of the 19th century. Expensive to build and maintain and often located in relatively inaccessible spots, they required constant oversight, live-in keepers, and regular deliveries of oil and later kerosene. With the advent of electricity, automating lighthouses became an increasingly attractive option for the federal government as it eliminated significant expenditures of manpower in both the keepers themselves and the staff required to deliver supplies and goods.

As Hudson River lighthouses began to be electrified in the 1920s, several lighthouses in dubious condition were demolished and replaced with automated beacons. Historic preservation was in its infancy at this time, and outcry from the public saved only a few structures during these years. When the Coast Guard assumed control of the Lighthouse Board in 1939, this process was accelerated.

The disregard for historic buildings and places became especially pronounced in the 1950s and 1960s during a period of enormous social and technological change. Federal assistance for new transportation infrastructure and so-called "slum clearance," branded euphemistically as "urban renewal," laid waste to the historic cores of many cities. The 1963 demolition of Penn Station in New York City shocked the public and led to the establishment of the National Historic Preservation Act of 1966. The act required federal agencies to consider historic properties in project planning and established the National Register of Historic Places as an inventory of the nation's historic places. This was by no means a panacea for historic preservation, but it gave new credibility and tools to promote preservation. A generation later, the National Historic Preservation Act was amended with the addition of the National Lighthouse Preservation Act, which provided a mechanism to transfer historic lighthouses to qualified local government or not-for-profit stewards.

Today, seven Hudson River lighthouses and the Statue of Liberty are all that remain of the over two dozen lights that once lit the Hudson. For information on how to visit these gems, visit www.hudsonriverlighthouses.org.

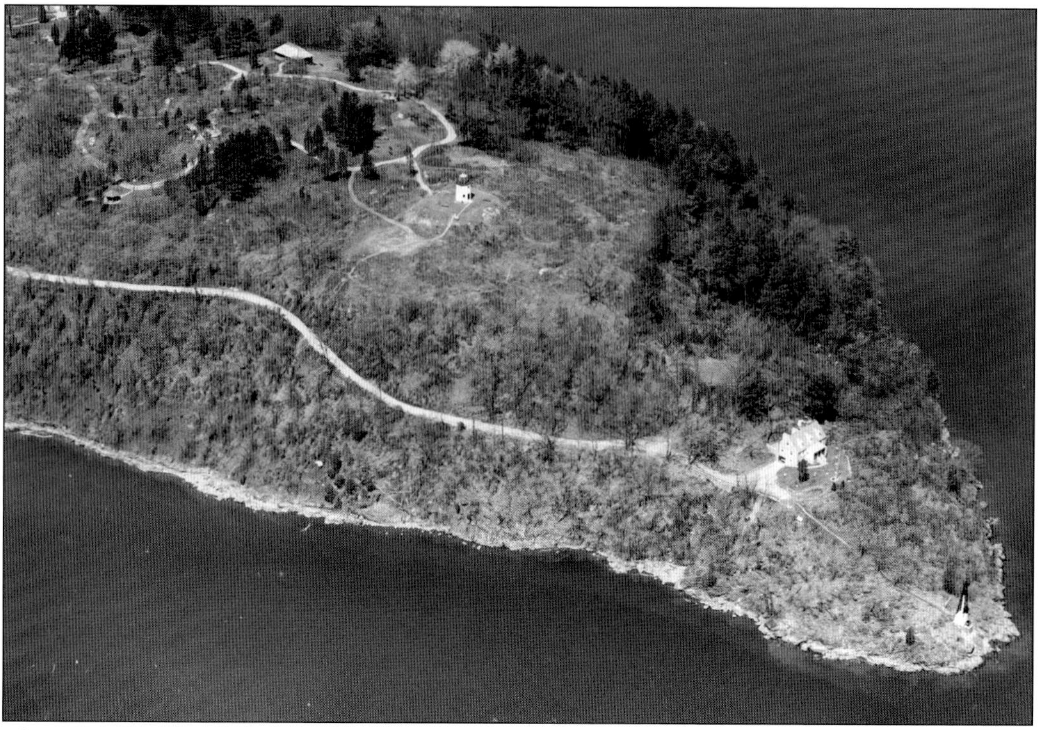

The Stony Point Lighthouse, which had been lit since 1826, was extinguished in 1921 and replaced with an automated tower at the base of the cliffs, near the original fog bell tower. Here, the path Nancy Rose had to walk to reach the fog bell can be seen. At the same time Stony Point was being extinguished, the Jeffrey's Hook Lighthouse was installed to replace a stake light. (SPB.)

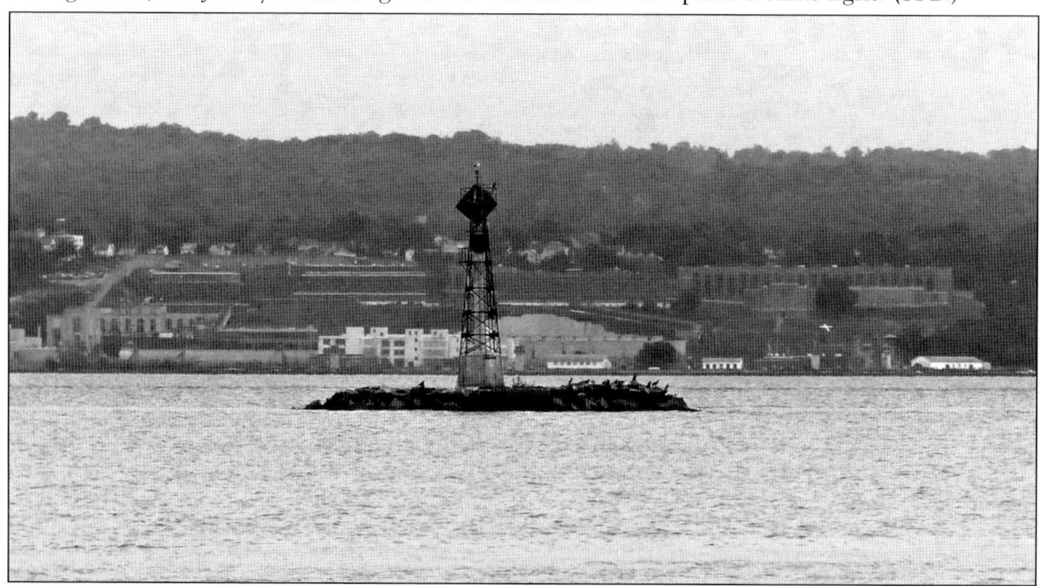

In 1923, the Rockland Lake Lighthouse was demolished and replaced with an automated light tower. Its precarious status on an eroding oyster bed made it ripe for demolition, as did the decreased marine traffic to Rockland Landing and the neighboring Knickerbocker Ice Company. (Joan Mayer.)

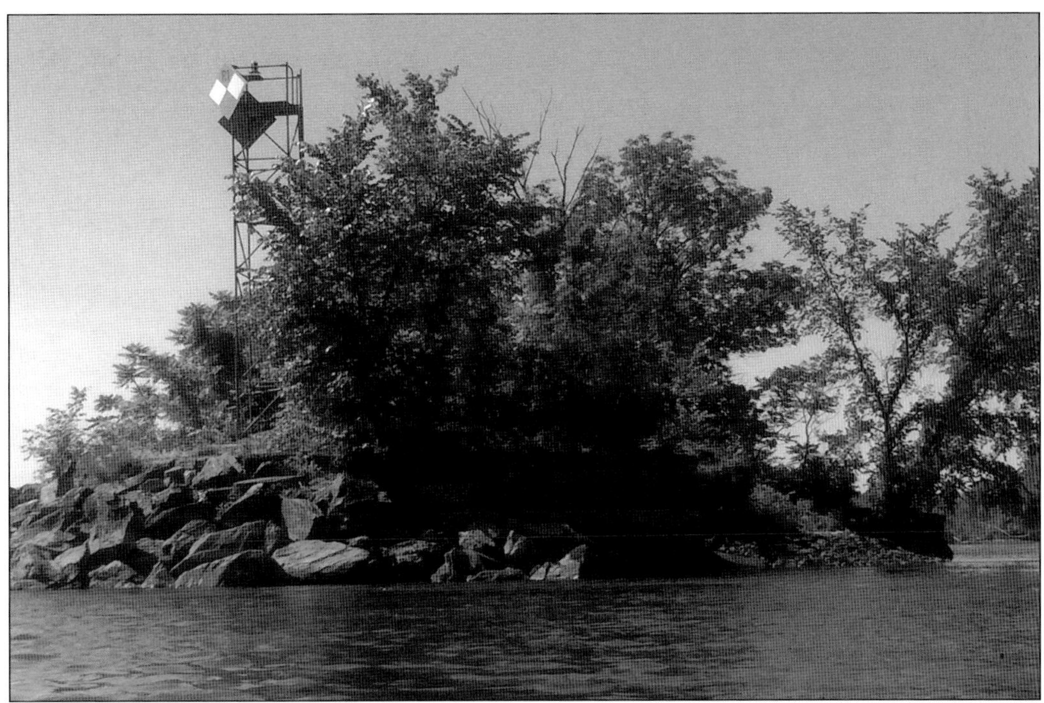

Four Mile Point Lighthouse was demolished in 1928, and the Coxsackie Lighthouse (above) was closed and demolished in 1939. The great round stone foundation of the Coxsackie light was left intact as it made a good base for the electric skeleton light that replaced the brick dwelling. Stuyvesant Lighthouse (below) was closed and demolished in 1932. As at the site of the Coxsackie Lighthouse, the stone foundation at Stuyvesant remains, but the skeleton light was placed on the riprap just to the side. Today, both foundations are so overgrown it is difficult to imagine that lighthouses once stood there. (Both, Mark Peckham.)

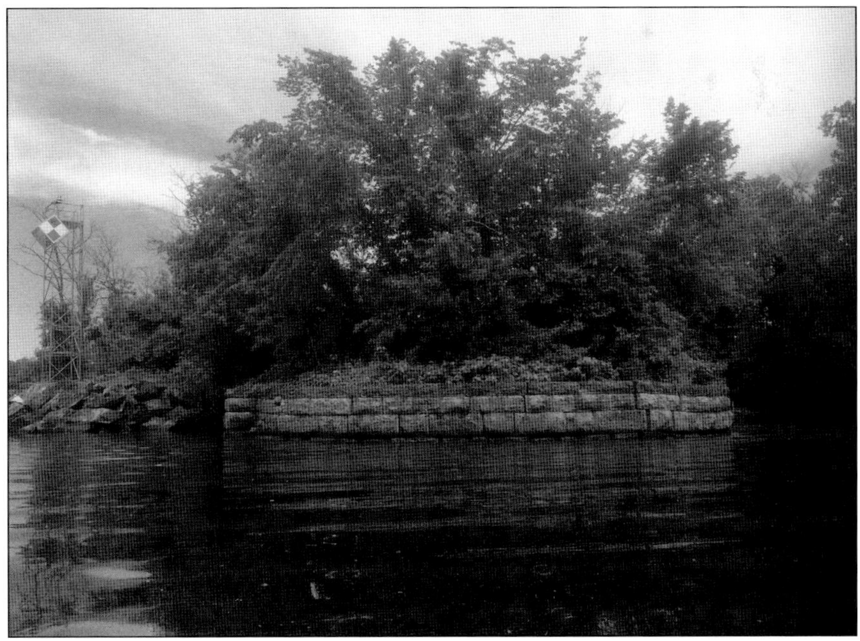

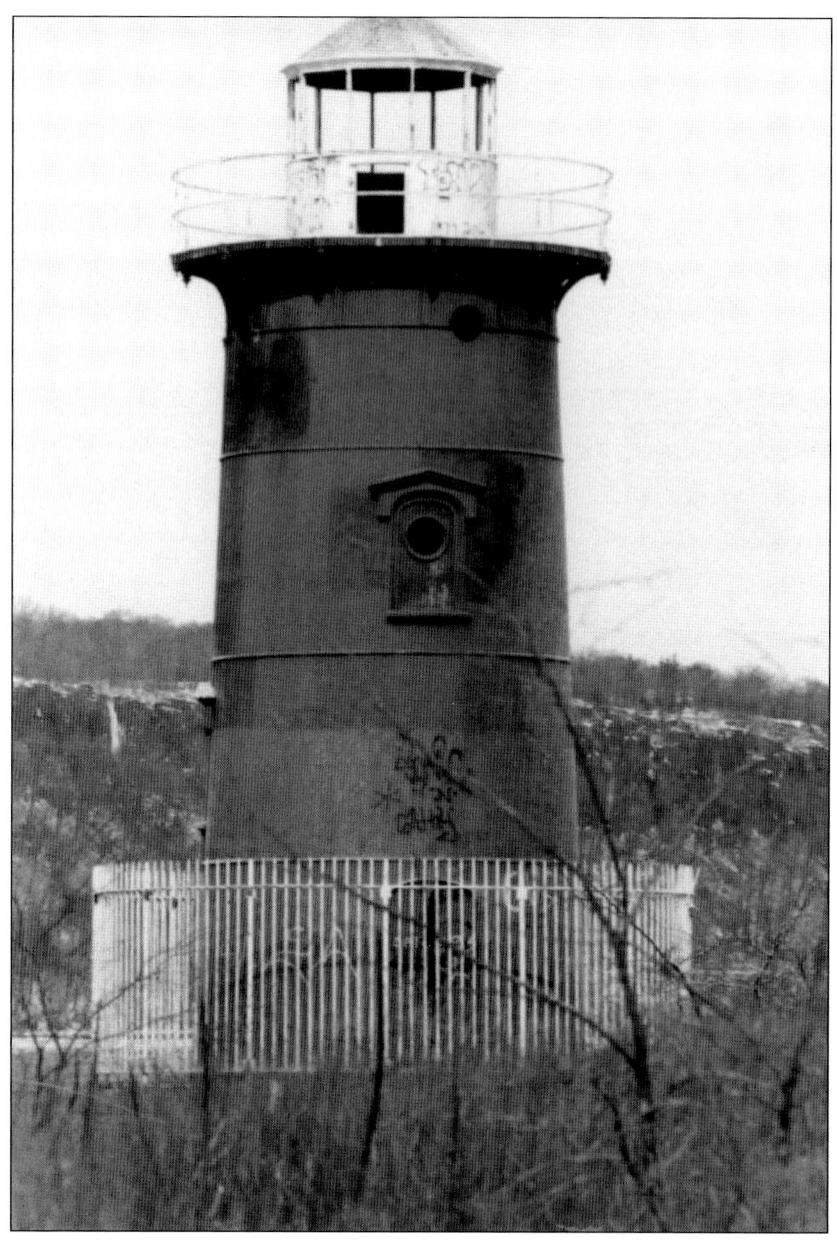

One of the first public pleas to save an obsolete lighthouse was inspired by the 1942 children's book *The Little Red Lighthouse and the Great Gray Bridge* by Hildegarde Hoyt Swift. The completion of the George Washington Bridge between Washington Heights and Fort Lee in 1931 and the installation of navigational lights on the bridge made the lighthouse in its shadow unnecessary. Swift's popular book, however, was all about how even the smallest lighthouse could make itself useful. The Coast Guard moved to demolish the lighthouse in 1948, but fans of the book, particularly children, wrote thousands of letters of protest and forced the Coast Guard to change its plans. In 1951, they announced the public sale and removal of the lighthouse structure, but protests ensued again, and the Coast Guard negotiated a transfer of the lighthouse to the New York City Department of Parks and Recreation for preservation that same year. For more information, visit www.nycgovparks.org. (NARA.)

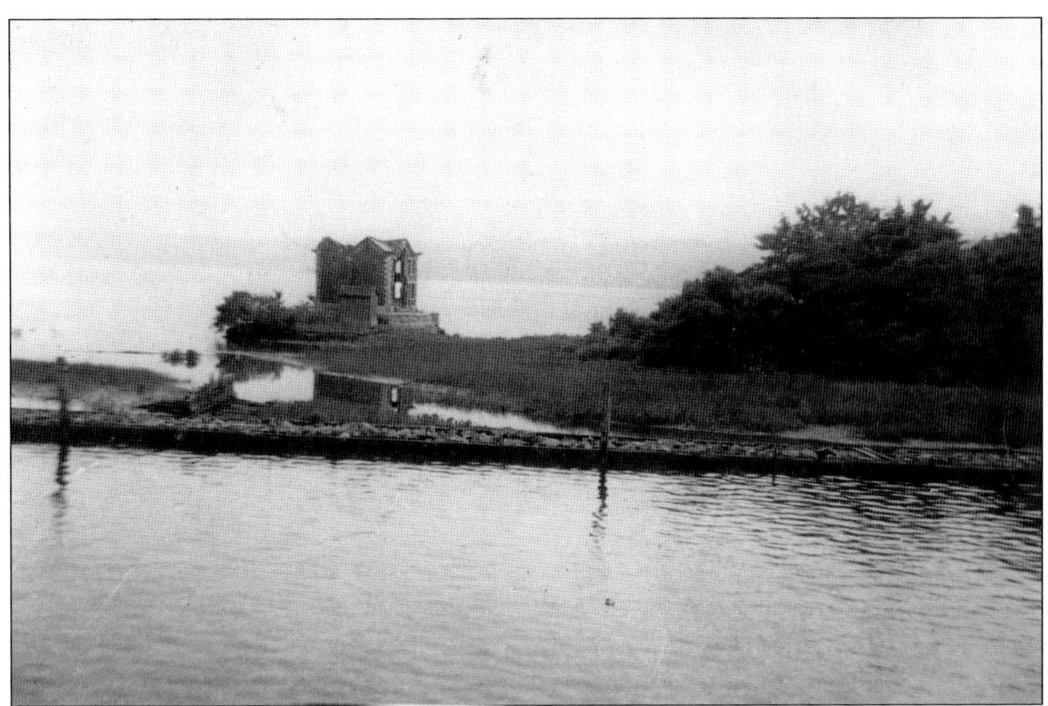

Other lighthouses were not so lucky. The 1867 Rondout Lighthouse, which had been abandoned in 1915, was in ruins by the 1950s. Attempts had been made to sell the structure early on, but removing the stone building to shore was too daunting for prospective buyers. In 1953, the remainder of the building was dynamited, and the rubble collapsed into the basement, where it remains today. (HRMM.)

In 1966, the Coast Guard proposed the demolition of the Saugerties and Esopus Meadows Lighthouses, both of which were in poor condition, and the sale of the decommissioned Tarrytown Lighthouse. These actions were postponed at the request of Gov. Nelson Rockefeller's Hudson River Valley Commission, which in 1967 published a report recommending the preservation of the river's remaining lighthouses through transfers to municipalities or not-for-profit organizations. Although this did not happen immediately, it ultimately became the model used in preserving the remaining lighthouses. (HRMM.)

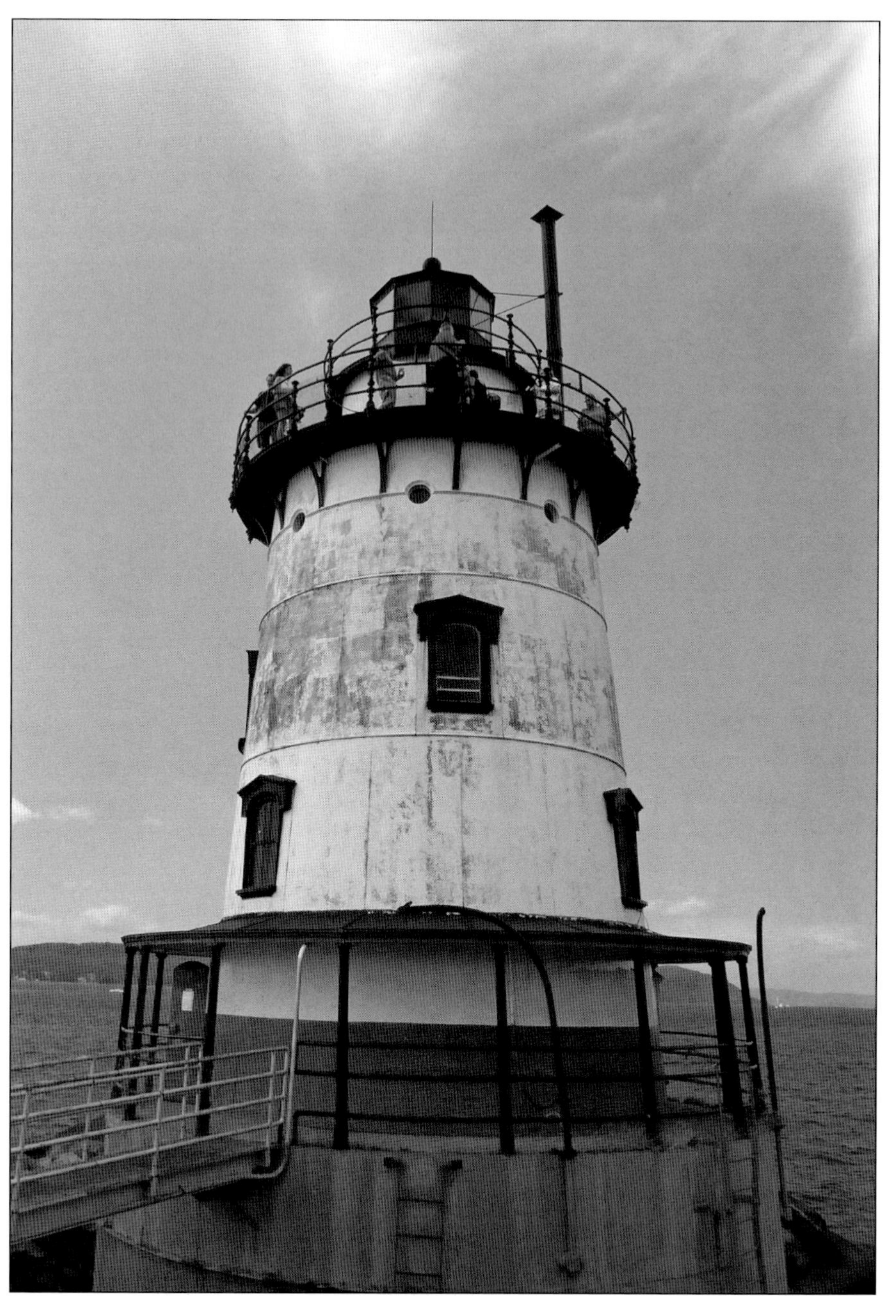

In 1969, the Westchester County legislature and county executive agreed to acquire the Tarrytown Lighthouse to preserve it for future generations. In 1977, the county built a footbridge from Kingsland Point to the lighthouse, but although preliminary restoration work began in the 1970s, it was not until 1982, just shy of the centennial celebrations in 1983, that the lighthouse was regularly open for tours. With live-in caretaker Christopher Letts, a commercial fisherman and environmental educator, the lighthouse was increasingly accessible throughout the 1980s and 1990s. Today, the lighthouse is operated by the Village of Sleepy Hollow Department of Recreation and Parks and receives some funding from the county toward maintenance. For more information, visit www.visitsleepyhollow.com/historic-sites/sleepy-hollow-lighthouse. (Joan Mayer.)

Additional attention toward the plight of these lighthouses was provided in 1969 with the publication of Ruth Glunt's book *The Old Lighthouses of the Hudson River*, which was reprinted in 1975 as *Lighthouses and Legends of the Hudson River*. Living adjacent to the deteriorating Saugerties Lighthouse and married to Chester Glunt, the retired superintendent of the Turkey Point Light Attendant Station, Ruth provided a glimpse at the way of life represented by these lighthouses. Her stories and anecdotes drew public interest in the remaining lighthouses and helped to inspire communities to step forward with plans to preserve them. It also encouraged the effort by New York State to nominate the lighthouses to the National Register of Historic Places in 1979, calling further attention to their significance and assisting in their preservation. (Both, HRMM.)

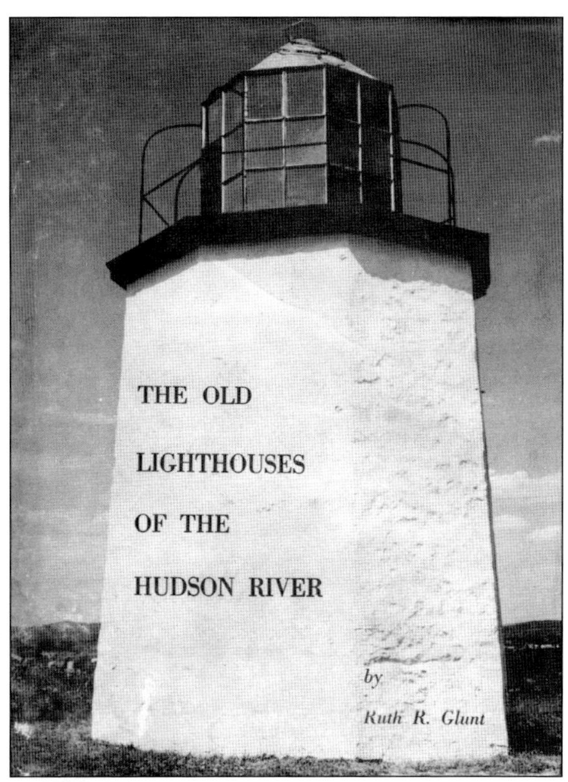

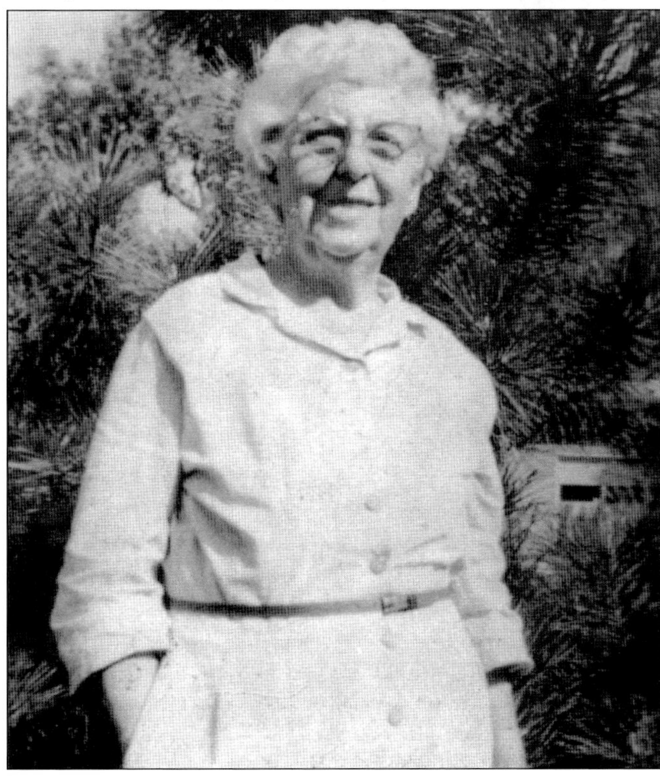

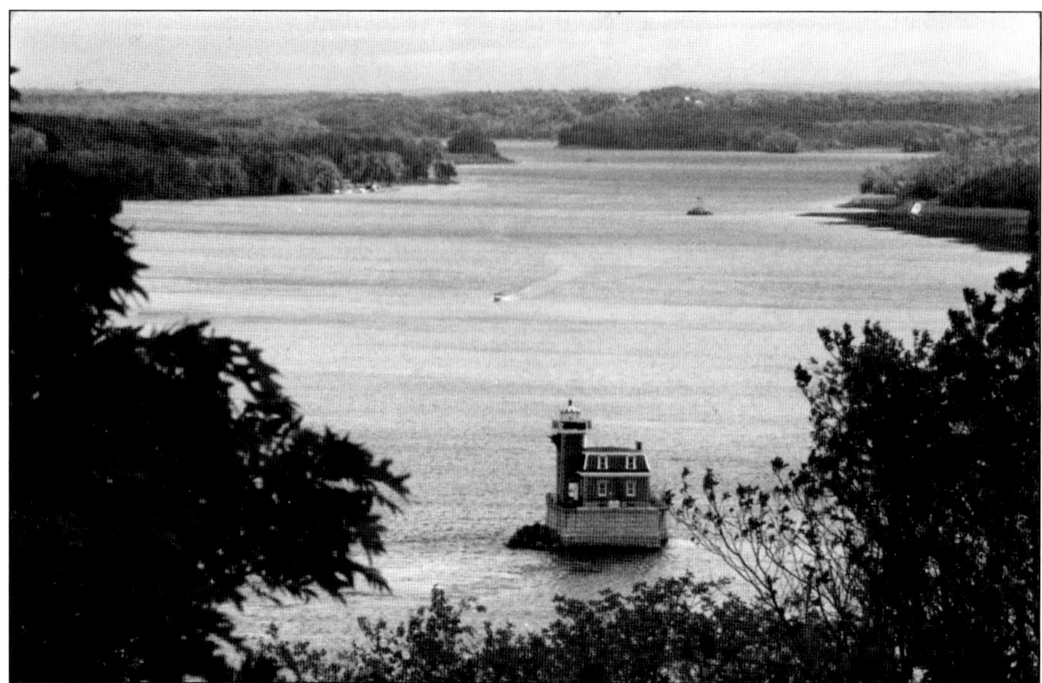

Compared to the other lighthouses, Hudson-Athens was in relatively good shape, having been used by the Coast Guard as a light and fog bell station into the 1970s. The Hudson-Athens Lighthouse Preservation Society was formed in 1982 and in 1984 entered into a 20-year lease with the Coast Guard, which ceded ownership in 2000. For more information, visit www.hudsonathenslighthouse.org. (Lynn Brunner.)

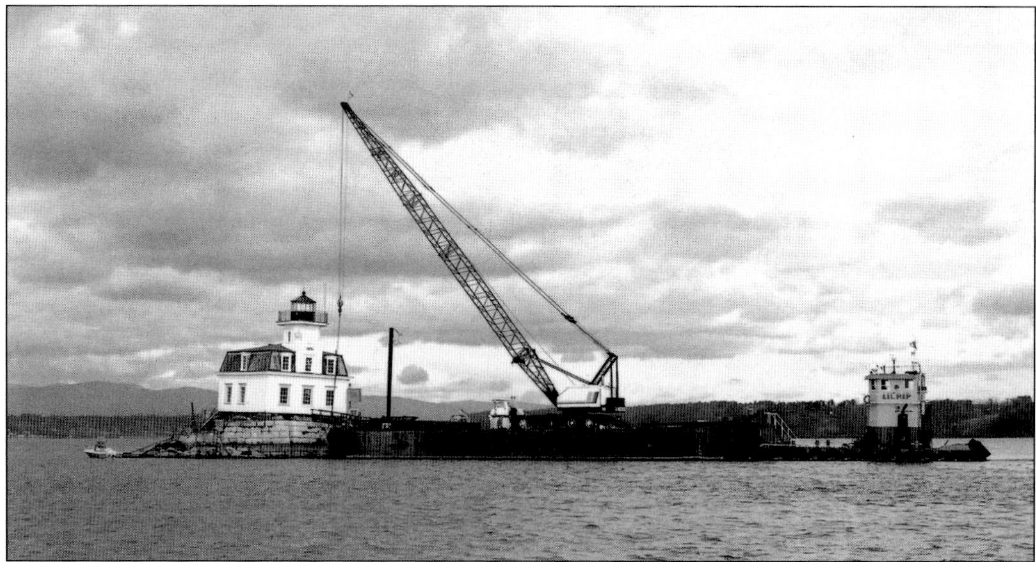

Due to impact damage from ice, debris, and even boats, the Esopus Meadows Lighthouse had acquired a serious tilt. Before any restoration work could be completed on the structure, the 17-inch drop needed to be addressed. In 2000, the house was raised by hydraulic jacks, and I-beams were slipped underneath to form a new foundation to replace the rotten sill plate and span the cracks in the top of the stone pier. (EML.)

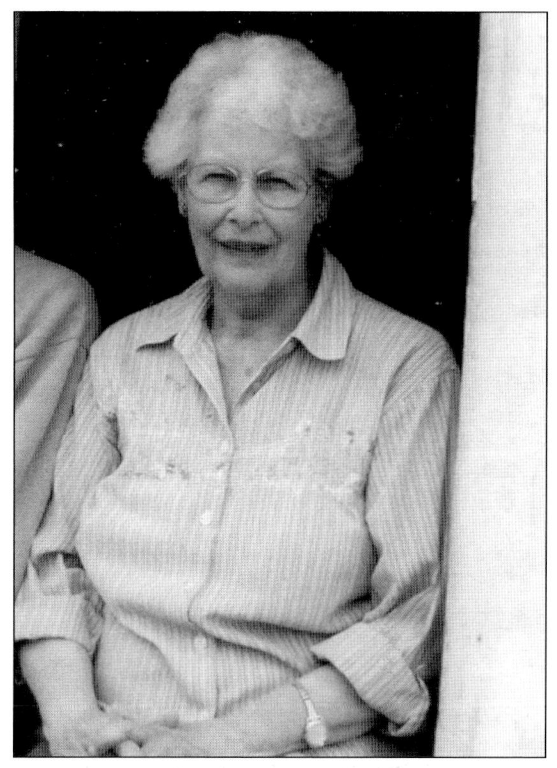

In 2002, the commission took ownership of the Esopus Meadows Lighthouse from the Coast Guard. The commission was lucky to have access to someone with a great deal of experience living in the lighthouse such as Doris McLintock (right). McLintock had spent her formative years in the lighthouse with her parents. Using her memories, the interior of the lighthouse was restored to the 1930s, with historic paint colors and donated furniture from that period. Below is the completed restoration of the original kitchen. For more information, visit www.esopusmeadowslighthouse.org. (EML.)

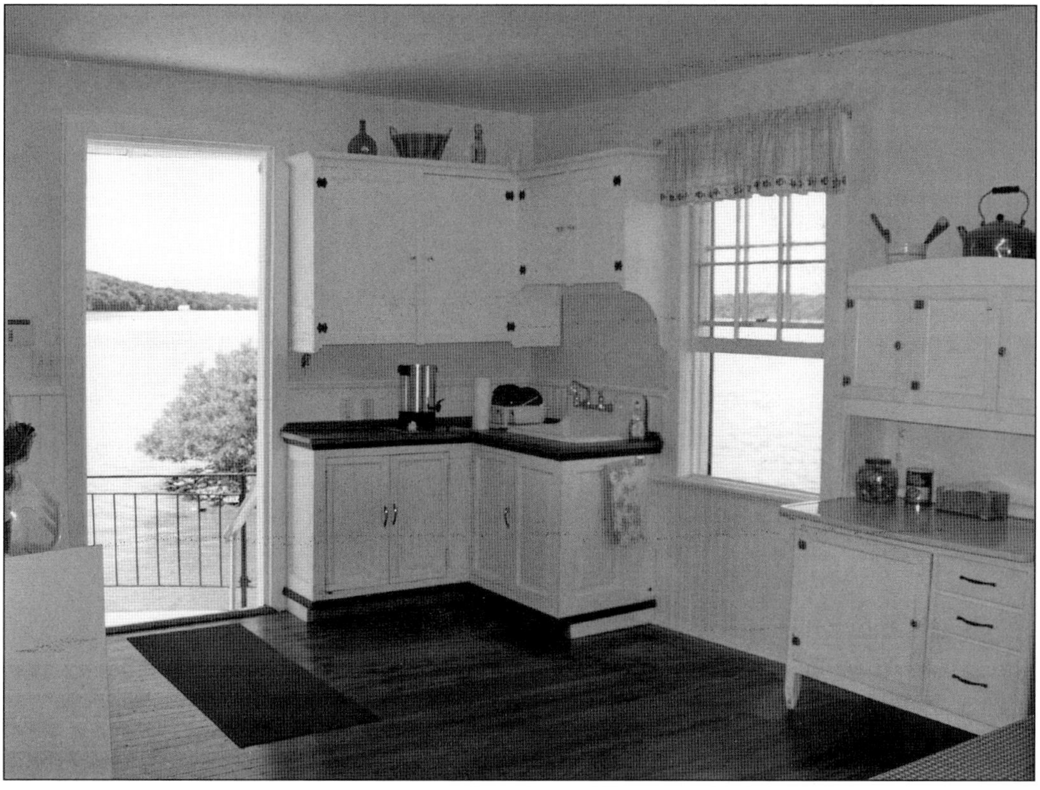

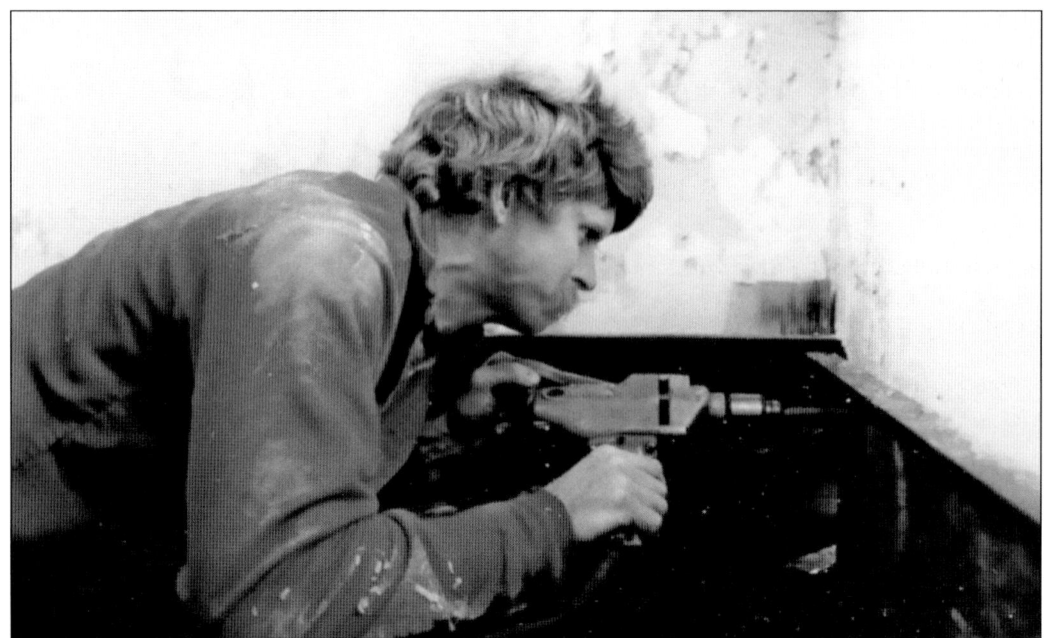

After automation of the beacon in 1954, the Saugerties Lighthouse sat vacant and neglected. As the condition of the lighthouse deteriorated, the light was removed from the tower in 1972 to a single pipe structure on the adjacent island. The Saugerties Lighthouse Conservancy was formed in 1985 with the purpose of acquiring the lighthouse and restoring it to its former glory. In 1986, Reid Bielenberg (above) and John Kurowski, both skilled craftsmen, were hired to stabilize the building. The situation was dire as the tower was ready to collapse into the river. Roofs and floors had rotted and caved in, so decisive intervention was needed. Alex Wade (below at left) was hired as architect and construction manager for the restoration. A barge was used to transport heavy materials to the building and to remove tons of rotten debris. (Both, SLC.)

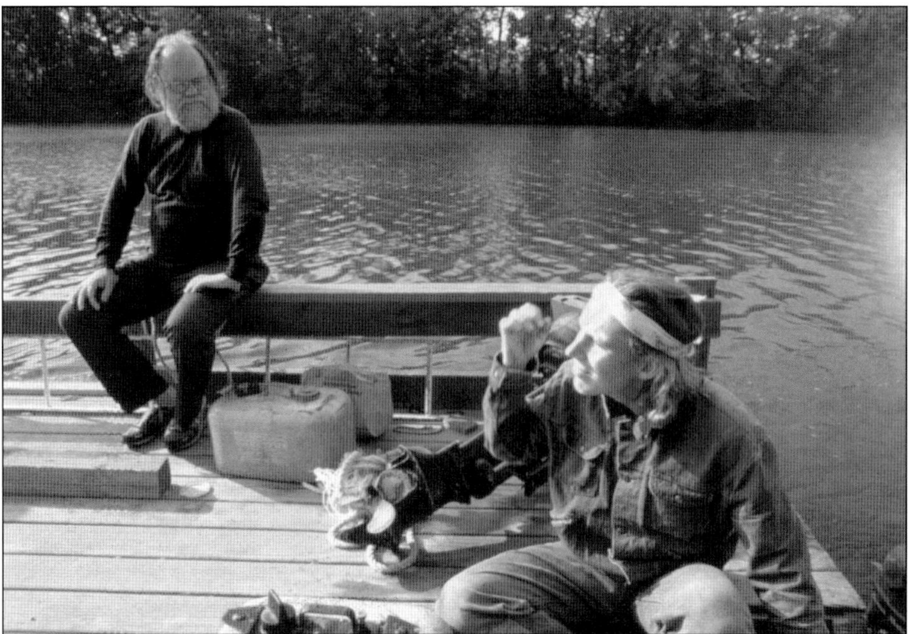

An elaborate scaffolding and shoring system was designed to hold up the tower and roof so that crumbling brick walls could be repaired. More than 10,000 new bricks were required to replace those that had crumbled to dust from moisture. The lantern room was restored to its original condition. On August 4, 1990, the beacon was reinstalled atop the tower, and the Saugerties Lighthouse was rededicated as an official aid to navigation again on the Hudson River. Today, the lighthouse is a bed-and-breakfast. For more information, visit www.saugertieslighthouse.com. (SLC.)

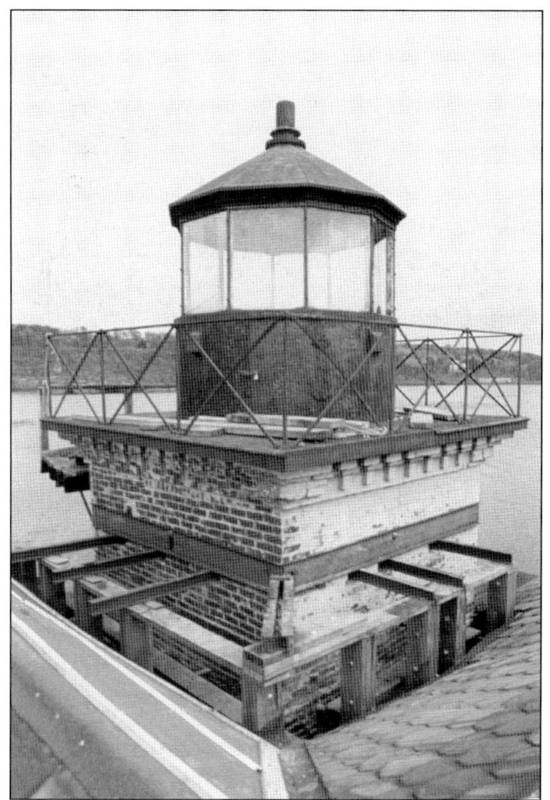

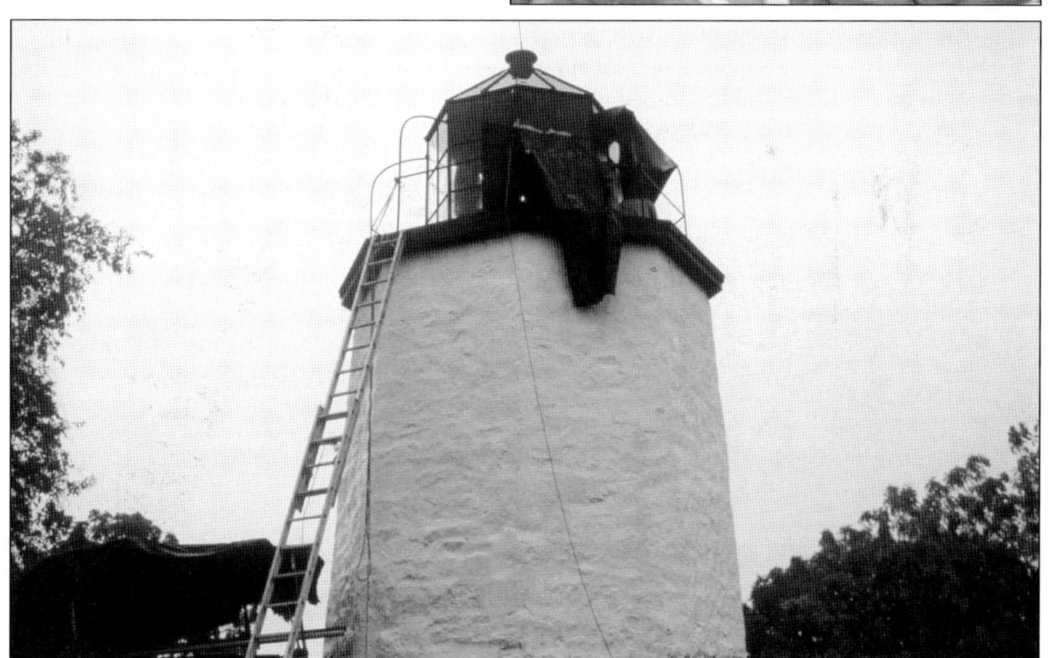

In 1986, the exterior of the Stony Point Lighthouse, long part of Stony Point Battlefield State Historic Site, operated by the Palisades Interstate Parks Commission, was repaired and repainted. Work was done to stabilize the interior of the tower, and the lantern windows were reglazed. (SPB.)

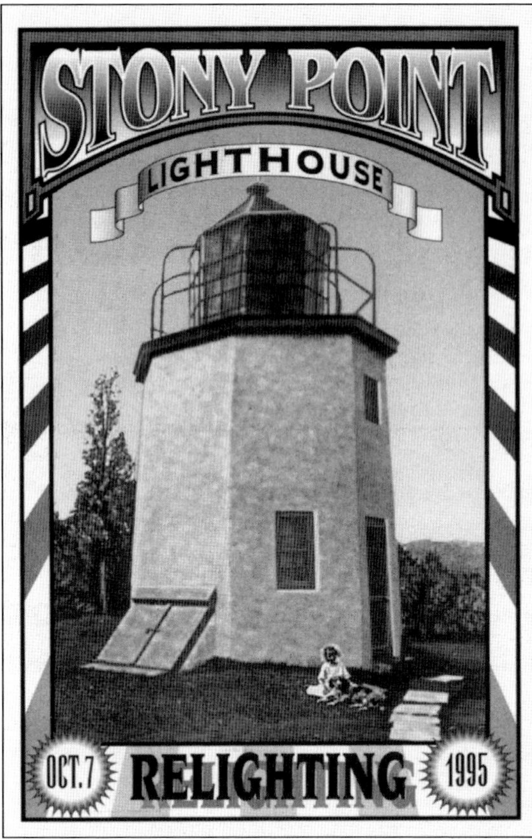

In 1995, the Stony Point Lighthouse reopened with a restored interior and exhibit, and on October 7, the light was lit for the first time since it was decommissioned in 1925. Today, the oldest lighthouse on the Hudson remains open to the public as part of the Stony Point Battlefield State Historic Site. For more information, visit parks.ny.gov/historic-sites. (Myra Starr.)

One of the youngest lighthouses on the Hudson, the Rondout Lighthouse was in much better condition than Esopus Meadows and Saugerties when it was listed with the rest of the group in the National Register in 1979. It was leased to the Hudson River Maritime Museum in the 1980s, refurnished, and opened for tours. In 1992–1993, the Hudson River Maritime Museum raised funds to replace the original slate roof on the lighthouse, which had been leaking. The City of Kingston took ownership of the lighthouse in 2005. (HRMM.)

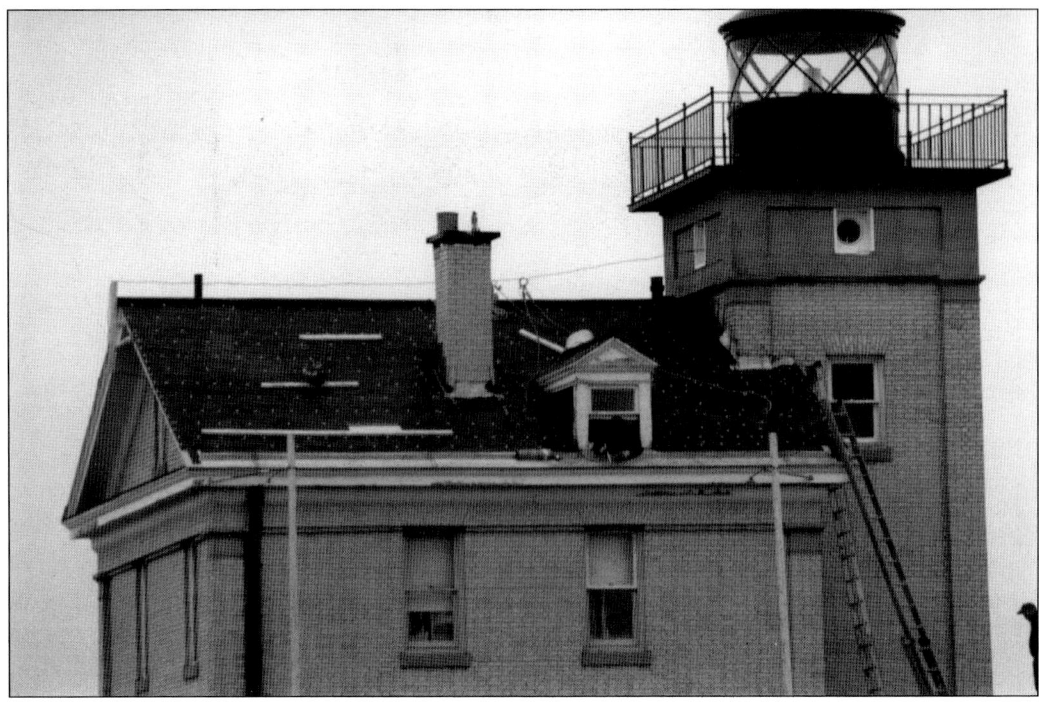

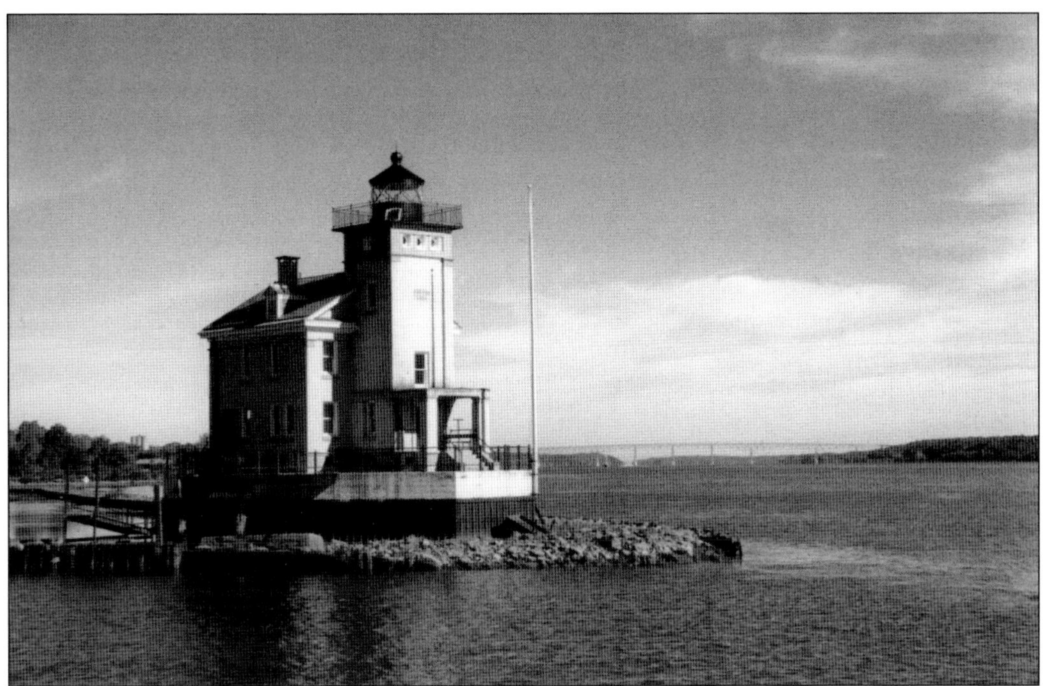

The Hudson River Maritime Museum and the City of Kingston have remained partners in keeping the lighthouse open to the public. Accessible only by boat, the Rondout Lighthouse is open for tours throughout the summer and fall months. For more information, visit www.rondoutlighthouse.org. (HRMM.)

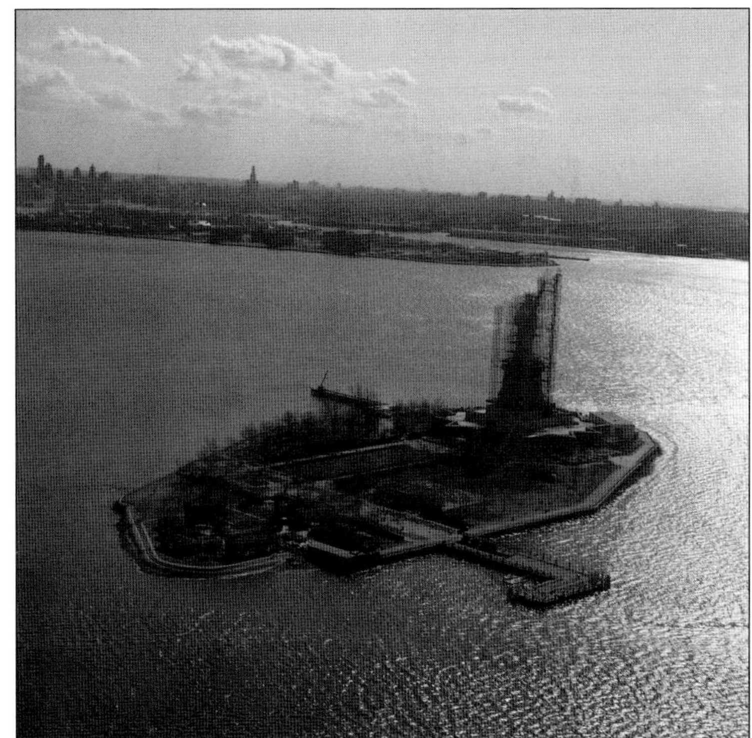

In anticipation of its centennial, a major restoration of the Statue of Liberty began in 1984. The interior iron grid was deteriorating and needed attention, and access to the crown and torch was becoming dangerous. Bringing scientists, historians, architects, engineers, and metallurgists together on an unprecedented scale, the restoration required construction of the largest free-standing scaffolding built at that time. (NARA.)

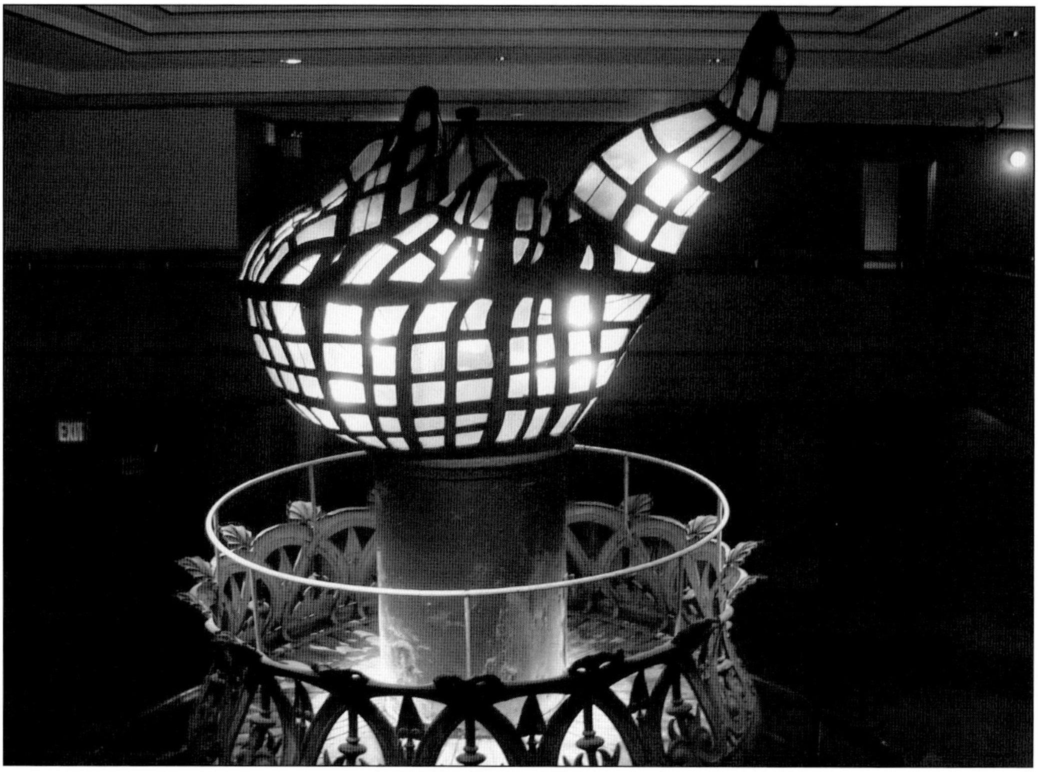

The restoration of the Statue of Liberty included the replacement of the original glass-paned torch, which was leaky and structurally unstable. Note the pyramidal red skylight in the center of the torch. The glass-paned torch was moved inside the onsite museum for preservation and viewing. That torch was replaced with a new one based on Bartholdi's original design, made of copper and gilded with gold leaf. (NPS.)

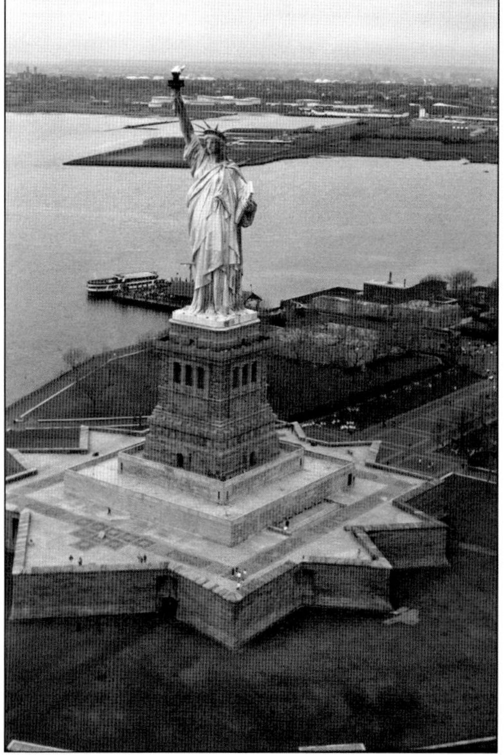

Completed in 1986 in time for the Liberty Weekend centennial celebrations around the Fourth of July, the newly renovated statue included a new torch and revitalized crown. Interior renovations including elevators serve to improve public access. The Statue of Liberty is open seven days a week to the general public. For more information, visit www.nps.gov. (NARA.)

About the Organization

The Hudson River Maritime Museum, located on the historic Rondout waterfront in Kingston, New York, was founded in 1980 by local steamboat enthusiasts to preserve the quickly disappearing maritime heritage of the Hudson River. Today, the organization operates a campus that includes a wooden boat school, a sailing school, and a rowing school as well as the museum and archive. It also works in conjunction with the City of Kingston to preserve public access to the Rondout Lighthouse. The Hudson River Maritime Museum's educational programs include annual exhibits, visiting vessels, history-based school field trips, lecture series, lighthouse tours, walking tours, history cruises, and more. In addition, the museum offers a wide range of rowing, sailing, and boating safety classes, boatbuilding and woodworking classes, and more.

The Hudson River Maritime Museum maintains an important historical archive of Hudson River history, with emphasis on the mid-19th to mid-20th centuries, including Hudson River steamboats, tugboats, lighthouses, ice boats, the Delaware & Hudson Canal, and river-related industrial manufacturing including bricks, cement, ice harvesting, shipbuilding, and more.

For more information about the museum, including class and event registration and online exhibits, please visit www.hrmm.org. In conjunction with the Hudson River Lighthouse Coalition, the Hudson River Maritime Museum also maintains www.hudsonriverlighthouses.org.

Consistent with our mission to preserve history on a local level, this book was printed in South Carolina on American-made paper and manufactured entirely in the United States. Products carrying the accredited Forest Stewardship Council (FSC) label are printed on 100 percent FSC-certified paper.

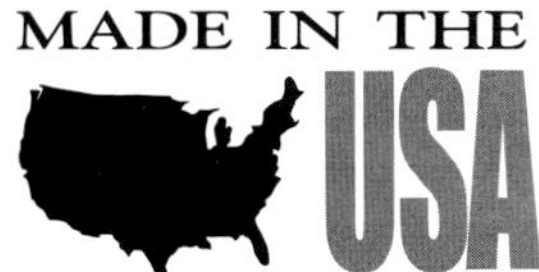